PRAGMATIC PLURALISM
AND THE PROBLEM OF GOD

AMERICAN PHILOSOPHY

Douglas R. Anderson and Jude Jones, series editors

PRAGMATIC PLURALISM AND THE PROBLEM OF GOD

SAMI PIHLSTRÖM

FORDHAM UNIVERSITY PRESS   NEW YORK   2013

Fordham University Press has no responsibility for the persistence or accuracy of URLs for external or third-party Internet websites referred to in this publication and does not guarantee that any content on such websites is, or will remain, accurate or appropriate.

Fordham University Press also publishes its books in a variety of electronic formats. Some content that appears in print may not be available in electronic books.

Library of Congress Cataloging-in-Publication Data is available from the publisher.

Printed in the United States of America

15 14 13   5 4 3 2 1

First edition

Contents

Preface

This book addresses fundamental issues in the philosophy of religion from a pragmatist point of view and will be primarily of interest to professional philosophers specializing in pragmatism or the philosophy of religion. It is not merely a specialized scholarly volume, however, as it can also be used as supplementary reading material in courses intended for graduate and advanced undergraduate students. Both pragmatism and the philosophy of religion have, obviously, been written on voluminously, but no previous book has applied pragmatism—or what I will call pragmatic pluralism—to issues in the philosophy of religion in the way this book will.

Philosophers have tended to view pragmatism either as a somewhat informal version of logical empiricism (given the resemblance between the pragmatic method and the verificationist theory of meaning) or as a radical postmodern critique of any kind of systematic philosophy (as in Richard Rorty's "antirepresentationalist" neopragmatism). Both ways of understanding pragmatism are misguided, as should become clear through the argument this book develops. On the other hand, scholarly studies on the classical pragmatists or their religious ideas rarely take neopragmatism seriously enough. A substantial look at both classical and recent currents in pragmatist thought is needed to evaluate the relevance of this extremely rich philosophical orientation to the philosophy of religion today and also to compare it to other traditions and perspectives.

Moreover, the relation between ethics and metaphysics, a major theme in this book, is becoming increasingly relevant in contemporary philosophy. Indeed, one of the goals of the present investigation is to show the deep integration of ethical and metaphysical themes in a pragmatically pluralist approach to major issues in the philosophy of religion, including the theism versus atheism controversy. Thus, it is my sincere hope that this volume will make a genuinely novel contribution to the on-going discussion not only on pragmatism but on key topics in the philosophy of religion generally, including basic ones concerning theism and atheism, as well as the religion versus science controversy, and more practical problems concerning, say, the problem of evil.

For this monograph, I've used some of my earlier articles as the basis for the chapters. The basic ideas for the introduction were presented at the "Brown Bag Seminar" of the Helsinki Collegium for Advanced Studies in November 2009. An early version of chapter 1 appeared in *The Pluralist* 5 (2010); copyright by the Board of Trustees of the University of Illinois, used with permission of the University of Illinois Press; a brief version of the chapter was presented at the 22nd World Congress of Philosophy in Seoul, Korea, in July–August 2008. Chapter 2 is based on my paper "Dewey and Pragmatic Religious Naturalism," published in *Cambridge Companion to Dewey*, ed. Molly Cochran (Cambridge: Cambridge University Press, 2010); copyright by Cambridge University Press, used with permission of the publisher. Parts of the chapter were presented in the Nordic Pragmatism Workshop "The Ethics of Belief" at the University of Jyväskylä, Finland, in December 2008; and in the workshop "Science and Religion" at the Forum Scientiarum, University of Tübingen, Germany, in February 2012. Chapter 3 incorporates material from a paper on Rorty's interpretation of Dewey's views on religion, presented in a conference on Dewey and Rorty at the University of Szeged, Hungary, in November 2009. An early version appeared in the proceedings of the conference in the e-journal *Pragmatism Today* 1, no. 1 (2010), www.prag matismtoday.eu. Chapter 4 is based on a paper delivered at a conference on William James and the "Transatlantic Conversation," organized at the Rothermere Institute of American Thought, University of Oxford in September 2010; there is also some overlap with my entry on James written for the *Encyclopedia of Ethics*, ed. Hugh LaFollette (Malden, MA: Wiley-Blackwell, forthcoming in 2013). Parts of the material were also presented as a guest lecture at New School University, New York City, in February 2011, and as the paper "Pluralism in Pragmatist Philosophy of Religion," presented in a symposium on religious pluralism and equality at the Helsinki Collegium for Advanced Studies in June 2011. Chapter 5 is based on papers presented at Columbia University, New York City, in February 2011; a meeting of the New York Pragmatist Forum at Fordham University, also in February 2011; and the international conference "Pragmatism and the Theory of Religion" at the Max-Weber-Kolleg, University of Erfurt, Germany, in February 2012; an early version was presented in a lecture series of the Helsinki Collegium for Advanced Studies in November 2010. A paper to some extent overlapping with the chapter is published in *Graduate Faculty Philosophy Journal* 33, no. 1 (2012). The conclusion includes some fragments adapted from my "Religion and Pseudo-Religion: An Elusive Boundary," published in *International Journal for Philosophy of Religion* 63 (2007).

I want to thank the respective publishers and journals for granting me the permissions to use copyrighted material.

I am deeply grateful to a number of colleagues whose help, support, and critical comments—often in the context of paper presentations that eventually turned into book chapters—have stimulated my writing of this book. These kind people who have helped me to understand not only what pragmatism or the philosophy of religion are all about but also what my own work on these topics is and can be about, include the following: Douglas Anderson, Hanne Appelqvist, Randy Auxier, Richard Bernstein, Niek Brunsveld, Vincent Colapietro, Alexis Dianda, David Dilworth, Russell B. Goodman, Judith Green, Dirk-Martin Grube, Leila Haaparanta, Jaana Hallamaa, Sara Heinämaa, Eberhard Herrmann, Larry Hickman, David Hildebrand, Ana Honnacker, Hans Joas, Lauri Järvilehto, Heikki Kannisto, Erkki Kilpinen, Heikki Kirjavainen, Simo Knuuttila, Timo Koistinen, Heikki J. Koskinen, Heikki A. Kovalainen, Alex Kremer, Arto Laitinen, Joseph Margolis, Hugh McDonald, Olli-Pekka Moisio, Don Morse, Ilkka Niiniluoto, Martha Nussbaum, Wayne Proudfoot, Joel Rasmussen, Michaela Rehm, Henrik Rydenfelt, John Ryder, Risto Saarinen, Carl B. Sachs, Thomas Schmidt, John R. Shook, Emil Visnovsky, Gereon Wolters, and Ulf Zackariasson. I am particularly grateful to the late Michael Eldridge, the late Peter H. Hare, and the late Juha Sihvola. Moreover, I should also like to thank the three reviewers who read the work for Fordham University Press and whose critical comments on the manuscript were enormously helpful: Wayne Proudfoot, Michael Raposa, and Roger Ward. In addition, Helen Tartar and her assistants at Fordham University Press have supported the project all the way from the start—and it was Doug Anderson who initially helped me to choose this particular book series for my work. Taavi Sundell assisted me in the final stages of completing the manuscript. Both the Department of Social Sciences and Philosophy at the University of Jyväskylä and the Helsinki Collegium for Advanced Studies have been ideal academic environments for my work. Finally, I remain most deeply grateful to my family for their continuing support.

PRAGMATIC PLURALISM
AND THE PROBLEM OF GOD

INTRODUCTION

Contemporary philosophy of religion is in a confusing state, as the different schools of thought seem to disagree not only about substantial questions such as God's existence but about the very nature and methods of the philosophy of religion. These disagreements do not just arise from the theism versus atheism dispute about the existence of God or from the currently popular science versus religion controversy, to which aggressive atheists like Richard Dawkins and Daniel C. Dennett have actively contributed. *Evidentialism* and *fideism* offer different metalevel views on the justifiability of religious faith and on its relation to science and reason: while evidentialism urges that religious beliefs (like scientific ones) require justification in terms of general, religiously neutral criteria of rationality, fideism draws a sharp distinction between faith and reason, advancing faith in the absence of evidence.

In addition to this primarily epistemological debate, a metaphysical and semantic disagreement concerns the nature of religious "reality" and our ability to refer to it linguistically. *Realists* affirm the existence of a mind-, concept-, language-, theory-, and discourse-independent world, maintaining that language can, in principle, be used to refer to such a reality and that truth is a matter of correspondence between linguistic items and the (generally) nonlinguistic elements of the world that "make true" our truths. *Antirealists*, in contrast, understand the nature of religious language—and language in general—in terms of its use within practices or forms of life, rather than any referential (representational) relations.[1] The major traditions in Western (analytic) philosophy of religion have been evidentialist and realist, but in the twentieth century philosophers inspired by Ludwig Wittgenstein were increasingly drawn toward fideist and antirealist views (though it is by no means clear that Wittgenstein's own ideas can be accurately interpreted in these terms).

The status of *pragmatist* philosophy of religion here is somewhat ambivalent. Generally speaking, pragmatists engage in the search for a *middle path* between extreme realism and antirealism, as well as between evidentialism and fideism, usually preferring to reconcile, integrate, or synthesize apparently conflicting perspectives instead of simply continuing to debate in those conventional terms. How exactly this is done in pragmatism must, however, be studied in detail, in critical comparison to other contributions to the relevant debates. Pragmatism is not always recognized as an important discussion partner in mainstream philosophy of religion; on the contrary, it is often quite strikingly neglected. Typical recent contributions to either analytic or continental philosophy of religion usually fail to even mention pragmatist alternatives.[2]

While the above-mentioned debates are concerned with the nature of religious beliefs and statements from the perspective of "theoretical philosophy," there are no less serious disputes in "practical philosophy." The relation between religion and morality, in particular, is both extremely important and highly unclear. Secular moralists sharply disagree with, say, divine command theorists on the ultimate grounds of ethical principles (and on whether any "ultimacy" is possible here). It remains particularly unclear what the place of religious values in "the good life" might be, and how this issue ought to be discussed in a largely secularized yet multicultural society promoting religious tolerance. Richard Rorty's proposal to treat religion as a private affair disconnected from the public use of reason, related to his suggestion that traditional philosophical issues should be redescribed as issues in "cultural politics" (i.e., issues about whether, and how, to use certain "vocabularies" or language-games), also raised considerable controversy in the early 2000s, continuing from a neopragmatist perspective the disputes over religion and society that John Rawls and others had initiated.[3]

However, long before Rorty's radical "ethnocentrist" neopragmatism, the tradition of pragmatism has sought to mediate between rival extremes in various areas of philosophy—and the philosophy of religion is no exception. Its problems can be fruitfully approached from a pragmatist perspective. This is what I hope to do in this book. I will not only demonstrate that a truly pragmatist approach in the philosophy of religion need not, and should not, be Rortyan—for Rorty's version of pragmatism in the end gives up normative criteria for adequately evaluating religious, or any, discourse (see chapter 3)—but also that a healthy understanding of religious thought presupposes a broadly pragmatist (practice-oriented) standpoint that is inherently *pluralistic*. There is no single, absolute, overarching perspective from which religious or theological issues ought to be viewed but a plurality of relevant philosophical points of view, reflecting the plurality of our practices and the rich variety of human needs, interests, and problems those practices respond to.

The problems of realism versus antirealism and evidentialism versus fideism, among others, receive new interpretations as soon as they are examined from a pragmatist point of view, because religion is then understood as a human practice (or set of practices) with certain inherent aims and goals, responding to specific human needs and interests, serving certain important human values, and seeking to resolve problematic situations that naturally arise from our practices themselves, especially our need to live with our vulnerability, finitude, guilt, and mortality. This by no means precludes rational criticism of religious ways of thinking; on the contrary, such criticism itself is served by better understanding the ways in which religion functions in our practices—or, better, *is* a practice. Pragmatist philosophy of religion is obviously committed to the *normative* task of the philosophy of religion generally, seeking to critically evaluate, and not just to explain and understand, religious beliefs and practices. The science versus religion dialogue, in particular, vitally needs a comprehensive and tolerant account of both scientific and religious practices and their somewhat diverging conceptions of rationality and intellectual (as well as ethical) responsibility. Pragmatism promises to advance such understanding. It promises to offer us pluralism and tolerance without succumbing to uncritical relativism, according to which "anything goes." This is why it is important—especially in the philosophically and more generally culturally confusing situation we now find ourselves living in—to take another look at what kind of resources pragmatism might offer for understanding religion.[4]

Moreover, pragmatism can mediate not just between (say) realism and antirealism (e.g., relativism) but also between analytic and continental approaches to the philosophy of religion. The hypothesis that pragmatism is able to lead us to a viable middle path in such controversies ought to be critically tested, however, and this is precisely what I plan to do in what follows. Indeed, my essentially pluralistic hypothesis—which can be understood as a specification of the general pragmatist hypothesis that the desired middle path is available—is that pragmatist philosophy of religion will be able to solve, or at least significantly moderate, several key tensions in the philosophy of religion, including particularly the tensions between realism and antirealism, on the one hand, and between evidentalism and fideism, on the other, thus enabling us to avoid not just dogmatic religious thinking but also other crude, unphilosophical views in this field (such as the currently popular attacks on religion by thinkers like Dawkins), thereby eventually yielding a more balanced understanding of the nature of religious life and values than the mainstream paradigms in the field are able to. It has been recognized—also by many nonpragmatists—that we need something like a middle ground between militant neo-Darwinian atheism and the attempts by some religious believers (including some philosophically very sophisticated ones) to "turn the clock backwards."[5] Pragmatism, I am confident, can help us in seeking and finding such a middle ground.

This book can therefore also be read as an extended effort to suggest that pragmatism can offer a new approach to the problem of how people or groups with very different worldviews, such as religious believers and atheists, can recognize or acknowledge each other not only as human beings with certain inherently valuable characteristics but as members of a common community of thinkers or inquirers. This challenge of mutual acknowledgment is presumably nowhere as urgent as in the question of whether the possibility of scientifically explaining religious experiences and beliefs—their emergence, spreading, and status in communities—conflicts with religious commitments. One could argue that the availability of plausible scientific (e.g., psychological, neurophysiological, sociological) explanations for religious experiences (as well as for the emergence and influences of religious beliefs and practices) makes religious worldviews irrational, as you cannot reasonably believe *both* that a religious experience arises, say, from neural or psychological sources *and* that it has been stimulated by a divine or transcendent reality. The pragmatist response to such a situation—a response we owe to William James, in particular—is, in brief, that we can contextualize the *same* matter (e.g., experience or belief) in quite different ways, as soon as we embrace a pragmatic pluralism (which could also be called perspectivalism or contextualism). One can still recognize the contextual (perspectival) validity of both contextualizations of the experience, the scientific and the religious; both could be "true" or "correct" from their quite different perspectives. This proposal comes close to the Kantian idea of reconciling the critique of rational proofs of theism with the practical (moral) commitment to theism (see chapter 1). One just has to learn to look at the "same" phenomenon from two different standpoints.

Accordingly, appreciating the possibility of two different and apparently conflicting views does not exclude the possibility of recognizing both as contextually acceptable and, even more importantly, of recognizing the subjects of those views as fellow thinkers or inquirers. The key methodological issue that arises here is whether the pragmatist (particularly Jamesian) pluralistic contextualism avoiding reductive "nothing but" categorization of religion could be developed into a novel methodology of religious studies that would truly enable the believer and the atheist to stand on a common intellectual ground—or even be united in a "common faith" in the capacities of human experience and intelligence (cf. chapter 2 on Dewey's *A Common Faith*).[6] The problem does remain, though, whether the believer and the atheist can truly recognize each other not only as individuals or groups possessing and employing contextually valid criteria of rationality but also as participants, with the same rights and duties, in a process of inquiry common to all human beings. This book is *not* an attempt to claim that pragmatism will easily remove all conflicts between different worldviews and orientations. Oppositions and tensions will undoubtedly remain as long as people continue to be interested in *weltanschaulich* issues.

What Is "Pragmatic Pluralism"?

A particularly relevant metalevel topic in pragmatist philosophy of religion is the relation between *metaphysical* and *ethical* issues, paralleling the distinction between *theory* and *practice*. The central pragmatist idea I will defend is that theory and practice in general, and metaphysics and ethics in particular, are deeply intertwined—both in the philosophy of religion in particular and in philosophy in general. This view is related to Hilary Putnam's defense of the fact-value entanglement[7]— and Putnam, of course, is another leading neopragmatist along with Rorty. Again, pluralism is a key to this debate: there is no overarching, metaphysically correct "absolute" view on the true nature of values and facts; there are different value-laden human perspectives on this question, and others.

A leading thought of this volume is that the theism versus atheism and religion versus science debates—no more than the more metalevel issues in the philosophy of religion—cannot be adequately settled from a single, privileged perspective but require a plurality of perspectives, pragmatically balanced and harmonized—and perhaps mutually recognized—in terms of their functional workability in the (would-be) believer's (or nonbeliever's) overall account of the ethico-metaphysical problem of God as a problem of her/his personal life and moral deliberation. These perspectives include, at least, the Kantian approach to theism in terms of the "postulates of practical reason"; Jamesian pragmatic pluralism, growing out of but significantly transforming the Kantian notion of the "primacy of practical reason"; Deweyan pragmatic naturalism (a very important development of pragmatism toward secularism); the Wittgensteinian quietist, mysticist standpoint, which, though nonnaturalist, might even be seen as analogous to the "natural piety" that Dewey's naturalism invokes; and neopragmatism, both in its Putnamian and Rortyan versions. All of these I will at least to some extent explicate and critically examine in the chapters to follow. I will defend the pragmatically pluralist idea that all these perspectives—even including Rortyan neopragmatism, albeit critically viewed—are needed and that the philosophy of religion, if pragmatically adequate, must hence be profoundly *antireductionist.*[8] Accordingly, not only should we, as pragmatists, be religiously tolerant; we should also philosophically tolerate many different (though not all) ways of understanding religion philosophically.[9] However, I will also have to show why, and how, pragmatism must block the apologetic projects defended by more mainstream philosophers of religion (or "Christian philosophers") like Richard Swinburne and Alvin Plantinga. The metalevel practical functionality of the above-mentioned perspectives, evaluated in Jamesian terms, must be shown to be superior to the latter ones (even though detailed critical evaluations of apologetic Christian philosophers' views are beyond the scope of the present book).

The Kantian background of pragmatism will, *contra* Rorty, be specifically emphasized in this book, but Kantian resources are certainly not sufficient for the pragmatist philosopher of religion. The plurality of pragmatically relevant approaches to the question of God's reality can be contrasted with Rorty's reductive picture of philosophy (of religion) as mere "cultural politics." Among the neopragmatists, Putnam's philosophy of religion, drawing from Wittgenstein and Kant in addition to the classical pragmatists, comes closer to the pluralist picture I defend than Rorty's does, but even Putnam's project will be found wanting because of its many unresolved tensions (see chapter 3). On the other hand, tensions may be unavoidable in truly pragmatist philosophy of religion. Among all human practices, religion may be the one in which the deep tensions and even contradictions involved in being human emerge most forcefully.

The different approaches to fundamental questions in the philosophy of religion I will be concerned with—as diverse as Kant's, James's, Dewey's, and the neopragmatists', with their Wittgensteinian aspects—are actually more unified than they might initially seem. All are versions of the idea that metaphysical positions, including those relevant to religion, ought to be *ethically evaluated.* Far from examining the "God of metaphysics" (to borrow the title of T. L. S. Sprigge's interesting book)[10] independently of ethical considerations, these views seek—or their creative pragmatic elaborator may and should seek—*an ethical grounding for (religious/theological) metaphysics.* To be sure, some of the pragmatist conceptions of religion to be discussed, notably Rorty's but arguably Dewey's as well, stop short of being metaphysical enough (or at all). To some extent this may be true about all the perspectives to be studied. The task of the pragmatist philosopher of religion is to push beyond such antimetaphysical prejudices. Pragmatic pluralism is a philosophy of tolerance and antidogmatism. We should not only advance religious tolerance as a socio-political principle; we should extend this tolerance, at a more "theoretical" level (yet avoiding any theory versus practice dichotomies) to different metaphysical ways of construing religious or theological outlooks, to different interpretations of what is crucial in religion—and to metaphysics itself. While advancing metaphysical inquiry, pragmatic pluralism is deeply committed to *fallibilism*. As inquirers, both in science, everyday life, and religion (and in all other areas of life, too), we are fallible beings. Any of our beliefs could be false, and we need continuous self-critical awareness of this fact. Pragmatist philosophy of religion is, perhaps better than most of its rivals, equipped to meet the challenge of critically discussing the value of religion in human life in a fallibilistic and tolerant spirit.

The concept of *pluralism*, invoked in the title of my book, deserves special discussion, because it is not immediately obvious what we should mean by this concept, even in the context of (Jamesian) pragmatist philosophy of religion. It has sometimes been suggested, relatively plausibly, that pluralism, in James's *A Pluralistic Universe* (1909), primarily amounts to a metaphysical theory, according to which there are "bits and pieces" of "pure experience" pretty much everywhere, and that it is therefore inseparable from James's radical empiricism. I agree that James's theory can be read in this way. However, in this book I will emphasize a quite different approach that departs from James's own usage of this terminology while in my view retaining his philosophical spirit (for more details, see especially chapter 4): perhaps pluralism, for Jamesian philosophers, is not to be construed primarily as a *metaphysical* doctrine but as a *metaphilosophical* one, highlighting the possibility of a plurality of different "correct" metaphysical positions, and thus coming closer to the argument of *Pragmatism* (1907), as well as the later defense of "internal realism" and "conceptual relativity" (or even explicitly "pragmatic pluralism") by Putnam, both in his writings in the 1980–90s and in the more recent ones cited above.[11] In fact, it is hard to see how the purely metaphysical doctrine, closely analogous to the view labeled "neutral monism," favored at some point by Ernst Mach and Bertrand Russell, among others, could be seriously regarded as "pluralistic." *Could* such a monism really be a form of pluralism? Shouldn't we, rather, maintain the possibility for monism (only) within a pluralism tolerating different metaphysical alternatives that are all pragmatically accountable within this more inclusive pragmatic pluralism? There is, then, a plurality of pluralisms. There are both metaphysical and (at the metalevel) conceptual, methodological, and metaphilosophical versions of pluralism, obviously needing further discussion and elaboration.[12]

Moreover, the pluralism issue manifests and even highlights the tensions inherent in pragmatist metaphysics more generally (in particular, tensions and challenges not yet adequately discussed in my previous works on these topics).[13] In what sense is a pragmatic theory or conception of reality "really" metaphysical? The relation between metaphysics and ethics must again be invoked here. As I will try to explain in chapter 4, pluralism, for James, is ethically superior to monism (particularly because monism leads to the problem of evil, which it cannot solve; see also chapter 5), yet genuinely metaphysical insofar as any view can be genuinely metaphysical for a pragmatist; the monism versus pluralism controversy *does* concern the way the world, for us, *is*. Key applications of the pluralism issue can be found in his philosophy of religion, e.g., in the "piecemeal pluralism" James defends in *The Varieties of Religious Experience* (1902) and elsewhere. The relation between pluralism and *relativism* must, however, be closely examined, at least insofar as we claim that pluralism is not simply a metaphysical position but a metaphilosophical legitimation of the plurality of rival, perhaps incompatible, yet equally justified approaches to metaphysics or to the philosophy of religion (or anything else).

Evil, Suffering, and Hope

In addition to general discussions of pragmatic pluralism—seeking a reevaluation of basic issues such as theism versus atheism, evidentialism versus fideism, and realism versus antirealism—more specialized treatments are needed on such religiously and theologically important concepts as evil and suffering. These topics are not among the main issues of this book, which seeks to defend pragmatic pluralism regarding the understanding of religious faith in general terms. However, the results of that general investigation will be applied to these topical issues in the final chapters of the book (see especially chapter 5). In particular, while it will be shown that a pragmatist—far from being a naïve optimist, religiously or otherwise—must take seriously the "dark" side of human life, including the ineliminable human potentiality for evil, a more positive outcome will also emerge from these considerations: the notion of *hope* can be made pragmatically relevant in a compelling manner in (Jamesian) pragmatic pluralism. One of the "undercurrents" of my discussion, therefore, is the attempt to develop a pragmatically viable concept of (religious) hope, to be carefully distinguished from the Rortyan neopragmatist deflation of this concept.[14]

One more special issue that pragmatic pluralism helps to conceptualize philosophically is the problem of "losing one's religion." How can religion be "lost," if religious identity is deeply constitutive of who (i.e., what kind of a person) one ultimately is, or what kind of culture or form of life one inhabits? The profoundly *antiessentialist* conception of religion based on pragmatic pluralism makes sense of this phenomenon, too. One may, *qua* someone or something slightly different from who/what one actually is—as seen and described in terms of some *other*, or perhaps some future, not yet realized but realizable, constitutive features of one's identity—lose one's religion and still remain (to some extent) the same person. The same applies to acquiring a (new) religious identity. As there are (for pragmatists) no essences of any kind, there is neither an essence to any particular religious orientation (e.g., Christianity) nor any absolute, external, ahistorical, transcendent sense in which one either is or is not committed to a particular religious orientation. Rather, religious values may be dynamically present in experience or one's life as a whole in many different ways, variously responding to natural human needs and interests, and thereby also changing in the course of experience, while simultaneously transforming that experience. Our religious identities, like *any* identities, are perspectival and contextual; hence, the pragmatist should be wary of any strict, dualistic categorization of individuals as simply believers or nonbelievers. The identity of religious values and ideas/ideals is similarly relational, contextually embedded, historically dynamic, and hence constantly in flux.

A problem inevitably arising here is whether a pragmatic pluralist can draw any normative distinction between "genuine" religious thought or life, on the one hand, and "pseudoreligion" or superstition, on the other. Does antiessentialism lead to relativism? I will take up this issue in my conclusion, where I will show that, just as the pragmatist need not give up metaphysics (either generally or in relation to religion in particular), she/he need not give up normative issues concerning the "genuineness" of a person's religious identity. Although religious identities are in constant transformation, their "true" nature can be contextually discussed. A key pragmatist criterion for the adequacy of a given philosophical approach to religion is the ability of the examined approach to satisfactorily respond to the self-reflective ethical question, "Is *this* genuine [sincere, serious, etc.] religiosity or not?"

It is, moreover, vital to direct that question toward oneself and *one's own* cultural practices and contexts in particular, instead of moralizing about others' religious commitments. Healthy criticism of others' commitments is naturally to be encouraged, but normative judgments should always first be directed to one's own position. Only thus—by recognizing the potential value of others' ideas and the potential weaknesses in one's own—can one fully take responsibility for one's critical contributions.

The Book's Contents in Brief

Chapter 1 proposes a reevaluation of the theism versus atheism controversy, and of the related metalevel dispute between evidentialism and fideism, from a Kantian transcendental perspective, connected with Jamesian pragmatism. If there is a morally vital human need to postulate the reality of God, and if this theistic postulation can be regarded as rational or legitimate from the perspective of "practical reason," then metaphysical and ethical aspects of the theism issue turn out to be deeply entangled with each other. A Kantian-cum-pragmatist philosophy of religion will inevitably approach the question of God's existence from a standpoint that thoroughly synthesizes ethics and metaphysics—just as

Kant's defense of theism as a postulate of practical reason did. A serious engagement with the theism versus atheism issue thus requires a plurality of philosophical standpoints, including the Jamesian pragmatic one and the Kantian transcendental one, and cannot be reductively accounted for in terms of a single overarching framework. Thus, I provide a preliminary formulation of the main theses of the entire book in this chapter. Furthermore, I introduce the religiously crucial notion of hope and emphasize its importance for both Kantian and Jamesian approaches.

A leading thought in my development of a Jamesian pragmatist philosophy of religion throughout this book is the one James shares with Kant: religion, or theism, may play a crucial role in our revolt against moral nihilism, against the threatening situation in which nothing matters and the moral perspective is a mere illusion. (This is biographically connected with James's famous nervous breakdown in 1871, after which he adopted the belief in free will along the lines of what he later came to describe as "the will to believe.") The metaphysical issue of theism is pragmatically relevant precisely because of its ethical relevance, its potential ability to lead us out of the absurdity of existence, into a vision of the world as somehow meaningfully organized (though this search for meaning must be dramatically qualified in order to avoid reading any obscene meaningfulness into evil: see chapter 5). Thus, James and other pragmatists writing on religion may be seen as "existential" thinkers, philosophers whose deepest concerns have to do with the significance of human existence. Yet, the success of religion or theism in this existential project is never guaranteed; as soon as we apply the pragmatic fallibilism endorsed by James as well as Peirce and Dewey to the case of religion, we must admit that there is no metaphysical or ethical security available.

Chapter 2 deals with the socially oriented, pragmatically naturalist conception of religious faith John Dewey developed in *A Common Faith* (1934) and elsewhere,[15] as well as Dewey's influence on pragmatist and naturalist currents in the philosophy of religion. In particular, I explain and discuss Dewey's distinction between "the religious," on the one hand, and actual religions, on the other. According to Dewey—the most important classical pragmatist following James—the religious aspects of experience can be appreciated without metaphysical commitments to anything supernatural. Here a problem arises: can the religious qualities of experience be fully naturalized by understanding them in a Deweyan manner as imaginative relations to human ideals, or will such naturalization inevitably reduce religious experience to something else?

Dewey's pragmatic naturalism thus leads us to reconsider the ontological status of religious "reality" (religious values, ideals, and other "entities"). Dewey, like Wittgenstein, can be read as reminding naturalistically and scientistically minded religious thinkers (and all others as well) that religious faith in God is *not* just a propositional belief in the existence of just another entity in the "household of reality." God is *not* a particular being in that sense, but "above" any particular beings there can be, or even "otherwise than being"—though here I am departing from Dewey's own terminology.[16] Yet, the issue of realism regarding religious experience and its objects (as well as scientific or philosophical studies of such experience and its objects) ought to be taken up as an analogy to the same issue regarding Dewey's conceptions of science and inquiry. This issue has potential applications not only for religious life but for theology and religious studies as well, that is, for any academic study of religion. From a Deweyan perspective, we may ask whether religious "reality," however different it is from mundane reality, is still somehow "really there" independently of us or whether it is constructed by us (our active pursuit of ideals). Finally, some comparisons to Wittgensteinian philosophy of religion and related currents of thought will be made in order to situate the Deweyan approach in the field of recent philosophy of religion.

Wittgensteinian "mysticism," in particular, may be compared to Dewey's notion of "natural piety." The religious standpoint is not just the constructive *activity* of the pragmatic (or transcendental) ego but also a kind of *passivity*, of being "spoken to" by, and being answerable to, something that we never constructed (such as, possibly, "nature"?). Accounting for such passivity, or inactivity, is obviously a challenge for any pragmatist theory. Dewey's natural piety may go some way toward articulating the relevant notion(s), but his views on religion do on the whole remain on the side of "activity theory." Further comparisons could be made to thinkers like Emmanuel Levinas, Paul Ricoeur, and Janet Soskice, but also to the early Wittgenstein's (somewhat Stoic) attitude to the world as a totality. However, even the activity versus passivity contrast is not as

simple as it may seem: we need to actively understand (construe) ourselves *as* passive in order to be able to adopt the religious standpoint. This
book and its chapter on Dewey can, however, only scratch the surface of
these deep problems; however, the possibility of comparing Levinas with
the pragmatists is noted in several places in the book.[17]

Like the classical pragmatists, neopragmatists like Rorty and Putnam
have consistently promoted the science-religion dialogue, albeit in very
different ways. While few neopragmatists can be primarily regarded as
philosophers of religion, neopragmatism as a philosophical framework
is readily applicable to the problem of understanding religion and its
relations to science. Thus, chapter 3 focuses on Rorty's and Putnam's
neopragmatisms, especially as they emerge as approaches to the relation
between science and religion. The Rorty versus Putnam contrast is crucial for understanding neopragmatism, also because it is an opposition
between secular and religiously engaged pragmatisms. In this chapter,
the discussion of the issue of realism in the philosophy of religion is also
continued, not only because the opposition between Rortyan and Putnamian pragmatisms largely centers around this issue but also because
there have been other neopragmatist, and closely related, recent contributions to the realism debate.[18] Finally, the concept of hope will be taken
up again: Rorty's deflationary account of this notion is contrasted with
James's (and Kant's) more substantial account(s) examined in chapter 1.

It must be noted, however, that we still lack the historical distance that
would enable us to properly evaluate neopragmatist philosophy of religion, or neopragmatism generally. I cannot discuss other neopragmatist
ideas in any detail; I will only be able to go through some of Rorty's and
Putnam's relatively familiar views in chapter 3. In fact this book itself is
an exercise in neopragmatist reflection, although, as the reader can easily notice, my favorite pragmatists are James and Dewey rather than the
currently influential neopragmatists. Only time will tell how neopragmatist suggestions will be received in the philosophy of religion.

Chapter 4 returns to James's pragmatist philosophy of religion with
special emphasis on its connections with his moral philosophy and the
ethical grounding of metaphysics available in Jamesian pragmatism and
pragmatic pluralism. It should be observed that the book is *not* structured chronologically: James is the last major pragmatist to be discussed

in detail because his overall view is closest to the one advanced in the volume. It is particularly important, given the main concerns of the book, to determine what exactly we should mean by "pluralism" (or "pragmatic pluralism"). James's version of pluralism will therefore again be revisited. This chapter suggests that Jamesian pluralism can be used—in its plural meanings—as a *(meta-)context* within which the different approaches to the philosophy of religion outlined above, especially to the issue of God's reality, can be nonreductively evaluated. Thus, it is a context intended to operate, or enable us to operate, against narrow-mindedness and dogmatism, especially when it comes to religion. However, no shallow eclecticism follows, as the Jamesian pragmatic method ties the different approaches together in a shared effort to understand our humanly natural search for religiously relevant meaning. Pragmatism is also a form of naturalism precisely in understanding this search as "humanly natural." Thus, the Jamesian approach I favor accommodates key Deweyan elements—and even Rortyan ones—while also finding Dewey's form of naturalism inadequate because of its ultimately monistic rather than genuinely pluralistic tendencies.

Pluralism and the *pragmatic method* are, I will argue, intimately tied to each other, especially in James but possibly also in other pragmatists (though not in Peirce, who firmly opposed James's pluralism). Indeed, pluralism itself can be defended by showing how to effectively apply the pragmatic method to key debates in the philosophy of religion, such as the one between evidentialism and fideism. Both evidentialist and fideist ideas are needed, and they can be seen to enhance our understanding of religion from their quite distinct and complementary perspectives, even though neither of them provides a complete picture of the situation. A truly pluralistic pragmatism should not simply abandon either evidentialism or fideism but set them in their proper place, critically *aufgehoben* (overcome yet maintained). Pluralism also promises a highly nonreductive picture of religious hope: genuine hope is only possible within a pragmatically pluralist account of the religiously relevant ideals we may pursue; one-sided, narrow-minded, and intolerant religious schemes destroy the very possibility of such hope. Again, we may see both apologetic religious thinkers like Swinburne and apologetic atheists like Dawkins as fostering such narrow-mindedness and intolerance, to be carefully avoided by pragmatism. Such apologetic writers all too easily crush the best values that religious worldviews may be able to promote.

Moreover, the Jamesian pragmatic method enables us to fruitfully return to the activity versus passivity issue raised earlier. The pragmatic method can be employed to articulate (at a metalevel, pluralistically) what it pragmatically means for us, in our experience, to be passive, to be a "listener," open to others. We may, to be religious, have to be passively open to a "presence of meaning" (in Ricoeur's sense), but we must actively, employing the pragmatic method, construe the meaning of this openness and passivity for us in our concrete experience.

Before concluding the inquiry, a pragmatic treatment of more "negative" ethico-religious concepts, such as evil and suffering, is necessary. Arguably, some versions of pragmatism (e.g., again, James's) may be better equipped to deal with the religious dimension of these features of human life than some others (e.g., Dewey's). I argue in chapter 5 that the problem of evil must be explored in a resolutely *antitheodicist* manner, without attempting in any way to justify or explain away the reality of evil. In this context I also raise the issue of genuine religion versus pseudo religion, which will be explicitly taken up in my reflections in the conclusion to this book. All the philosophical approaches examined in the previous chapters (with the exception of Rorty's) seem to draw, in their different ways, a contrast between "genuinely" or "truly" religious ways of thinking, on the one hand, and ways of thinking that fail to be genuinely religious, possibly representing something like "superstition" instead, on the other. It is important to examine whether this normative contrast has any pragmatic content. Again, the issue must be studied by connecting religious thought and life intimately with the human practices within which it takes place and the practice-embedded problematic situations it responds to. The pragmatic pluralist should argue, with James, that there is no essence of religious thinking (thus once again arguing against monism and dogmatism of all kinds), but it does not follow from such pluralism that the problem of distinguishing between genuine religiosity and its pseudoreligious corrupt forms is not at all relevant. Rather, the challenge is to make this distinction—again both metaphysically and ethically—pragmatically relevant and substantial.

Special emphasis must be drawn on the question of whether, pragmatically speaking, there might be (pseudo)religious or theological ideas (e.g., regarding the "justification" of evil) that are culturally or humanly "unthinkable," or ethically—and *therefore* also metaphysically—simply unacceptable.[19] The pragmatic cash-value of religious beliefs can arguably be appreciated by focusing on suffering and related phenomena: religion may, though it also may not, offer us (contextual, never absolute) security, help, consolation, spiritual salvation, etc., also leading up to a "morally strenuous" attitude to life. In chapter 5, I argue that religious metaphysics offering such consolation, as a certain kind of response to problems arising from our practices and life situations, *may* be pragmatically acceptable, given that it avoids justifying or explaining away evil in a "theodicist" manner.[20] The problem of evil and suffering cannot, for ethical reasons, be regarded as theoretically solvable.[21]

Having elaborated on no less than five quite different perspectives on the nature of religious faith, especially in relation to scientific and generally rational discourse—that is, the Kantian, the Jamesian, the Deweyan, the Wittgensteinian, and the neopragmatist—I conclude, drawing my inspiration mainly from James but also from the other authors considered, that pragmatist philosophy of religion must be inherently pluralistic and antireductionist. There is no reason to suppose that the major problems of the philosophy of religion could be settled, or even interestingly discussed, from a privileged point of view, from any single absolute perspective. Kantian, Jamesian, Deweyan, Wittgensteinian, and neopragmatist—and presumably many other—resources are vitally needed for a truly pragmatic understanding of what truly religious life and religious practices are like. A genuinely religious life, or a genuinely religious intellectual outlook, incorporates aspects from all of these. Moreover, it incorporates both passivity and activity, dialectically connected, understanding the religious person's attitude as irreducible to either of these two poles.

ONE

PRAGMATIC ASPECTS OF
KANTIAN THEISM

Is God real? What do we, or what should we, mean by this question? How, if at all, might the question, given that its meaning(s) can be clarified, be settled or even rationally discussed? Is there any chance for a reasonable, scientifically minded person to believe in God, or is atheism the only intellectually responsible option for us today? Is theism inevitably committed to the antiscientific absurdities of creationism, the "intelligent design theory," and other unfortunately increasingly influential fundamentalisms?

The purpose of this chapter (and this book, for that matter) is not to resolve these vast issues in the philosophy of religion. Nor will I engage in the science versus religion controversy in any detail. I do, however, hope to illuminate the traditional issue of theism from a specific philosophical perspective.[1] The kind of questions listed above help to describe the problem framework we are entering, as well as the sidetracks to be avoided in serious philosophy of religion (e.g., the debate between creationism and Darwinism, which is hardly either scientifically or philosophically interesting).[2] Furthermore, my remarks will not be restricted to the opposition between *theism* and *atheism* as such.[3] As already preliminarily explained in the introduction, the metalevel contrast between *evidentialism* and *fideism* opens up another basic dispute in the modern debate over theism, perhaps even more important philosophically than the theism versus atheism dispute itself, as it concerns the criteria in terms of which the latter dispute is to be adjudicated, and the kind of reasons that may be invoked to support (or attack) theism.[4] It seems to me, for reasons that will properly emerge in due course, that there is a desperate need for a middle ground or synthesis between these two extremes in contemporary philosophy of religion, and the present chapter will go some way toward providing such a synthesis by redescribing the problem of theism in both Kantian and pragmatist terms. In short, evidentialism is, in most cases, inadequate as an interpretation of religious people's views on God, because religious faith needs no rational (religiously neutral) evidence, and can be neither defended nor criticized in terms of such "scientific" evidence. Religion, in short, is a human practice quite different from science, and though it may be related to science in various ways—that is, it is not completely autonomous and self-standing—it cannot be adequately evaluated by means of criteria internal to scientific practices. Fideism, in turn, is highly problematic, because it tends to lead to relativist and irrational views sharply distinguishing between faith and reason and by advancing the view that reason has no role at all to play in religious issues. Fideism, thus, sees science and religion as too autonomous from each other, while the evidentialist's error is the opposite one.[5]

The proposal I will explore and (with some reservations) defend in the following inquiry is a reconceptualization of the theism versus atheism and evidentialism versus fideism issues in an explicitly *ethical* manner—though obviously only some selected perspectives on such an enormous task can be taken up in a single chapter. Indeed, both evidentialism and fideism, arguably, turn out to be insufficiently ethical responses to the problem of theism versus atheism. The traditional alternatives themselves—that is, theism and atheism, when characterized as opposed metaphysical standpoints regarding the question of God's existence—suffer from the same insufficiency. Philosophical debates over these matters have unfortunately often ignored the ethical, hence pragmatic, aspects of the problem of God's reality;[6] or, more precisely, philosophers of religion have traditionally been interested only in the ethical implications theism (or atheism) might have, instead of considering whether theism (or atheism) might itself be grounded in ethical premises, or whether such metaphysical issues might in the end be inevitably entangled with ethical ones. It is to these ethical issues at the heart of the theism debate that I suggest we should turn our attention. This suggestion amounts to a Kantian—and pragmatist—rearticulation of what the question is ultimately about. However, while Immanuel Kant's doctrine of the "postulates of practical reason" and William James's pragmatist defense of the legitimacy of religious faith will function as my starting points, this chapter is not a historical study of either Kant's or James's philosophy of religion. Rather, I will use these two classics as sources of inspiring perspectives on the complexities of the theism issue. My primary purpose is not to get either Kant or James (or any of their interpreters) right but to say something right, or at least something worthy of further consideration, about the systematic problem of theism (and atheism) with the help of these important thinkers. (James will be more comprehensively discussed in chapter 4.)

In particular, I will employ Kantian and Jamesian insights in order to argue that the theism issue is not exhausted by the narrowly intellectual (evidentialist) considerations one might advance in favor of either theism or atheism. Accordingly, theism should not be reduced to the mere metaphysical theory that God exists. Rather, we need the resources of what Kant called "practical reason"—the kind of reason that James, the pragmatist, saw as (in a certain sense) pervading human reason-use generally—in order to arrive at any humanly acceptable solution to this problem. It is, in short, not only philosophically narrow-minded but downright *unethical* to leave the ethical aspect out of such a major metaphysical problem as the one of (a)theism. Theism *might*, I will suggest, be rationally acceptable in terms of practical reason, or more generally from the standpoint of the vital human needs and interests embedded in our practices of life, and this *is* a kind of rational justification; nevertheless, it is very different from the kind of justification standardly aimed at in the evidentialist discourse on theism and atheism. Moreover, justification in terms of practical reason might be the *only* rational justification available for the religious believer. From a Kantian and Jamesian point of view, the religious believer's faith in God need not be made scientifically acceptable, or warranted in terms of religiously neutral criteria of reason (that is, either empirically verifiable or epistemically justified in a broader sense), because it is ultimately not a matter of science or reason (at least not primarily); the important thing is to make it *ethically acceptable* in the face of evil and suffering that we, believers and unbelievers, experience in the world we live in (see also chapter 5).

This chapter, by itself, will not defend either theism or atheism—nor will it defend either evidentialism or fideism. Rather, I will examine some central conceptual background assumptions a proper scrutiny of which I find necessary for any philosophically adequate account of the complex situation we face when considering the problem of God—and the problem of what a proper human response to this question ought to be. The major suggestion for revision regarding the assumptions we habitually make here amounts to a rethinking, an ethical reorientation, of this problem framework. Far from dispensing with the metaphysical status of the theism versus atheism dispute, however, I see the proposed rethinking of the ethical (pragmatic) aspects of theism as a rethinking of the relation between ethics and metaphysics. In this sense, our explorations in the philosophy of religion will provide us with a case study of the relations between two traditionally separate philosophical subdisciplines that we should, in my view, seek to integrate. Yet, such integration should not sacrifice pragmatic pluralism about the multiple perspectives we pragmatically need for an adequate understanding of religion.

First, I will briefly explain, on Kantian grounds, why we should reject traditional (metaphysical) versions of theism, especially the kind of rational "proofs" of God's existence that pre-Kantian philosophers—and even some contemporary philosophers—have employed. I will then present the Kantian (and pragmatist) "moral argument" for theism, drawing particular attention to the question of whether this argument should be understood as metaphysical, ethical, or both. Next, I will continue the discussion of the relation between these aspects of theism in terms of the Kantian idea of the primacy of practical reason. Finally, I will briefly take up the problem of evil in this context, before providing some concluding remarks on relativism and pluralism, which will pave the way for further discussions of these matters in subsequent chapters. (The problem of evil will be revisited in more detail in chapter 5.)

The Dialectical Illusions of Traditional Theism

Even though I do not want to downplay the importance of David Hume as a major critic of theism, in my view Kant is obviously a turning point in the history of the philosophical criticism of traditional metaphysical theism. In the first *Critique*, Kant effectively challenged the legitimacy of the standard arguments (ontological, cosmological, and physico-theological) for God's existence.[7] There is no need to go through this familiar terrain here in detail. It is sufficient to note that, according to Kant, the most serious flaw in the "ontotheological" proof—according to which God must exist, because God is the greatest imaginable being and a necessary component of such maximal greatness is existence—is the confused assumption that existence is a "real predicate," denoting a property in the same way as predicates like "red" or "heavy" denote properties of individuals. The idea of an *ens realissimum*, a being with all perfections (that is, all positive predicates), is in the ontological proof illegitimately "hypostatized" into an object, although such a mysterious, transcendent object can never be given to us in experience. Reason naturally, inevitably, arrives at this idea, but the crucial error is made when the existence—indeed, necessary existence—of the corresponding entity is inferred. The "cosmotheological" proof (or family of proofs), in turn, relies on the ontological one by identifying the assumed necessary ground of all contingent beings with the *ens realissimum*. Whether the cosmological argument is formulated in terms of causal concepts (i.e., by invoking God as the "first cause") or merely, as Kant does, in terms of the supposed need to postulate a noncontingent being to ground all contingently existing ones, it amounts to a breach of the transcendental bounds of reason Kant has defended in the bulk of the first *Critique*. Finally, the physico-theological (or teleological) "design argument" fares no better, and few philosophers today take it seriously, given the obvious ways in which the universe does not seem to be well designed.[8] And even if it did so seem, the Kantian response is to point out that the one who postulates a cosmic designer for the totality of the world again illegitimately steps out of the bounds of sense set by the transcendental inquiries of the *Critique*. The "natural theology" of the physico-theological proof is as speculative and as seriously guilty of unjustified and unjustifiable transcendent assumptions as the "transcendental theology" involved in the ontological and the cosmological proofs.

The traditional theistic proofs are examples of reason's natural tendency to seek the "unconditioned" beyond the series of conditioned entities and events we come up with in the empirical world. Insofar as we remain at the level of mere "ideas" (concepts), there is no problem, and our tendency to form the idea of the unconditioned—in its various forms—is unavoidable. Problems arise when reason finds itself compelled to postulate the unconditioned object of such an idea. Such a move to the metaphysical unconditioned is, Kant tells us, simply beyond the capacities of human cognition. Human reason's habit of formulating ideas leading to "transcendental illusion" is natural and inevitable, but the theistic proofs are fallacies a critical thinker can and ought to avoid. According to leading contemporary interpreters of Kant, such as Henry Allison and Michelle Grier, the actual source of these fallacious inferences, in addition to the unavoidable transcendental illusion, is the (avoidable) commitment to *transcendental realism*, the doctrine that the world as the object of (possible) experience is the world as it is in itself. This doctrine fails to draw the crucial transcendental distinction between things as they are in themselves (that is, things as they would be when abstracted, *per impossibile*, from the conditions required for representing them) and appearances, the form of which is constituted by the human cognitive faculty (sensibility and understanding).[9]

If Kant is right, there is no rational hope for constructing either purely conceptual (a priori) or empirically premised ("design") "proofs" of the existence of God. It would be irrational, or uncritical at least, to build one's religious faith on the basis of such hopeless demonstrations. Kant's critical system as a whole has been rejected by many, perhaps most, contemporary philosophers, but even strongly anti-Kantian thinkers usually find Kant's attack on theistic metaphysical speculation convincing. Many have concluded that theism is not rationally defensible at all, and that atheism ought to be maintained instead. Others have concluded that, given the impossibility of defending God's existence by reason, faith should be adopted "irrationally," or perhaps "arationally," quite independently of reason and its capacities. This is the fideist solution, intended to contrast with evidentialists' demand for proof, evidence, and rational legitimation.[10]

It is this post-Kantian dialectics between evidentialism and fideism that I want to, at least to some extent, question here. In short, I will argue that while it is both intellectually and religiously illegitimate—even superstitious or pseudoreligious[11]—to seek religiously neutral rational proofs or evidence for God's existence, the theism versus atheism issue should not, and cannot, be reduced to an "arational" choice, either, into a mere matter of faith totally independent of reason. A critical, both intellectually and religiously respectable, perspective on this issue may be found, I will argue, if we are prepared to view the problem as *both ethical and metaphysical*, in a way that draws no principled dichotomy between these aspects of the problem.

Thus, I will take my lead from Kantian considerations of practical reason. Obviously, I will suggest that we can learn a great deal from Kant's reflections on theism and its relation to morality. It is only from the perspective of our moral life, that is, from the perspective of what Kant called practical reason, that theism arises as a rationally legitimate (and potentially religiously legitimate) response to the problems we experience. Nevertheless, we clearly need to *go beyond Kant*, toward something like the pragmatism defended by William James and some of his followers, if we want to fully trace out the pragmatic, ethico-metaphysical aspects of theism. As this book as a whole will argue, though, we should *not go too much beyond Kant*, definitely not along the slippery slope from James's pragmatism to Rorty's neopragmatism (see chapters 3 and 5).

Transcendental Arguments for Theism

Kant himself was a religious believer. Furthermore, he was not a mere "deist" in an Enlightenment style—in the manner of, say, Voltaire—but a theistic believer in a "living God." We may even say that he maintained the metaphysical view that there is a living God, even though (as we just saw) he vigorously attacked previous "pre-critical" metaphysicians', especially Leibniz's and Wolff's, desperate attempts to prove the existence of such a transcendent deity. I am neither interested in the details of Kant's own religious or theological views here nor in his Christian (specifically Protestant) background, but in his *postulates of practical reason* (namely, the freedom of will, the existence of God, and the immortality of the soul). It is, in particular, from the perspective of my proposal to (re-)entangle ethics and metaphysics in the philosophy of religion that this Kantian topic deserves scrutiny. We may ask, for instance, whether the postulates are defended by Kant (in the second *Critique*) by means of a *transcendental argument*, and if so, how that argument differs from the arguments defending the categories and other "epistemic conditions"[12] of objective cognition in the first *Critique*. Even more importantly, we should ask whether the defense of the postulates in "Dialectics" of the second *Critique* leads to a metaphysical position according to which God exists. I want to approach this question by suggesting that Kant's postulates are *both* metaphysical *and* ethical—indeed, in a way in which their metaphysical and ethical aspects are inextricably intertwined.

Even a paradigmatic case of a metaphysics built on ethics can be found in Kant's doctrine of the postulates of practical reason. Although this is not Kant's own way of putting the matter, we might say that this doctrine presupposes *transcendental idealism*: the world is not absolutely independent of us but is responsive to our ethical (or more generally valuational) needs and interests, or "in the making" through such needs and interests.[13] *We* structure reality in terms of what the moral law in us requires; there is no prestructured, "ready-made" world that we could meaningfully engage with. Notably, what I am here labeling transcendental idealism is a broader doctrine than the one defended in "Transcendental Aesthetic" of *Critique of Pure Reason*, because I am not merely following Kant in regarding space and time as properties of appearances (rather than as properties of things as they are in themselves) but more widely suggesting that the reality we find ourselves living in is structured by us—not merely by our "cognitive faculty" but also by our various practical interests and purposes. But *is* this structuring really metaphysical, or should we simply confine ourselves to an ethical, pragmatic, account of the Kantian postulates? Is there "really" a God, or are we just entitled to act "as if" there were one?

I cannot examine in any detail the way in which Kant constructs his famous "moral argument" for the existence of God and the immortality of the soul in the "Canon of Pure Reason"[14] and in "Dialectics" of the second *Critique*.[15] Rather, I will take up the question concerning the metaphysical status of Kant's postulates. It is clear that, as mere ideas of pure reason ("transcendental ideas"), the concepts of God and the soul lack "objective reality." At best, these ideas can be employed *regulatively*, not *constitutively*. This, however, is only the point of view that theoretical, speculative reason offers to the matter. From the perspective of practical reason—which, famously, is ultimately "prior to" theoretical reason in Kant's system[16]—there is indeed some kind of "reality" corresponding to these concepts (or ideas). The epistemic status of these concepts, when transformed into postulates of practical reason, is, to be sure, quite different from the status of the actual constitutive, transcendental conditions of any humanly possible experience, such as the pure concepts or categories of the understanding and the forms of pure intuition (space and time), explored in the "Transcendental Analytic" and the "Transcendental Aesthetic." We may say that the latter kind of concepts necessarily structure, according to Kant, the (or any) human, experienceable, cognizable world, that is, any objects or events we may conceivably encounter in this world. There would be no world of objects at all, at least no world we would be able to represent cognitively, in the absence of such structuring principles and categories. However, the postulates of practical reason also structure—in an analogical though definitely not identical manner—the human world as a world of ethical concern, deliberation, and action. The key idea here is that this "structuring" is not "merely ethical" but also metaphysical. Another key idea is that this structuring is, because of its uniquely ethical and metaphysical status, also transcendental.

In a recent article, Frederick Beiser has offered one of the most insightful interpretations of Kant's defense of "moral faith" as a genuinely metaphysical perspective on the reality of God and the immortal soul. He insists, against a number of commentators viewing Kant's philosophy of religion in a deflated "thisworldly" and immanent manner, that Kant's notion of the highest good, or *summum bonum*, is irreducibly

theological, quite explicitly derived from the Christian tradition, especially Augustine and the idea of a "City of God."[17] These notions, after
all, refer to a situation in which there is a harmony between the duties set
by the moral law and the happiness of moral agents acting on the basis
of, or out of respect toward (i.e., not merely in accordance with), this
law. Beiser accurately summarizes Kant's argumentation as follows:

1. We have a duty, set by the moral law, to promote the highest good
   (*summum bonum*).
2. We have to presuppose the conditions for the possibility of the highest good.
3. God's existence is a condition for the possibility of the highest good.
4. Therefore, we have to presuppose the existence of God.[18]

This argument, on Beiser's reading, is an argument *absurdum practicum*, as distinguished from an argument *absurdum logicum*. Unlike the
latter, that is, unlike traditional arguments of the form *reductio ad absurdum*, it does not purport to show that denying the conclusion would
yield a logical contradiction or lead to incoherence but that denying the
conclusion would result in a breach of one's moral duty (which, according to Kant, is itself a necessary demand of reason). According to Beiser,
the Kantian moral law and the moral faith based on the concept of the
highest good are, though epistemically independent of each other (in the
sense that one can, and indeed must, be committed to the duties morality sets us entirely independently of the highest good, and thus independently of theism), nevertheless logically dependent: the possibility of
acting on the basis of the moral law presupposes moral faith, because it is
a condition set by the law itself. We can know, independently of any religious standpoints, that the moral law binds us, i.e., that we are absolutely
committed to the duties it sets for us, but according to the *absurdum
practicum* argument we cannot really act on the basis of that law unless
we presuppose God's existence and the immortality of the soul.[19] As the
moral law requires us to pursue the *summum bonum*, it necessarily requires us to pursue whatever is required for this goal to be possible (pursuable) for us, and here both God's existence and the immortality of the
soul enter the picture. The harmony of morality (moral virtue) and happiness could never be achieved, and would not even be a possible goal, in

the absence of God. Moreover, this would not be a pursuable goal if there were no (potentially) "infinite progression" toward such a harmony in immortal life.

This is an argument I find essentially pragmatist, and indeed it resembles James's reflections on the will (or right) to believe and on the pragmatic need to postulate a divine reality. Beiser, however, in my view too sharply differentiates Kant's views from James's, construing the latter (in a typically misleading fashion) as "merely pragmatic" and immanent, thus not genuinely metaphysical in the sense in which he reads Kant's views as metaphysical.[20] He fails to see that James, too, can be interpreted as a pragmatically theistic metaphysician pretty much along Kantian lines, if we understand his "pragmatic method" not as a method of simply getting rid of metaphysical pseudoissues (in which case this method would be little more than an early version of the logical positivists' verificationist theory of meaning) but as a method of making explicit, of "distilling," the pragmatic core of metaphysical disputes that would otherwise remain obscure and interminable.[21]

When holding, with Kant, that God's existence and immortality are postulates of practical reason, we mean, roughly, that they are some kind of necessary auxiliary presuppositions needed for morality to be and mean what it is and means for us, presuppositions without which the highest good, which is set as a duty to us by the moral law, could not be realized. For Kant, these presuppositions are both subjectively necessary needs or interests of reason and objective requirements of morality arising "from within" the moral law dictated by reason itself. We can never know anything about God or the soul as they are in themselves, *qua Dinge an sich selbst*; we cannot know anything about them in the sense in which we can know something (a lot) about the empirical objects and events constrained by the transcendental conditions of possible experience, either; we can only "know" (or, rather, must postulate) them as objects required for the purposes of practical reason—purposes which, however, are, famously, primary to those of theoretical reason. I believe Beiser is correct when he emphasizes that Kant's defense of the postulates is not merely pragmatic or "immanent" in the sense of being detached from metaphysics and from the Christian, specifically Protestant, tradition that Kant had inherited and to which he contributed. The moral world in which the highest good is ultimately realized is readily comparable to the heavily metaphysically loaded notions of the City of God and *corpus mysticum*.[22] Kant is, then, genuinely a theist, a theistic metaphysician, and maintains that the very possibility of morality in the sense in which it is set to us as a task—more precisely, the possibility of pursuing what the moral law necessarily requires—really presupposes a metaphysical commitment to the existence of God, even though this commitment can rationally and legitimately only be made from the perspective or standpoint of practical (instead of theoretical) reason. It is important to notice that metaphysics and ethics are deeply entangled here. Somewhat controversially Beiser argues, furthermore, that the hot scholarly debates over whether Kant's ideal of the highest good is noumenal or phenomenal, or transcendent or natural, or other-worldly or this-worldly, are misguided, presupposing a false premise according to which these are mutually incompatible alternatives; insofar as we are dealing with a truly Christian ideal here, both alternatives can be realized, as the world will eventually be completely transformed through Christ's second coming.[23]

We hardly need to go that far, whether or not Kant himself did. Yet, we have to realize that Kant's defense of the postulates and of "moral faith" through them is still a *transcendental* justification for a kind of metaphysics, though not a justification for any *transcendent* metaphysics postulating mysterious objects for the contemplation of (mere) theoretical reason.[24] However, the transcendentality at work in the arguments for the postulates is now found within our practices of moral deliberation under the guidance of the moral law, or the categorical imperative. If theistic metaphysics (or immortality as another component of such metaphysics) is understood as requiring justification from the point of view of speculative, theoretical reason, then all that results will be paralogisms and the errors involved in the traditional proofs for God's existence, criticized in the first *Critique*. The true Christian metaphysician avoids *such* metaphysics, but she/he need not—and should not, if Kant is right— avoid ethically inspired pragmatic metaphysics. Practical reason may, according to Kant, legitimately widen the scope of the ideas left problematic by theoretical reason and render their objects real;[25] the concepts and objects postulated by practical reason may even be constitutive, instead of being merely regulative, as the ideas of pure reason must remain in their only theoretically legitimate employment.[26] Thus, practical reason may turn reason's ideas from a merely regulative use into a constitutive use, which does not, however, make those ideas dogmatic principles to be avoided by critical metaphysicians.[27] In a fully transcendental sense (though not, again, exactly in the same sense in which the categories and the *Anschauungsformen* are transcendental), the postulates must be invoked to "structure" the world we—morally speaking—live in. The need to embrace these postulates, particularly theism, is something that arises, to use J. J. Valberg's expression, from within "our horizon," which for us opens up the world.[28]

The Kantian argument for God's existence, even though it is a moral argument, remains transcendental in the sense of examining necessary conditions for the very possibility of certain humanly given phenomena (in this case, morality). I would even go as far as saying that Kant, or the Kantian metaphysician (including even James, when seen as an unorthodox quasi-Kantian pragmatist metaphysician), argues transcendentally for the need to postulate transcendent objects or principles (such as God), even though the transcendence involved in them can only be legitimately postulated (immanently) "from within" the practices of morality that transcendentally require them. It is possible to defend a transcendent postulation, or the postulation of transcendence, by means of transcendental reasoning or reflection.

Some people will at this point undoubtedly protest that such transcendence is not transcendent enough, that it is a mere pale shade of the real thing. Well, this is all we can have in the Kantian setting: no illegitimate speculation about the metaphysics of pre-given, dogmatic principles or entities (structured prior to our moral point of view) is needed or even possible. The crucial conclusion at this point is that Kant's defense of "moral faith"—as a form of theism—is both metaphysical and ethical. In an adequate account of theism, these aspects of theism should be synthesized in a Kantian manner. Jamesian pragmatism, though different from Kant's transcendental philosophy in obvious ways, joins in this synthesizing effort.

The Primacy of Practical Reason

I thus, finally, arrive at the basic argument of this chapter. This argument has already emerged in my reflections above: if we want to employ the Kantian strategy in defending theism in terms of, or from the standpoint of, practical reason, then we need to soften the boundary between metaphysics and ethics. The metaphysical aspects of theism must be fully integrated into its (possibly even more fundamental) ethical aspects. Alternatively, the ethical aspects of the problem can be seen as fundamental by seeing *them* as metaphysical in an important sense: it is, precisely, the way we ought to structure the world we live in that will lead us to embrace, or perhaps rather avoid, theistic postulations. The metaphilosophical status of the issue of theism must, hence, be thoroughly rethought in terms of this metaphysics-ethics entanglement. To paraphrase Kant, a theistic (or, indeed, atheistic) metaphysics without ethics would be blind, whereas a merely ethical reconceptualization of the issue—in which the metaphysical element would be totally lacking—would be empty.

In addition to Kant's doctrine of the postulates, another crucial example of the entanglement of metaphysical and ethical perspectives on the issue of theism is available in James's pragmatism.[29] James has not usually been read as a Kantian thinker, but we have already seen that his position, especially regarding theism and immortality, can be fruitfully compared to Kant.[30] From a pragmatist point of view, as much as from the Kantian one, ethics and metaphysics are profoundly entangled. Moreover, in our Kant-James comparison, it is extremely important to emphasize the primacy of practical reason, as has been done above. Religion, or theism, is pragmatically legitimated as a postulate needed for morality, for our ethical life and practices. Yet, no theological ethics in the style of, say, divine command theory can be rationally accepted by a critical moral philosopher. Claiming that ethics can be grounded in or based upon theology (or religious revelation) would seriously misrepresent the relation between ethics and religion. What we need, according to both Kant and James, is *moral theology*—a theology based on ethics, rather than vice versa. Any attempt to base ethics on theology, or religion, would be an example of heteronomy instead of autonomy (in Kantian terms), but the only critical and rational way to provide a basis for theology is the ethical way.

There is a problem here, though. Is theism (or the "theological postulate")[31] here practically (pragmatically) legitimated a priori, by reason's capacities only (as it definitely is in Kant), or does it receive its legitimation empirically or psychologically, as an attitude de facto "energizing" moral life, because we are the kind of beings we are (as the matter seems to be in James)?[32] My suggestion here is that just as Kantian transcendental (critical) philosophy more generally synthesizes the precritically opposed epistemological doctrines of empiricism and rationalism, and just as pragmatism, especially in neopragmatist writings such as Hilary Putnam's, attempts to bridge the gap between facts and values,[33] we should try to reconcile Kantian (transcendental) and Jamesian (pragmatist, empirical, psychological) ways of justifying theism ethically. I am not saying that such arguments will inevitably or immediately succeed; that would be a much more ambitious claim. What I am suggesting is that the Kantian aspects of theism need pragmatic rearticulation, and that the thus rearticulated pragmatic aspects of theism must not be thoroughly disconnected from the Kantian transcendental work of practical reason. Both the Kantian and the pragmatist see theism as, primarily, a problem of human life. For both, the ultimate question is the moral basis of metaphysics, especially theistic metaphysics. For neither can the theism issue be resolved in total absence of ethical considerations.

I have in the preceding section freely spoken about transcendental arguments when discussing Kant's strategy of defending theism as a postulate of practical reason. We should of course be extremely careful here, and I have already pointed out that the argument we may identify in the second *Critique* is not transcendental in the same way in which Kant's arguments for (say) the objective reality of the categories in the first *Critique* are. In fact, Kant himself quite explicitly renounces transcendental arguments in theology. For him, transcendental arguments are above all designed to demonstrate that (and to show how) certain conceptual assumptions are required as preconditions of any humanly possible experience. A transcendent God, if he exists, will inevitably fall beyond such experience. No argument can, as we have seen, justify one's belief in God in the same way in which our belief in, say, causality is rationally justified, or even transcendentally demonstrably true—that is, according to Kant, apodictically certain. Thus, in Kant's own sense, the "transcendental argument" for theism as a postulate of practical reason is not a transcendental argument, at least not properly speaking. Kant (who occasionally himself conflates the transcendent and the transcendental, while of course officially keeping them strictly apart) says explicitly that we should not resort to any transcendental arguments in theology, and he even uses the very expression, "transcendental argument," in this context, even though it was for a long time widely believed that he never employed this exact wording (which became standard usage only after P. F. Strawson and other twentieth-century transcendental philosophers).[34]

Even so, let us reconstruct the Kantian argument for theism in the following explicitly transcendental shape:

1. Human moral pursuits (that is, pursuing what the moral law requires, or more specifically, pursuing the highest good) are possible *only if* (we believe that) God exists (and, *mutatis mutandis*, if we [believe that we] possess an immortal soul).[35]
2. Moral pursuits are possible (because actual).
3. Therefore, (we should believe that) God exists (and, *mutatis mutandis*, we possess an immortal soul).

It should be clear that theism, even though it is a transcendent hypothesis, is here arrived at through a transcendental-sounding reasoning concerning the conditions necessary for the very possibility of a given human actuality, namely, the pursuit of morality (on the basis of what the moral law requires). This argument yields the properly transcendental aspect of what we may call Kantian theism. Insofar as Kantian theism is "pragmatic," at least in the sense of relying on the *absurdum practicum* argument identified by Beiser, what we have here is a transcendental aspect of pragmatic theism. The crucial transcendental reflection needed in support of the argument must, obviously, focus on the major premise (1). The minor premise will be denied only by moral nihilists, whom we would not expect to be interested in a Kantian defense of theism in the first place; at any rate, Kant himself is hardly seriously concerned with defending the possibility (or even the actuality) of morality, which he sees as obvious enough, in need of no philosophical defense. It is the "transcendental how" question[36] that he—here as much as in the theoretical philosophy—is asking, and God's existence, theism, emerges as a response to that question. We may see Kant's "Dialectics of Practical Reason" as an attempt to offer the support needed for the first premise, though as a reading of Kant this must remain controversial.

For comparison, I will attempt the following reconstruction of what might be seen as the Jamesian argument for theism:

1. Human moral pursuits (that is, "morally strenuous living" or the "morally strenuous mood" of life) are possible, in a full, serious, and "energizing" sense, *only if* (we believe that) God exists.
2. Human moral pursuits are possible (because actual).
3. Therefore, (we should believe that) God exists.

James, and to some extent even Kant, is characteristically ambivalent about the two versions of this argument made explicit in the parenthetical additions of doxastic operators. God's existence is argued to be necessary for ethics either as a mere belief or as a reality. Both readings are preserved in the argument schemes above, because I do not here want to take a definite stand on the correct interpretation of either Kant's or James's position in this regard. However, this very distinction may itself be a problem for a properly Kantian transcendental philosophy—and for a properly Jamesian pragmatism. After all, the way the world is— including the reality or unreality of God—may itself to some extent depend on our categorizing perspectives, to which our beliefs, especially those beliefs that we find ourselves ethically compelled to endorse, may crucially contribute. James occasionally speculates with the possibility of God's being dependent on our believing. As a straightforward causal claim, this sounds absurd—or atheistic at best—but as a Kantian-like transcendental claim about all our ontological postulations, including religious or theological ones, being transcendentally dependent on our human epistemic and ethical perspectives it is much more plausible.[37]

In the Jamesian case, premise (2) is not indubitable, at least not in the way it is in Kant, because we might be in real danger of arriving at a kind of moral nihilism, if we take seriously the "scientific," materialist view of the world according to which there is merely the "dead," physical universe without any "higher" or "spiritual" elements. The Jamesian pragmatist—or the philosopher who wants to introduce Jamesian pragmatic aspects into the Kantian defense of theism—cannot take the reality of the moral point of view for granted. Morality *may* turn out to be an illusion. This is a genuine threat in our permanently insecure human existence. There can be no metaphysical guarantees of a "happy end" for the universe we inhabit or even for the significance of a single moment of a human life within it. We can never be absolutely sure, purely intellectually speaking, that there truly is a place for such a thing as morality in our lives.[38] However, it is right here that the Kantian (or quasi-Kantian) transcendental aspects of theism—and of morality—return to our picture. It is precisely because of the highly uncertain situation in which we humans must face the world we live in, precisely because we cannot take for granted that there is a place for (genuine) morality in our lives, precisely because nihilism and universal death might be the "be all and end all of all things" (as James sometimes worries), that we *are*, ethically speaking but metaphysically as well, justified in adopting the theistic belief, which then, *ex post facto*, will (if anything will) be able to render our lives morally significant, after all. It is our very human insecurity, the problematic circumstances we continuously find ourselves in, the precarious yet ethically demanding structure of our lives, that justifies our employing all the pragmatic methods we might find at our disposal in order to secure the moral significance of our existence. What we have to do here is to employ our active will to believe in the reality of God—to make a Kierkegaardian leap of faith—in order to liberate our moral energies to viewing the world and our lives as ethically meaningful.

It is along these lines that we should, for instance, read James's defense of theism—and the corresponding criticism of materialism or atheism—in the third lecture of *Pragmatism*. The argument can even be seen as (quasi-)transcendental, or transcendental in a pragmatized and naturalized sense, if we start from the premise that human life as we know and experience it *is* morally significant. That is, if we treat this presupposition as non-negotiable—if we simply refuse to adopt moral nihilism—then we can argue for theism as a precondition of such a "given" actuality of our life that we cannot call into question. The argument will be relativized to contingent situations of human life and to historically transformable facts about what we find significant in our lives—that is, what *we* find negotiable and non-negotiable—but it will be a transcendental argument at any rate, at least if we are prepared to soften our notion of a transcendental argument and to blur the boundary between transcendental and pragmatic arguments, which is often regarded as sharper than it needs to be.[39] However, if we do find moral nihilism a "live option" for us (to use Jamesian language once again), then we cannot argue for theism in this transcendental manner. Then we are only justified in adopting theism as the "energizing" source for our moral life, as an empirical and psychological "hypothesis" that may, but need not, enable us to view our lives as morally significant in a manner we are (or at least may be) unable to view them if we start from atheism.

A lot depends, then, on whether or not we regard moral nihilism as a plausible, or even possible, starting point for our ethical and metaphysical reflections. If we do, then there is no hope for a transcendental argument, even for a pragmatic transcendental argument, in favor of theism. Such an argument can never succeed, if its critic can resort to moral nihilism. Even then, theism may be defensible as the "energizing" solution to life's moral dilemmas (as James would put it), though. But, more importantly, if we do not find moral nihilism a possible starting point— that is, if our rejection of such nihilism is non-negotiable, as it surely is in Kant, and if, in short, such a nihilism is for us a nonstarter—then the Kantian transcendental and the Jamesian pragmatic arguments for theism, in the forms in which I have analyzed them, seem to coincide. In this case, there certainly are crucial pragmatic aspects in the form of theism I have labeled Kantian (whether or not anything I have said does justice to any of these two thinkers).

In both cases, what we arrive at through the ethical transcendental argument is a form of moral theology, instead of any theological ethics, as was already explained above. God's reality is based on the needs and interests of our moral life. Furthermore, in order for such a grounding of a metaphysical thesis in ethical premises to be possible, some kind of (pragmatic) transcendental idealism must presumably be embraced. The metaphysical reality of God cannot, we have seen, be settled independently of ethical considerations. Whether or not there is a God, whether or not a "moral salvation" of the world is possible, whether or not life is meaningful and significant in some deep sense—these issues are not decidable in the absence of moral deliberation and the ethical perspectives we bring into our world and lives. This is what I mean by the suggested "rethinking" of the relation between metaphysics and ethics in the philosophy of religion. Such a rethinking was initiated by Kant in his very important doctrine of the postulates of practical reason, examined above, but it was through James's pragmatism that a new page was turned in this process. My results in the present inquiry are, hence, indebted to both Kant and James, though I have not sought to interpret any of these two philosophers in any great scholarly detail in this chapter.[40]

It is roughly in this sense that I am advancing the "primacy of practical reason," an idea vigorously defended by Kant and inherited by James—though everything James took from Kant he took, so to say, against his own will, because he abhorred Kant's complex system and heavy transcendental terminology. We must, however, go beyond both Kant and James in arguing not simply for the *primacy* of practical reason in relation to theoretical reason (in the case of theism in particular, or in ethics and the philosophy of religion more generally) but for the deep *entanglement* of practical reason with its theoretical counterpart. There is, after all, only one human reason. It is, in Jamesian terms,[41] the "whole man in us" (James's sexist language use here notwithstanding) that is at work whenever we set out to settle such morally and religiously vital issues as the one concerning God's existence. There can in the end be no neat separation between the theoretical and the practical faculties of this "whole man." This is what has in fact been argued above under the rubric of the entanglement of metaphysics and ethics. This is also, accordingly, what I have meant by saying that the defense of theism as a postulate of practical reason (Kant) or as a pragmatic commitment designed to "energize" our moral lives (James) is not "merely pragmatic" (immanent) in the sense of being detached from metaphysics—the realm of theoretical reason—altogether.[42] It is both ethical and metaphysical, and it is right here that the theoretical and practical concerns of reason interpenetrate and (transcendentally) condition one another.

We should not simply—reductively—say, then, that religion (or religious metaphysics) is ethically grounded, according to Jamesian pragmatism. Rather, it can be suggested that there is something like a *reciprocal containment* or *holistic mutual adjustment* between religion and ethics. Ethical considerations ground religious commitments as postulates of practical reason in the Kantian sense explicated above. The latter, however, then make the ethical pursuit itself possible as the truly motivating pursuit it must be in order to be ethical at all. Both are needed for the other to be possible in a fully human manner. Thus, in a way, the ethical grounds of religion and religious metaphysics are integrated.[43]

After all, we might even regard this holistic entanglement of theory and practice, or perhaps better their inseparability, as a defining characteristic of pragmatism, particularly James's version of it. The pragmatist, when reasoning about theism or about anything else, does not naively set practice prior to theory but theorizes in and through practice—and, conversely, attempts to practice whatever she/he theorizes about. Theism, in particular, will then be a truly "live" issue to be lived and examined. It will be a genuine option, and thus a potential candidate for an issue to be resolved through the will to believe strategy, though any human opinions we may arrive at concerning such a major problem of our (theoretical-cum-practical) reason must remain fallible and controversial—and it is simple pragmatic wisdom to recognize this fallibility.

The Problem of Evil

A redescription of the problem of evil—another traditional problem in the philosophy of religion and, moreover, a problem often taken to haunt theism, in particular—is also needed, if one emphasizes the Kantian and the pragmatic aspects of the theism issue in the way I have done. The metaphysics of (a)theism, when approached through the kind of pragmatic and transcendental arguments sketched in the previous section, is inevitably a humanized metaphysics of good and evil, given the essential connection between the postulation of God and the concerns of moral life, or the requirements of the moral law.[44] However, it is clearly not only the theist who can provide moral reasons for her/his belief; the atheist may offer, and many atheists have in fact offered, a straightforward, and very powerful, ethical argument against God's existence—a kind of "atheological" argument—by relying on the obvious, familiar, undeniable fact that there is apparently unnecessary evil in the world we experience and live in:

1. If God exists, he is supremely powerful (omnipotent), omniscient, and benevolent.[45]
2. A supremely powerful, omniscient, and benevolent being would remove or prevent all unnecessary evil and suffering.
3. There is unnecessary evil and suffering.
4. Therefore, there is no supremely powerful, omniscient, and benevolent being.
5. Therefore, there is no God (as traditionally understood).

Here, the empirical and factual premise (3) is usually taken to be obvious enough, although there are theistic believers who famously attempt to develop theodicies by denying that the evil and suffering we undeniably seem to find in our world are unnecessary. I will not discuss this line of thought here, because I find it implausible and misleading not only in philosophical but also religious terms.[46] Nor will I discuss those suggestions, such as James's, that deny premise (1), postulating not an infinite but a limited, finite God.[47] Despite the undeniable interest of such ideas, they are so far removed from any theism that people in the Christian tradition would find a genuine option that they need not be considered at this point.

The crucial issue here, as in the previous sections, is the relation between ethics and metaphysics in the problem framework of evil. In traditional theism, evil poses a logical or evidential challenge.[48] Thus, the existence of evil challenges the metaphysical view called theism, which operates with the notion of an omnipotent, omniscient, and supremely good being. It is supposed that this metaphysical view can be evidentially tested and evaluated independently of ethical considerations, simply by weighing rationally available evidence for and against it. The reality of evil is taken to be evidence for atheism, or at least evidence against theism (and perhaps in favor of agnosticism rather than atheism). Now, if my argumentation is even partly plausible, it is a fundamental mistake to view evil in this way. What we are dealing with when dealing with the so-called problem of evil is not simply an evidential (let alone a purely logical) challenge to the rational acceptability (or simply coherence) of the theistic metaphysical hypothesis. What we are dealing with is a fundamental ethical problem concerning the ways we humans interpret (or "structure") the world we live in. The problem of evil is, above all, an ethical problem, and as such a dramatic challenge to our human form(s) of life, to the ways we interpret and experience our world, and it is precisely for this reason that it is a metaphysical problem as well. It is a problem about how we ought to, or how we can, construe the basic structures of the reality we inhabit. Should we, or can we, morally speaking, postulate an infinitely powerful, supremely benevolent being as the agent finally responsible for all *this*? Should we rather reject such a theistic (and, possibly, theodicist) postulation?[49] Employing the pragmatic method outlined by James, we should always ask what such questions come down to in practical terms, that is, in terms of the potential practical effects their possible answers, or our commitment to such answers, might have in our lives. The "cash costs" (in terms of possible human experience, especially moral experience) of a theodicist postulation of an omnipotent, omniscient, and absolutely benevolent deity ultimately responsible for the horrible sufferings of innocent human beings, including children, just because those sufferings are not "real" after all, or are necessary elements of a plan that is generally good, are in my view much higher than the "cash value" such a postulation might have because of its ability to solve certain logical or evidential dilemmas.

A theistic commitment in a world in which there undeniably is unnecessary evil is a very difficult commitment to make, but it *might* render a believer's life meaningful in a profound sense, and thus help her/him in living further, and in facing the evil there is, even in desperate circumstances. On the other hand, the believer might also find her/his faith being fragmented through experiences of evil and suffering.[50] There is no easy solution available here; everything depends on the overall moral shape one's life takes. We again arrive at the conclusion that the metaphysics of theism cannot be regarded as an abstract intellectual matter to be decided in terms of evidence, such as the existence of evil. Rather, the existence of evil constitutes a framework within which we, as moral agents, ought to carefully consider the ethical aspects of any metaphysical commitments we make. We might "structure" reality into such a metaphysical shape that it becomes ethically unbearable; indeed, this is what happens, in my view, in theodicist attempts to "defend God" and his scheme of things in the face of "merely apparent" suffering. Philosophical, speculative, rationalizing theodicies are, at worst, an insult against all those who suffer, and philosophers defending them should go back to their libraries and open a couple of crucial passages in *The Brothers Karamazov*.

The hopelessness of any philosophical theodicy is not only a conviction shared by Kant and James but a natural outcome of our Kantian-cum-pragmatic reasoning about theism.[51] If the very possibility of arguing for or against theism requires a morally serious framework, a situation of both individual and social life in which the moral perspective on one's own agency is taken fundamentally seriously, then one cannot just treat evil as a merely evidential concern. The kind of theism that emerges as a possible result of the pragmatic argumentation examined in the previous sections—that is, the kind of theism that *might* be defensible as a postulate of practical reason in Kant's sense (or, with some qualifications, in a Jamesian sense)—does not leave room for a theodicist consideration of the evidential pros and cons of theism in relation to evil. It is, indeed, much more religiously sensitive to detach the topic of evil from the issue of theism altogether, to approach it as an ethical and political problem rather than a theological one,[52] than to confuse religious thinking by treating the problem as an evidential challenge. If you cannot think about evil within your religious outlook without lapsing into theodicy, then you better not think about it within that outlook at all. Paradoxically, a secular approach to evil may thus be the more genuinely religious one (cf. also chapter 5 and the conclusion).

The problem of evil, then, requires rethinking along the lines of the ethics-metaphysics entanglement, just as much as the problem of theism versus atheism does. In both cases—and the prior case is in a way a special instance or an outgrowth of the latter—a pragmatic approach yields a morally sensitive picture of how we ought to think about such matters of vital importance. This picture maintains a touch of transcendentality, in a (quasi-)Kantian sense, given the role played by transcendental considerations of what is possible or impossible, or what makes and does not make sense, within human moral life as we know it "from within." It is worth recalling that James was never insensitive to the experiences of evil that human beings had to go through in their lives; on the contrary, he saw Leibnizian and Hegelian theodicies as crudely morally insensitive.[53] The unacceptability of theodicism, the ethical unbearability of the alleged need and value of theodicies in the philosophy of religion, is part and parcel not only of the ethics but also of the metaphysics of theism, pragmatically considered.

The discussion of the problem of evil in this chapter has been only preliminary, however. A more extended, equally Jamesian-inspired discussion of why this particular problem should encourage us to see our philosophical theoretical activities of inquiry and reflection as seriously limited will be provided in chapter 5.

Final Reflections

The immediate goal of this chapter has been to illuminate some basic issues concerning the status of theism (and the theism versus atheism dispute)—as well as the metalevel contrast, evidentialism versus fideism—from the perspective of the question concerning the relations between metaphysics and ethics. I have proposed that pragmatism and Kantianism should be integrated, and that their synthesis is most valuable especially because it enables us to pay attention to the emergence of another, even more important synthesis, namely, the one between metaphysics and ethics. Any "Kantian" or "pragmatic" form of theism worth the name must be an inseparable mixture of metaphysical and ethical commitments—or, better, it must be an ineliminably metaphysical position defended (and in the end only defensible) by means of ethical considerations starting from our moral practices and from the requirements morality sets us (that is, the moral law and the highest good, in Kant, and the need for a strenuous moral mood, in James—though, I must hasten to add, none of this requires us to commit ourselves to the particular moral philosophies defended by these two philosophers).[54]

It is from the perspective of the synthesis of ethics and metaphysics that I hope we might be able to view theism as a rationally justifiable option for a genuinely religiously inclined person in her/his life circumstances. This inevitably contextual and "aspectual" justification a believer might arrive at is very different from the kind of justification the evidentialist hopes to be able to provide. Theism, or any religious faith, can never be justified or rationally defended in terms of the same religiously neutral, fully objective general criteria of rationality that are used, for example, to ground our scientific theories about the empirical world. Theism can only, if at all, be "justified" within the moral life we must (an ethical "must"!) lead in any case—and this, again, is an irreducibly ethical commitment that is not based on any prior, or more important, considerations. This insight does not lead us to any unproblematic happy end in our reflections, of course. If it is only from within a life already experienced as morally demanding or challenging that we can so much as hope to reasonably defend theism (or *any* serious view in the philosophy of religion), then one might argue that only someone already committed to something like theism (in a Kantian or Jamesian sense) can be sufficiently open to the arguments I have sketched. If morality is possible only within a framework colored by the theistic assumption, then it might seem that anyone who really takes morality seriously will already have to be a theist, in which case the argumentation referring to the moral status of the theistic worldview would be futile. If, on the other hand, the argument is to be relevant from the perspective of a nonbeliever, then we must at least agree that the nonbeliever can take life morally seriously—even struggle to achieve the morally strenuous mood in her/his own secular way—in which case it is simply not true that theism is required for serious moral life, after all (although, even in this case, theism might be a legitimate option for a person seeking fundamental seriousness in her/his moral orientation).

This problem is closely connected with the issue of *relativism* in the philosophy of religion. I am invoking this problem not in order to solve it but only in order to conclude this chapter with an acknowledgment of our need to live with it, and to live up to its depth. The worry may arise that it is only from within a religiously informed perspective that arguments in favor of religious belief can rationally emerge in the first place.[55] This chapter cannot settle, or even conceptually illuminate, the problem of relativism, to which we will repeatedly return in the following chapters, both explicitly and implicitly (with no possibility of offering any theoretical resolution to the problem, though), but I may already have been able to give a glimpse of its urgency in the philosophy of religion, even though I have arrived at this particular problem only through an indirect route, by considering the possibility of synthesizing ethical and metaphysical aspects in Kantian-cum-pragmatic defenses of theism. I conclude by re-emphasizing our need to live, as harmoniously and "strenuously" as possible, with the haunting prospects of relativism, with the fact that we may never be able to justify our religious (or nonreligious, or any *weltanschaulichen*) commitments in a fully objective manner, to all parties potentially concerned. We have to take seriously the moral task of justification itself before we can even start arguing for, or against, theism. This is, above all, to accept the primacy of the moral point of view we are continuously challenged to occupy—and thus the autonomy of morality in relation to everything else, including religion—but it is this very primacy that renders that point of view deeply metaphysical, inseparably and ubiquitously embedded in everything that goes on in our human lives, in everything (including God) we may be able to find real from within those lives.

Instead of ending up with radical relativism, as fideism threatens to, the present discussion may have taken some steps toward a healthy pragmatic *pluralism* in the philosophy of religion. The theism versus atheism issue cannot be adequately settled from a single, privileged perspective but requires a plurality of perspectives, pragmatically balanced and harmonized in terms of their functional workability in the (would-be) believer's overall account of the ethico-metaphysical problem of God as a problem of her/his personal life, moral deliberation, and reflective ethical understanding. These perspectives include, as I have argued, both the Kantian approach to theism in terms of the postulates and Jamesian pragmatism (growing out of the Kantian notion of the "priority of practical reason"), but others might be invoked, too: for example, John Dewey's pragmatic naturalism (a development of pragmatism toward secularism that nevertheless retains a deep respect for the possibility of "naturalized" religious experience, as explained in chapter 2), and the Wittgensteinian quietist, mystical attitude to the world *sub specie aeternitatis* (which, in turn, may be seen as a version of the "natural piety" that Dewey's naturalism invokes). I believe we must defend the pragmatically pluralist metalevel view that all these perspectives—and perhaps others, including neopragmatist ones, which I won't take up until chapter 3—are needed and that the philosophy of religion, if pragmatically adequate, must hence be thoroughly *antireductionist*.

This antireductionism is ultimately also a key distinguishing feature between Kant and James. Kant's transcendental philosophy, while being a precursor of pragmatism, is more reductive than James's in the sense that everything must ultimately be based on the universal structure of human cognition and the moral law, as analyzed by Kant. James, clearly, is *not* a Kantian transcendental thinker in the sense of invoking such an immutable structure or even in the sense of explicitly presenting any transcendental arguments (though some of his arguments can be reconstructed as quasi-transcendental, as shown in this chapter). Yet, the basic Jamesian idea of examining the ethical conditions for the possibility of a pragmatically adequate metaphysics of theism is Kantian, or transcendental, in the sense that our commitment to the requirements of morality are the only possible ground of any religious views we may reasonably, or with full legitimation, maintain.

In this chapter, I have thus emphasized the Kantian background of pragmatism, but neither Kantian nor Jamesian resources *alone* are sufficient for the contemporary pragmatist philosopher of religion (nor are they sufficient in other fields of pragmatist philosophizing). I must, therefore, turn to the other important pragmatist standpoints I need to illuminate the phenomena of religion and religious experience from a practice-embedded, ethically engaged perspective: Deweyan naturalism (chapter 2) and Rortyan as well as Putnamian neopragmatism (chapter 3). I will return to issues such as the problem of evil (chapter 5) and the demarcation between "genuine" religiosity and pseudoreligiosity (Conclusion), only very preliminarily examined in this chapter. However, while James will not be the primary figure of the next two chapters, his pragmatic method—which I will return to more substantially in chapter 4—should be constantly kept in mind. The other pragmatist accounts to be considered next are explored within the context of a Jamesian-inspired pragmatist investigation of the ethically engaged relevance of the various philosophical perspectives we may adopt on religion, even when James himself is barely mentioned.

TWO

DEWEYAN PRAGMATIC
RELIGIOUS NATURALISM

John Dewey is often regarded as a purely secular thinker, a "naturalist" and "humanist." In most commentaries, Dewey's pragmatism—
including his moral, social, and educational thought—is barely, if at
all, connected with his views on religion,[1] in contrast to William James,
whose explorations of religious themes, emphasizing the value of individual believers' experiential perspectives, continuously attract scholars'
attention.[2] This chapter, however, deals with the socially oriented, pragmatically naturalist conception of religious faith Dewey developed in *A
Common Faith* (LW9:1–58)[3] and elsewhere, as well as Dewey's influence
on pragmatist and naturalist currents in the philosophy of religion.[4] In
particular, Dewey's distinction between "the religious," on the one hand,
and actual religions, on the other, will be emphasized. According to
Dewey, the religious aspects of experience can be appreciated without
metaphysical commitments to anything supernatural. Here a major
problem arises: can the religious qualities of experience be fully naturalized by understanding them in a Deweyan manner as imaginative relations to human ideals, or will such naturalization inevitably reduce

religious experience to something else (e.g., scientific, ethical, aesthetic, or political experience)?

Dewey's pragmatic naturalism thus again leads us to consider the ontological status of religious "reality" (religious values, ideals, and other "entities"). Hence, the issue of *realism* regarding religious experience and its objects (as well as scientific or philosophical studies of such experience and its objects) can be taken up as an analogy to the realism issue in Dewey's conceptions of science and inquiry.[5] This issue has potential applications not only for religious life but for theology and religious studies as well, that is, for any academic study of religion. From a Deweyan perspective, we may ask whether religious "reality" is "really there" independently of us or constructed by us—by our active pursuit of ideals. Finally, some comparisons to Wittgensteinian philosophy of religion and related currents will be made in order to situate the Deweyan approach in the field of recent philosophy of religion. One may examine the relation between Deweyan pragmatic naturalism and the radically antimetaphysical interpretations of religion offered not only by Wittgensteinians and neopragmatists like Rorty, but also by so-called continental thinkers such as Vattimo.[6]

I will not study the evolution of Dewey's views on religion. For example, his early involvement with the absolute theistic idealism represented by thinkers like Edward Caird cannot be discussed here.[7] Roughly, Dewey's work on religion can be divided into his early writings in the 1880–90s, the period from the mid-1890s to the late 1920s (during which his naturalism evolved and "religious issues tended to recede into the background"[8]), and his views in the 1930s (and later). According to Steven Rockefeller, Dewey had by 1894 rejected most religious teachings unique to Christianity, yet maintaining much of Christianity's ethical concerns[9]— and he never entirely gave up the idea of God, though he abandoned it in its traditional theological shape.[10] I will mainly focus on Dewey's mature position, especially *A Common Faith*, though I will refer to his writings prior to that book. The Deweyan approach to religion will, I hope, considerably enrich the Kantian-cum-Jamesian position that I started to develop in the previous chapter and to which I will return in chapters 4 and 5.

Deweyan Pragmatic Naturalism

Dewey was a naturalist in the sense of maintaining that the natural world—with its immense riches and varieties—is all there is.[11] There is nothing outside this all-encompassing nature. Human beings are natural creatures along with everything else. But nature may be much more than is dreamt of by scientific materialists and reductionists. Dewey's naturalism was never a crude form of materialism; Dewey understood "human nature" in an inherently teleological manner.[12] Even so, his pragmatic naturalism has usually been taken to diminish rather than highlight the importance of religion.[13]

Dewey urges that classical philosophical dualisms—such as mind and body, experience and nature, knowledge and action, science and technology, facts and values, or theory and practice—should be abandoned. Our human world is a mixture of these. In particular, the "experimentalist" attitude in inquiry rejects the traditional assumption, prevalent since Plato, that theoretical knowledge and practical action are fundamentally distinct. As soon as we abandon the "quest for certainty" characterizing this tradition, we realize that knowledge *is* action and theory *is* practice.

While nature, for Dewey, is everything, there is no privileged standpoint from which the fundamental metaphysical structure of nature "in itself" could be determined. Deweyan naturalism is thoroughly nonreductive. No scientific (or any other) discipline stands in an "absolute" position in describing and explaining reality. The Deweyan pragmatist, appealing to what is natural to human life, insists that such scientifically problematic things as values, freedom, purposiveness, and other culturally emergent features distinguishing us from mere animals belong to our "human nature." They do not lie beyond the natural world. On the contrary, our concept of nature must be modified in order to accommodate the undeniable fact that we naturally engage in normative evaluation of our actions.[14] It is through our participation in cultural practices, in value-laden forms of life, that we become fully human. This enculturation is a completely natural development. Hence, Deweyan naturalism is compatible with a richly "culturalist" conception of humanity,[15] maintaining that human life takes place in a "normative order" constructed and reconstructed in cultural practices.

From Dewey's perspective, the reductive (or eliminative) naturalists who seek to reduce, say, values to mere facts, to something nonnormative and allegedly more fundamental (or, more radically, seek to eliminate them from the scientific worldview), are not good naturalists. Naturalism ought to take seriously what belongs to the natural world. It is a central element of human nature that we are normatively concerned creatures, beings continuously engaged in evaluation. Our actions are guided by values, goals, and ideals. Thus, a full-blown naturalism is a pragmatic naturalism. It does not deny the reality of values and normativity, because they are crucial to our self-understanding as agents. While naturalism, as a general philosophical orientation, has often been criticized because of its tendency to lose normativity, this criticism does not apply to the nonreductive naturalism of the Deweyan stripe, which is, in a way, more thoroughly naturalistic than its reductive rivals. By embedding his nonreductive naturalism in pragmatism (or experimentalism, as he often preferred to call it), Dewey was able to accommodate values, for pragmatism starts from an action-centered picture of humanity, refusing to call such a picture into question on the grounds of an allegedly more fundamental scientific image of reality. Even natural science, the chief inspiration of reductive naturalism, is possible only within valuationally structured human life, as a goal-directed practice. As soon as we realize that the pragmatic, experimental way of thinking typical of science is by no means restricted to scientific inquiry, we may extend it to nonscientific inquiries, including ethical, social, and even religious "inquiry" arising the relevant "problems of men" in these fields. These, too, may reveal natural features of human practices.

Although Dewey argues against Cartesian epistemology (and, generally, against the Western tradition beginning with Plato's theory of eternal, immutable Forms as the objects of knowledge), it is not implausible to suggest that his naturalistic pragmatism is, like James's, (quasi-)Kantian: he inquires, from within our natural practices, into what constitutes those practices, regarding normative evaluation as a (naturalized) condition for the possibility of certain humanly important phenomena, including science.[16] In this sense, most contemporary naturalists have moved far away from Deweyan pragmatic naturalism, though some, including McDowell, have in their critiques of reductive naturalism taken steps toward Dewey.[17] It is against the background of nonreductive pragmatic naturalism that Dewey's remarks on religious qualities in experience must be understood. Dewey's naturalism is broad, inclusive, and tolerant enough to accommodate humanly natural experiences of and valuational perspectives on reality that can be, and perhaps ought to be, characterized as religious. Therefore, the nature versus culture dualisms sometimes emerging in discussions within contemporary philosophy of religion—for example, in the context of the realism debate[18]—are simply unpragmatic and largely irrelevant from the perspective of Deweyan naturalism.

The Message of A Common Faith

In interpreting Dewey's religious views, it is important to apply his pragmatic naturalism to religious values, ideals, and qualities of experience. The background here is the apparent clash between science and religion. This tension was a formative factor for Dewey's philosophy as a whole, a crisis to which he promised a pragmatist remedy.[19] In his (few) writings on religion he tried to resolve it by navigating between the perils of supernatural religions and religiously inspired moral conservatism,[20] on the one hand, and militant atheism, on the other, arguing that both lose religious qualities of human experience, reducing experience to something poorer and narrower than what it may become.

As Dewey puts it in *A Common Faith*, religious values can be "inherent in natural experience" (LW9:20). "Any activity pursued in behalf of an ideal end against obstacles and in spite of threats of personal loss because of conviction of its general and enduring value is religious in quality" (LW9:19). "The religious" must be liberated from the supernatural commitments of actual historical religions, from dogmas and doctrines that are, pragmatically, unnecessary. The values and ideals belonging to the religious attitude are not imaginary but real; they are "made out of the hard stuff of the world of physical and social experience" (LW9:33). The religious is, through this rearticulation, rendered part of nature—which, for Dewey, is all-encompassing.[21]

The basic contrast thus lies between religions and "the religious" (that is, religious experience, or religious qualities or aspects in experience).

The *proton pseudos* of both traditional religions and militant atheism is the identification of the religious with the supernatural, which disentangles religiosity from life.[22] Religion must be brought down to earth, to what is "common" between us.[23] Supernaturalism—especially the claim that religions have a monopoly of supernatural means to further human ideals—is an obstacle in pursuing the natural changes that are in our power to bring about; hence, religious values need emancipation (LW9:19–24, 38–39, 45, 50–53).[24] This is how Dewey contrasts his proposal to the quarrels between religious and scientific ideas:

> I shall develop another conception of the nature of the religious phase of experience, one that separates it from the supernatural and the things that have grown up about it. I shall try to show that these derivations are encumbrances and that what is genuinely religious will undergo an emancipation when it is relieved from them; that then, for the first time, the religious aspect of experience will be free to develop freely on its own account. (LW9:4.)

Thus, Dewey is about to tell us what is "genuinely religious"— apparently in contrast to what is pseudoreligious or superstitious. The key to this normative distinction lies in the difference between (a) religion(s) and the religious. A religion is "a special body of beliefs and practices having some kind of institutional organization," whereas "religious," as an adjective, does not denote any specific entity but "attitudes that may be taken toward every object and every proposed end or ideal" (LW9:8). Many elements of actual religions survive from "outgrown cultures" (LW9:6); we should leave such baggage behind. Religions largely "prevent . . . the religious quality of experience from coming to consciousness and finding the expression that is appropriate to present conditions, intellectual and moral" (LW9:8)—particularly to modern scientific thinking. Dewey, then, is not proposing *a* religion but "the emancipation of elements and outlooks that may be called religious" (LW9:8).

Dewey is above all speaking about religious experience, which is well in line with his more general project of raising experience into the status of a fundamental philosophical category.[25] However, Deweyan religious experience is social—his conception of the religious articulates a "common faith"—rather than individual, as in the equally experience-centered

philosophy of religion of his fellow pragmatist, James.[26] More importantly, religious experience, for Dewey, is not a special type of experience.
It is not *sui generis*.[27] As a quality of experience, "religious" can be connected with aesthetic, scientific, moral, or political experience,[28] as well as
with experiences of companionship and friendship (LW9:9). Whenever
there is "a change *of* will conceived as the organic plenitude of our being,"
there is a religious attitude, outlook, or function (LW9:13). Thus, "whatever
introduces genuine perspective is religious" (LW9:17). Since, for Dewey,
religious experience cannot be self-sustaining but requires other experiences (scientific, moral, social, political, aesthetic),[29] one might, in contemporary philosophical jargon, read him as saying that religious qualities of
experience *supervene* on those other, more fundamental, qualities, or that
they *emerge* from the latter.

As Deweyan religious experience is in and of nature, the attitude
which "attributes human achievement and purpose to man in isolation
from the world of physical nature and his fellows" is "essentially unreligious" (LW9:18). Thus, for Dewey, a paradigmatic case of a non- or even
pseudoreligious way of thinking is an individualist, supernaturalist account of spirituality isolated from other individuals. Conversely, the paradigmatic case of a social enterprise carrying religious qualities is science,
whose methods Dewey sought to incorporate into moral and political
"inquiries." "Faith in the continued disclosing of truth through directed
cooperative human endeavor is more religious in quality than is any faith
in a completed revelation," Dewey argues (LW9:18). Our "faith in intelligence" may, then, become religious in quality (LW9:19).[30] Here Dewey arrives at his famous definition, concluding the first chapter ("Religion
versus the Religious") of *A Common Faith*: "Any activity pursued in behalf
of an ideal end against obstacles and in spite of threats of personal loss
because of conviction of its general and enduring value is religious in quality" (LW9:19). The pragmatic "test" of the value of any religious endeavor
is, then, ultimately ethical—as it is in Kant (cf. chapter 1).

In the second chapter, "Faith and Its Object", Dewey repeats his trust
in the "new methods of inquiry and reflection" as having become "the
final arbiter of all questions of fact, existence, and intellectual assent"
(LW9:22–23). The scientific method can accept nothing as sacrosanct, beyond critical testing (LW9:27–28). There is no return to any prescientific

revealed religion. Dewey characterizes "faith" as "the unification of the self through allegiance to inclusive ideal ends, which imagination presents to us and to which the human will responds as worthy of controlling our desires and choices" (LW9:23). In moral faith, we are "possessed" by our imaginative vision of ideals; when this moral faith has a "unifying function," it may be called religious.[31] Again, there is no need to view the ideal ends "possessing" us as supernatural: "The assumption that these objects of religion exist already in some realm of Being seems to add nothing to their force, while it weakens their claim over us as ideals, in so far as it bases that claim upon matters that are intellectually dubious" (LW9:29; cf. 32–33). Yet, the "reality" of ideal ends and values is unquestionable. Dewey offers a pragmatic argument: it is "unnecessary" for the religious attitude to rely on supernatural dogma. Values arise from nature, having their roots in "natural conditions", emerging through imagination's "idealizing" existence (LW9:33). Dewey is a pragmatic realist about values and ideals when he notes: "The aims and ideals that move us are generated through imagination. But they are not made out of imaginary stuff. They are made out of the hard stuff of the world of physical and social experience" (LW9:33).

One of the imaginatively projected ideals dear to many is the idea(l) of God, reinterpreted by Dewey as the "*active* relation between ideal and actual" (LW9:34). Dewey adds, however, that he would not insist that the name "God" must be given to this (or anything) (LW9:34–35). He seems to suggest that *if* we speak about God, this is how we should do it: scientifically, naturalistically, immanently, rather than dogmatically or supernaturalistically, or through an illegitimate postulation of anything transcendent. Dewey's position is, then, compatible with our not using the concept "God." Yet, Dewey wanted to make room for our use of that concept, to understand people who cannot help using it.[32] The concept of God as a relation between the ideal and the actual also helps us to overcome the "lack of natural piety" that "militant atheism" suffers from: "A religious attitude . . . needs the sense of a connection of man, in the way of both dependence and support, with the enveloping world that the imagination feels is a universe. Use of the words 'God' or 'divine' to convey the union of actual with ideal may protect man from a sense of isolation and from consequent despair or defiance" (LW9:36). This way of conceptualizing divinity enables Dewey to connect his reflections with his more general view of continuous *growth* as our highest goal in experience. The growth of knowledge in scientific inquiry, or "growth in understanding of nature," may also be religious in its aims and aspirations (LW9:38). After all, the study of the mysteries of creation has often been viewed as a fundamentally religious activity.

In the third and final chapter, "The Human Abode of the Religious Function," Dewey considers at more length the social relevance of his conception of faith. He argues that there is no need to "shut religious values up within a particular compartment"—to draw a sharp division between the religious, on the one side, and the secular or profane, on the other (LW9:44–45).[33] The liberation of the religious from narrow supernaturalism is ethically and socially, even politically, relevant:

> I cannot understand how any realization of the democratic ideal as a vital moral and spiritual ideal in human affairs is possible without surrender of the conception of the basic division to which supernatural Christianity is committed. Whether or not we are, save in some metaphorical sense, all brothers, we are at least all in the same boat traversing the same turbulent ocean. The potential religious significance of this fact is infinite. (LW9:55–56)

We should appreciate our creative potential to grow and transcend our actual selves, struggling together toward the actualization of ideals, instead of assuming that our ideals are "already embodied in some supernatural or metaphysical sense in the very framework of existence" (LW9:56). Dewey's philosophy of religion is antimetaphysical (in a sense to be explored below): there is no such thing as "the very framework of existence," because existence itself emerges in and through human ideal-driven inquiries. Yet there is a tension here. Dewey, as a good naturalist, does seem to subscribe to something he describes as "the mysterious totality of being the imagination calls the universe" (LW9:56). There is, after all, the natural universe, giving rise to any human values and ideals there may be. Religious qualities of experience are inherently related to this mysterious nature, or the awe we feel when realizing that we are parts of it, and its growth.

I have quoted at length from *A Common Faith* in order to emphasize the naturalist aspects of Dewey's philosophy of religion. This book, though Dewey's most sustained articulation of a philosophy of religion, is not the only work in which he discusses religion. Some of his writings prior to *A Common Faith*—which was published when he was already seventy-five years of age—contain brief excursions to religion and religious experience.[34] For example, in *Human Nature and Conduct* (1922), Dewey says that the function of religion is "caricatured rather than realized" if religious consciousness is strictly separated from morality and science (MW14:181). He continues: "The religious experience is a reality in so far as in the midst of effort to foresee and regulate future objects we are sustained and expanded in feebleness and failure by the sense of an enveloping whole" (MW14:181). In the concluding pages, he returns to the issue:

> Religion has lost itself in cults, dogmas and myths. Consequently the office of religion as sense of community and one's place in it has been lost. In effect religion has been distorted into a possession—or burden—of a limited part of human nature, of a limited portion of humanity which finds no way to universalize religion except by imposing its own dogmas and ceremonies upon others; of a limited class within a partial group; priests, saints, a church. Thus other gods have been set up before the one God. Religion . . . has been perverted into something uniform and immutable. . . . Instead of marking the freedom and peace of the individual as a member of an infinite whole, it has been petrified into a slavery of thought and sentiment, an intolerant superiority on the part of the few and an intolerable burden on the part of the many. (MW14:226–227)

Views familiar from *A Common Faith* were, thus, already present in Dewey's earlier works.[35] The crucial point is that religion should return to an intimate connection with our other social pursuits: the "religious spirit" will, Dewey tells us in *Reconstruction in Philosophy* (1920/1948), be "revivified" when it is brought into "harmony with men's unquestioned scientific beliefs and their ordinary day-by-day social activities" (MW12:200). Then, poetry and religious feeling "will be the unforced flowers of life" (MW12:201). In *The Quest for Certainty* (1929), furthermore, Dewey characterizes the "religious attitude" as "a sense of the possibilities of existence and as devotion to the cause of these possibilities, as distinct from acceptance of what is given at the time," and urges the liberation of this attitude from "unnecessary intellectual commitments" (LW4:242–243; cf. 242–247). The potential energy of this attitude ought to be "released for positive activity in behalf of the security of the underlying possibilities of actual life" (LW4:243). The "unnecessary intellectual commitments" Dewey refers to are, again, the otherworldly ideas inherent in religious traditions. Such a postulation of an "other-world" is "a refuge, not a resource" (LW4:244).

After the publication of *A Common Faith* in 1934, a controversy over Dewey's religious views followed. Some traditional religious thinkers welcomed Dewey's "new" religiously inclined ideas, whereas others saw them as falling short of the real thing. For example, Reinhold Niebuhr claimed, in his review of Dewey's book, that Dewey was closer to traditional religion than he supposed.[36] In particular, Henry Nelson Wieman's comments in *Christian Century* caused some debate.[37] From Dewey's perspective, Wieman illegitimately hypostatized the *functional* unity of forces contributing to the good (forces he was prepared to call "God") into a "prior organic unity," reading his own views into Dewey.[38] Secular readers of Dewey, in turn, insisted that Dewey should not be interpreted as a theist in any traditional sense. In addition to reviews, several journal articles and book chapters on Dewey's religious ideas were published within a short period of time,[39] and doctoral dissertations on this topic soon appeared.[40] Dewey himself reviewed in the mid-1930s, before and after the appearance of *A Common Faith*, several books on religious and theological topics.[41] The discussion, succeeded by more general debates over the meaning of "naturalism,"[42] continued well into the 1950s and 1960s, and novel contributions (which I can barely mention here) are continuously published.

In the criticisms and interpretations following the publication of *A Common Faith*, a number of religious thinkers attacked Dewey's naturalization of religion. For example, J. W. Buckham pointed out that "religion has no vitality" without genuine faith in an actually existing personal deity.[43] In the 1939 Schilpp volume devoted to Dewey, Edward Schaub argued that Dewey was not entirely fair to supernaturalism, to which Dewey replied that "*A Common Faith* was not addressed to those who are content with traditions in which 'metaphysical' is substantially identical with 'supernatural.' It was addressed to those who have abandoned supernaturalism."[44] Naturalists wondered, on the contrary, why Dewey had to use the term "God" at all, given that his "God" "has so little relationship in function or content with the gods of old,"[45] and whether it wouldn't be more natural to see him as an atheist, after all. According to Corliss Lamont, Dewey is in no sense a theist, "but an uncompromising naturalist or humanist thinker who saw the value of a shared religious faith free from outworn supernaturalism and institutional fanaticism."[46] A more recent secular interpreter even claims that Dewey's "God" is something like the combination of social intelligence, democracy,[47] and science, and that the central issue of A Common Faith is social and political rather than religious.[48] As Horace Kallen put it in 1950, democracy and science are "the sacra and sancta of a common faith," which seeks peace and freedom and a universal respect for human rights.[49] And as Rockefeller in the 1990s points out, Dewey was not a theist, because he rejected any transcendent God, treating "God" as "a preferential term that could be employed as a poetic symbol to identify those forces and values in experience that are of ultimate concern to a people in their quest for well-being."[50]

A crucial issue to be examined next is the metaphysical status of the Deweyan divinity. I cannot deal with the commentators'—either Dewey's contemporaries' or more recent ones'—views in detail, but it is important to note that, from a traditional religious (Christian) perspective, Dewey's "God" lacks the attributes of a genuine theistic divinity, whereas from a naturalist perspective, it is hardly necessary to invoke such a pseudodivinity at all, because nature and its own, entirely this-worldly forces and dynamics are sufficient to account for human ideas and ideals as well. So *why* do we need, *if* we do, a Deweyan God? In what sense, if any, is the Deweyan God *real*?

Religious "Reality"—Ready-made or Constructed?

The pragmatically naturalist picture of religious values and qualities developed in A Common Faith seems to make the religious aspects of experience dependent on our ways of experiencing. This is a good reason to take a brief look at Dewey's perspective on the issue of realism and apply it to the religious case. The apparently sharp contrast between secular and theistic readings of Dewey may be based on the ignorance, on both sides, of the depth of the realism versus constructivism (idealism) tension in Deweyan pragmatism (and pragmatism generally).[51] The problem posed by *A Common Faith* is not just the contrast of *naturalism* versus *supernaturalism* but, implicitly, *within* his general naturalist approach, the *realism* versus *constructivism* tension: is religiously relevant "reality," even God (as an ideal), humanly "constructed" through intelligent thought, activity, imagination, and inquiry, or is such a divine reality "ready-made" out there in the (transcendent) world itself? The fact that this problem lies at the core of Deweyan philosophy of religion helps us to appreciate the fundamentally Kantian nature of his philosophical problems, analogously to the Kantian pragmatism already preliminarily developed in chapter 1, although he departed from Kant in obvious ways (even more obviously than James did).

Hence, we should connect Dewey's concern with "the religious" with broader issues of inquiry, particularly the problem of the reality of the objects of inquiry. Here Dewey's philosophy of religion touches his general pragmatist thought. Dewey's pragmatic "instrumentalism" (also called "experimentalism" or "operational thinking") accommodates an intriguing tension between standard realisms and antirealisms about the objects of inquiry. Dewey cannot be classified in the traditional terminology of the realism debate; yet, noticing a connection to this debate places his philosophy of religion in a proper perspective, often overlooked by his critics and sympathizers alike.[52]

Dewey's position in the philosophy of science is instrumentalist, more generally empiricist, although his talk about instrumentalism should *not* be equated with later philosophers' of science narrower treatment of the doctrine carrying the same title. In *The Quest for Certainty*, Dewey celebrates the operations and interaction needed for scientific knowledge, thereby rejecting the gap traditionally thought to lie between knowledge and action. This seems to lead to a form of antirealism:

> [The] scientific conceptions, like other instruments, are hand-made by man in pursuit of realization of a certain interest.... [W]hen the physical sciences describe objects and the world as being such and such, it is thought that the description is of reality as it exists in itself.... [However, the] business of thought is not to conform to or reproduce

the characters already possessed by objects but to judge them as po-
tentialities of what they become through an indicated operation. . . .
[T]o think of the world in terms of mathematical formulae of
space, time and motion is not to have a picture of the independent
and fixed essence of the universe. It is to describe experienceable
objects as material upon which certain operations are performed.
(LW4:109–10)

Science, accordingly, has no more privileged relation to "the real" than
(some) other human practices—including, perhaps, religious experience.
"Scientific conceptions" are not "revelations of antecedent properties of
real Being and existence" but "instrumentalities which direct operations
of experimental observations" (LW4:153–54). Natural laws, similarly, are
"intellectual instrumentalities," "*formulae for the prediction of the prob-
ability of an observable occurrence*," not statements about "ultimate and
rigid uniformities of being" (LW4:164–65). A law that was supposed to
"govern phenomena" ought to be understood as "a way of transacting
business effectively with concrete existences" (LW4:165). Similarly, in *Experience and Nature*, Dewey equates the objects of science with "nature
in its instrumental characters."[53] The key move for a pragmatic naturalist is to stop treating the objects of science as complete, absolute, or self-
sufficient; such metaphysical realism will only result in the insoluble
problem concerning the relation between perceptions and the "real objects" they are supposed to be about, with two incompatible kinds of
knowledge and of the objects of knowledge. Dewey's "instrumentalism,"
then, is not a theory about personal utility or satisfaction in knowing,
but about what the proper objects of science are.

Dewey's commitment to instrumentalism is relatively obvious when
he argues that the problem of the "two tables" (the "Eddington tables") is
illusory, because the table we perceive and use is "the only table", "for it
alone has both individuality of form . . . and also includes within itself a
continuum of relations or interactions brought to a focus" (LW4:191).
Maintaining that reality is what is given—or actively "taken"—in experience, Dewey disagreed with the "new realists" of his time.[54] He writes:

The world as we experience it is a real world. But it is not in its primary phases a world that is known, a world that is understood, and is
intellectually coherent and secure. Knowing consists of operations

that give experienced objects a form in which the relations, upon which the onward course of events depends, are securely experienced. It marks a transitional redirection and rearrangement of the real. It is intermediate and instrumental. (LW4:235)

If Dewey holds that the scientific table, or the "scientific image" in which the table is not a concrete, perceived, practically manipulated object, but a collection of microphysical particles, is unreal or illusory, he is subscribing to an instrumentalist antirealism, which several philosophers of science, especially scientific realists, have powerfully called into question. If this instrumentalist reading of Dewey is correct, it may be extended to the religious "objects" of experience, yielding a *theological instrumentalism*. Then, God and other religious "entities" would, qua ideals, be some kind of instruments of thought. Alternatively, if Dewey, rather, subscribes to *idealism*, or to what is today called *constructivism*, when maintaining that objects are not independent of inquiry but pragmatic constructions arising out of an intelligent use of the methods of inquiry,[55] his view may again be applied to our "construction" of God. In religious experience, too, the ultimate reason for postulating a divine reality is the functional role played by such an ideal in human life.

Despite the instrumentalist and constructivist elements of Dewey's views, it would be overhasty to read him simply as an antirealist in either his philosophy of science or his philosophy of religion. He uses the terminology of "objects," "concepts," "conceptions," "theories," "hypotheses," etc., more loosely and thus more confusingly than is customary in recent analytic philosophy of science and religion. Moreover, we should remember that Dewey was, primarily, a naturalist, arguing that experience and knowledge, including the production of scientific knowledge (and its objects), are natural phenomena in a natural world in which we try to settle our problematic situations. As noted, this naturalism goes well together with humanism and culturalism. Whatever is natural to *our* practices of inquiry—our culturally developed habits of settling indeterminate situations by critically using the intelligence that itself naturally arises as a human capacity of reacting to such situations—is to be accepted and understood in empirical detail, rather than treated with philosophical suspicion. Philosophical skepticism about, say, the existence of unobservable theoretical entities postulated in our most advanced and successful scientific theories (or practices) would be an utterly *unprag-matist* and *unnatural* attitude from Dewey's perspective. Rather, we should take seriously the natural practices of inquiry we engage in. It was the actual practice of inquiry itself that Dewey appealed to when, for instance, attacking the ancient ideal of certainty and the "spectator theory of knowledge" (LW4:163–64, 195). Now, could the Deweyan naturalist say that there are equally natural practices of religious experiencing, yielding their own ontological postulations, such as God, and that there is no prior philosophical reason for being skeptical about such postulations? At least such an analogy of naturalism could be further examined in the philosophy of religion.

The Deweyan pragmatist is definitely *not* a scientific realist, *if* scientific realism is defined as the thesis that scientific theories provide us with the only true picture of reality, or that the "scientific image" is ontologically prior to the "manifest image" we are more directly acquainted with in ordinary experience.[56] Nor is the Deweyan pragmatist a *theological realist* if this means an analogous postulation of an ultimate religious reality knowable only through mysterious experience or revelation. But a Deweyan may be, and arguably Dewey himself was, a scientific realist in the sense of rejecting unnatural doubts about the reality of theoretical entities postulated in the actual course of scientific theorization, as long as such theorization is rooted in its humanly natural practical contexts, that is, the transactional processes of settling problematic situations arising in the course of experience. He *might* also have been, or the contemporary Deweyan might be, a pragmatic theological realist in the sense of accepting whatever the naturally religiously inclined "inquirer" finds necessary to postulate within her/his genuinely religious experience.

Of course, pragmatists should admit that any specific postulations of theoretical entities in science may prove ill-founded, and this applies to the postulation of "religious entities," too. But, as fallibilists, we should adopt such a critical, open attitude to *any* human claims and ideas whatsoever. The key pragmatist move in the philosophy of science is to liberate not only science but also scientific realism—and any other philosophical interpretations of science we might practically *need*—from essentialist, foundationalist, and noncontextualist pursuit of certainty, and other remnants of "first philosophy." Similarly, the pragmatist move in the philosophy of religion is to liberate both theism and theological realism—and other philosophical interpretations of religious experience—from foundationalist dreams of an ultimate, absolute perspective on reality. Pragmatism offers a middle path (or several paths) between realism and instrumentalist antirealism, and realism and constructivism—both in the philosophy of science and the philosophy of religion—demonstrating that the Deweyan approach to such controversies need not be hostile to realism in either field. The contextualization of the reality of both scientific and theological postulations to specific aims and purposes of inquiry has the advantage of keeping one's realism thoroughly pragmatic.

What I am suggesting is that this Deweyan pragmatic contextualization of the realism issue to practices of inquiry applies with full force to religious and theological inquiries. There is no need to suppose that there is (or is not) a ready-made divine reality out there, in a transcendent world order, waiting for us to penetrate into it either through religious experience, dogmatic revelation, or theological sophistry. There is, rather, a human value-laden pursuit of religiously conceptualizable ideals, an ongoing struggle for the good in the natural world of material and social existence, and the "objects" of this struggle may be pragmatically regarded as "religiously real." *This* is the (or at least *a*) message of *A Common Faith*, connected with an understanding of naturalized pragmatic realism emerging from Dewey's major works.

Only few commentators, early or late, have emphasized this combination of pragmatic realism and constructivism in *A Common Faith*. Howard Parsons is an exception:

> The reality of God is not just the world, nor is it man; it is the dynamic, unifying, and creative conjunction of the two. It includes both man and nature as creative. God must be activity for Dewey, for activity is the universal category of nature; but in Dewey's thought God appears to be a unique kind of activity. . . . Yet, as such, the activity of God is not distinguished, in Dewey's thought, from that of man. . . . [Dewey sometimes] leaves the impression . . . that the divine activity is nothing more than the work of man. Yet there are numerous indications in Dewey's writings that there is a creativity in human life other than man's own creativity.[57]

This is a basic tension in Dewey. Is God (or divine activity) dependent on us, our "construction"? Or is there something external to us, upon which *we* are fundamentally dependent? Dewey seems to hold that, through religious experiences, a process and force of creativity superior to our own emerges; nevertheless, this remains *our* postulation in and through our natural experience and practices. Interpreters have trouble with finding a way out of this tension, worrying whether Dewey is led to a merely epiphenomenal picture of God.[58] Douglas Anderson labels Dewey's postulation a "half-God,"[59] while William Rowe sees Dewey as a humanist whose "God" is a human achievement, produced by our intelligence and imagination.[60] Here, a (quasi-)Kantian reading *can* find a way out by construing the "dependence" of God, or divine creativity, on us (our postulations, experiences, practices, etc.) "transcendentally."[61] We do not causally or factually produce God (nor scientific objects); what we do produce is the experiential practice or framework within which religiously meaningful ideals and the possibility of an "active union" of the ideal and the actual arise. *From within* such religious practices, God may be real enough. Our ideals are not illusory but among the truly real elements of the world we live in, producing real effects in our actions.[62] If divinity arises in the functionally established harmony of the ideal and the actual, it need not be epiphenomenal or illusory; it may be an emergent and, hence, *pragmatically real* structure within a (quasi-)transcendentally constituted practice-laden framework. This of course requires that we more generally maintain that "pragmatically real" structures are constructions arising out of human practices—a view analogous to, or even a pragmatist version of, Kantian transcendental idealism.

Dewey and American Religious Naturalism

I will return to the issue of how metaphysical or antimetaphysical Dewey's philosophy of religion is. Meanwhile, however, I will discuss briefly how, following Dewey—and, in theological circles, the Chicago School of liberal theology, especially its leading figure, Wieman—"religious naturalists" have defended thoroughly non- or antimetaphysical theories of religious experience and language.[63] Religious statements do *not*, they claim, refer to any metaphysical fundamental reality, especially not to any supernaturally structured reality; rather, they express our emotions or attitudes. Nature is the only ultimate, self-sufficient reality, to be understood scientifically without appeals to any supernatural intelligent design.[64] Thus, we find recent religious naturalists speaking about, say, "grace" or "the sacred" as human modes of existing in *this* world, instead of referring to anything transcendent. Yet, while everything that can be explained can be scientifically explained, science will never tell us anything *deep* about the meaning or significance of the world or life—about grace or "the sacred." Religious language may be needed to articulate our sense of meaning (or meaninglessness), one of our modes of existing. There are, as J. A. Stone puts it, "religious aspects of this world that can be appreciated within a naturalistic framework."[65]

In a Deweyan manner, Charley Hardwick argues that the sacred, or God, cannot be found "in the ontological inventory of what exists," because religion must not be construed referentially. Faith should be understood "*exhaustively* as an existential self-understanding."[66] God is real for us "only in moments of transformation," in a faith "enacted ever anew"—not "objectively real."[67] Thus, one is "free to locate religious content in value, not ontology," yielding not a metaphysical theism but a *valuational theism*, in which "*God* or *God exists* can serve as a complex meta-expression for a form of life that is expressed as a theistic seeing-as. . . . Though *God* is not in the inventory of what exists [because that inventory is purely physicalist], *God exists* can be conceived valuationally in terms of the source of good."[68]

There could hardly be a clearer statement of an antimetaphysical religious naturalism.[69] Hardwick may even be taken to offer a reconstruction of Dewey's account of God as the active union of the actual and the ideal, though Dewey might have resisted the idea that God's existence is a "source" of good. The traditional theist will, unsurprisingly, remain unconvinced by this naturalist harmonization of religious discourse with a scientific worldview. Something is lost, such a theist will argue, if the supernatural element of religion—referring to something *beyond* human life and ideals—is abandoned. In particular, no doctrine of a *personal* God can be maintained in this kind of naturalism—either Hardwick's or Dewey's.[70] Even the treatment of the sacred and grace seem to be watered-down versions of their truly religious alternatives. As John

E. Smith explains, discussing Wieman's theology, "the avoidance of a total naturalism" becomes a problem: if we try to maintain the transcendence of God while rejecting supernaturalist doctrines, God may become "but a name for the humanization of the social order and the process of growth in value experience, both individual and social."[71] Hardwick also admits that the interesting challenges to religious naturalism are theological: how to develop a "full-blown religious perspective on naturalist terms," "how to relate to a specific religious tradition," and so on.[72] These are also challenges for the Deweyan theologian or philosopher of religion.[73]

The overall concern of these thinkers—both Dewey and his naturalist followers, whether or not they see themselves as "Deweyans"—is to render religious faith and discourse acceptable not by legitimating it metaphysically but by reinterpreting it as being essentially about values, about what is good or "ideal" in life, about ideal aims and goals, etc. The obvious response—today as much as in the 1930s when the controversy surrounding *A Common Faith* was intense—is that something important which has traditionally been a defining mark of the religious has been left out.[74] A critic may argue that both religion and science will be turned into superficial pseudoinquiries, if religion is rendered "scientifically acceptable" or intellectually warranted. This is too easy a harmony. We cannot turn religion into a scientifically acceptable discourse simply by saying that we are physicalists or naturalists when getting to the ontological business. If we seriously hold that the physical world is all there is, it is difficult to defend any religiously relevant "source" for the values invoked in religious discourse. Within such a naturalized religion, one's commitment to religious values is a kind of make-believe. As Rockefeller puts it: "If religious faith is basically moral faith, why use the word religious at all? What is distinctively religious about Dewey's concept of religious faith?"[75] Christian theologians like Niebuhr felt, with good reason, that "something was missing" in Dewey's naturalized God.[76]

Given that Dewey's naturalism was nonreductive even in ontology (assuming that Dewey does, albeit unorthodoxly, engage in ontological reflection), his position may be superior to that of the recent religious naturalists, however. Dewey needs no sharp separation between values and ontology, because there is no such thing as *the* ontology of the real world. Any ontology we may be justified in accepting is value-laden. If so, valuational religious perspectives on what there is may be as natural and, therefore, as warranted as nonreligious ones. This "perspectival" justification of religion needs further scrutiny, but here I can only continue to examine its relation to metaphysics.

Dewey and Wittgenstein

The "Wittgensteinian" philosopher of religion may, despite obvious differences, be vulnerable to the same kind of critique as the religious naturalist. Wittgenstein himself declared that the believer and the nonbeliever may share the same worldview, thus maintaining exactly the same factual beliefs. The value or meaning of the world is not to be found *in* the world, according to Wittgenstein. Therefore, the Wittgensteinian alternative in the philosophy of religion may come close to the antimetaphysical, naturalist line of thought just outlined, even though some of Wittgenstein's writings (particularly *Tractatus Logico-Philosophicus*) may also be seen as belonging to the genre of mystical literature.[77] Wittgenstein would never have approved of Dewey's or other religious naturalists' way of rendering religious qualities of experience scientifically acceptable. Nor would Dewey have sympathized with the emphasis on religious ritual in Wittgensteinian philosophy of religion, or the view (which may not have been Wittgenstein's own) that religious language receives its meaning simply from its use in ritualistic contexts; in many cases, rituals may just be superfluous remnants of traditional religions that are to be dropped out of activities enhancing genuinely religious qualities of experience. Yet, Wittgensteinian insights into the practice-based character of religious language may enrich the Deweyan separation between religious experience and the dogma of traditional religions, especially if one fears that Dewey leaves religious experience without determinate content. An obvious similarity between Dewey and Wittgenstein is indeed their common emphasis on religious practices and their role in human forms of life.[78]

The comparison between Deweyan and Wittgensteinian perspectives may be continued by invoking the notion of *genuine* religious experience, as contrasted to pseudoreligious or superstitious dogma. Indeed,

Dewey's charge against traditional religions in *A Common Faith* might be understood as an argument against their pseudoreligious tendencies. Truly religious values and qualities must, he repeatedly argues, be emancipated from the pseudoreligious domination of supernaturalist assumptions. Yet, it is difficult to draw the line between the religious and the pseudoreligious.[79] Though Wittgenstein would have resisted the reconciliation of science and religion, he might have agreed that supernaturalist, dogmatic religions are pseudoreligious in treating essentially valuational statements as metaphysical statements about the essence of reality. Such supernaturalism breaks the rules of truly religious language use.

Equipped with this insight, I return to the issue of metaphysics versus antimetaphysics in Deweyan philosophy of religion. At a general level—in relation to Dewey's conception of experience and nature—there has been considerable debate over whether Dewey engages in metaphysics, and if so, in what sense.[80] I will not continue this debate but only note, again, that it can be applied to religion. We may ask whether Dewey is really talking about religious qualities or religious reality, or *only* about human attitudes, practices, experiences, etc. Is there a possibility for a "religion after metaphysics,"[81] or will such a "religion" be merely a deflated pseudoversion of the real thing? Could a naturalized account of divinity suffice for a religiously adequate conception of "ultimate meaning"[82]—or is such a notion a remnant of foundationalist metaphysical theology? Obviously, these questions arise in the context of Wittgenstein's and his followers' philosophy of religion, too.

These problems go back to Kant. Both Kant and Dewey rejected dogmatic, transcendent, theistic metaphysics; both approached religiosity from an ethical point of view, Kant in terms of practical reason and Dewey in terms of values and ideals. For Dewey, the pursuit of "ultimate meaning" and value in a supposed isolation from other human beings and nature is illusory.[83] However, Dewey's view on religious qualities in experience may be too deflated for a Kantian taste. After all, Kant attempted to save elements of traditional Christian theism, even metaphysical theism, though in a form subordinated to ethics (see chapter 1). As Shook observes, Dewey's God, even in the early idealist phase, was never fully theistic in the sense of being external to human nature; it was "immanent in human nature."[84] Perhaps, however, we may see Dewey's

God as an *ethico-metaphysical* principle, if we understand metaphysics itself (religious metaphysics included) as subordinated to, or inextricably entangled with, ethics (moral values, ideals, and commitments).[85]

There is a form of metaphysics that might be maintained even in the Deweyan—and, *mutatis mutandis*, Wittgensteinian—framework, with no commitments to supernatural dogmas. This is a metaphysics emphasizing the *mystery* of the natural world, requiring a kind of humility and recognition of our indebtedness to nature for everything there is and for everything we are, or can ever hope to be. J. P. Soneson argues that such a "combined sense of mystery and indebtedness" characterizes the Deweyan "religious quality of experience,"[86] and that if this is appreciated, we may even view Dewey as "fundamentally a religious thinker."[87] The primary context for this understanding of Dewey is the "precariousness" or "instability" of existence—our insecurity and contingency—he emphasized not only in his writings on religion but especially in *Experience and Nature*.[88] Life is always potentially tragic, because we may at any time lose things we hold dear. As Soneson reflects:

> The tension between tragedy and hope, I want to argue, is the womb in which the religious function, as Dewey understands it, is nurtured and born. There is no need for the religious function apart form the tragedy of life. On the other hand, the religious function is not possible apart from the potential for growth that grounds the hope that circumstances can change for the better, that fulfillment or satisfaction—salvation, to use the more traditional term—is possible amid the tragedy of life.[89]

Deweyan philosophy of religion by no means denies the reality—the full, painful reality—of evil and tragedy.[90] A recognition of their reality *is* a kind of metaphysics—a metaphysics of the fundamental (though historically changeable) traits of human existence in a precarious natural world full of contingency, a world that is a source of tragic collapses as well as of liberating, enabling, energizing hope. Soneson is, I believe, right to point out that Dewey *is* a metaphysician in a Kantian sense. For both, "the task of metaphysics is to state the conditions for the possibility of knowledge," though for Dewey, such conditions are not apodictic a priori ones.[91] Metaphysics "reflect[s] upon what our talk about things implies about the kind of world or context in which we live."[92] It is roughly in this sense that we may view Dewey's treatment of the religious aspects of experience as metaphysical in a quasi-Kantian manner. The dualism between metaphysics and the criticism of metaphysics, like the one between religious and secular views or experiences, collapses in Deweyan pragmatism—as it does in Wittgensteinian reflections on the ways in which "essence lies in grammar."[93] The true pragmatist has no practical use for such sharp dichotomies, even in theology.

Yet, arguably, Dewey might have paid more attention to evil and suffering as both metaphysical and religious or theological problems. Despite the devastating loss of two sons, he maintained a generally optimistic (melioristic) attitude to life, while recognizing the reality of tragedy.[94] The question is whether his recognition of the tragic sense of life is deep enough. For instance, James's depiction of a "sick soul" in the *Varieties* may, in the end, be religiously more adequate. In chapter 5, I will return to the problem of evil as a major issue in pragmatist philosophy of religion—though not generally recognized as such by most pragmatists, with the key exception of James—but it is important to note already here that, despite its major achievements, it is right here that Dewey's *A Common Faith* must be found wanting. There is indeed something missing when the depth of the problems of evil and suffering is not addressed. I am not claiming that Dewey never addresses these topics at all; I am only suggesting that deeper insights into them may be found in Jamesian pragmatism.

Final Reflections

I have compared Dewey's project to the metaphysics versus antimetaphysics contrast as it emerges in other twentieth-century currents in the philosophy of religion, especially the Wittgensteinian one. A number of other comparisons might have been offered; consider, for instance, the crucial influence on Dewey that Peirce's and James's pragmatisms had. In contrast to these pragmatists' more supernaturalist tendencies—even Peirce's, given his speculative evolutionary cosmology—Dewey is the sober naturalist. It is his resolutely antimetaphysical orientation which motivated me to compare Dewey to Wittgenstein. On the other hand, it would be mistaken to view Dewey as simply subscribing to what has become known as Wittgensteinian philosophy of religion. The Wittgensteinians' virtually exclusive emphasis on religious language use is misleading from a Deweyan perspective. Nor can we accept the interpretation that Dewey is thoroughly antimetaphysical in his philosophy of religion—or in his philosophy generally—although there are strong antimetaphysical tendencies in his thought. He constructs a new, pragmatic metaphysics irreducible to old, nonpragmatic ones—just like he reconstructs our ways of thinking about the religious. Perhaps we should, then, see Dewey as a philosopher pragmatically destroying yet another traditional dichotomy, the one between metaphysics and the criticism of metaphysics. He is engaged in both, entangling the two. Similarly, his religious naturalism obviously attacks the traditionally sharp dualism between the spiritual and the secular or profane.[95] Deweyan religiosity embodies an attitude of "natural piety" toward the totality of nature, the universe that both overwhelms us and is a source of our values and ideals, connected with a unifying moral faith in those ideals; moreover, this attitude is comparable to the Wittgensteinian one of seeing the world *sub specie aeternitatis*, even though we can never fully meaningfully adopt such a perspective and can never fully linguistically express the kind of experience related to it.[96]

What we should find most valuable in Dewey's work on religion is his painstaking effort to harmonize scientific and religious thought. Consider, in conclusion, how he closes *A Common Faith*:

> Ours is the responsibility of conserving, transmitting, rectifying and expanding the heritage of values we have received that those who come after us may receive it more solid and secure, more widely accessible and more generously shared than we have received it. Here are all the elements for a religious faith that shall not be confined to sect, class, or race. Such a faith has always been implicitly the common faith of mankind. It remains to make it explicit and militant. (LW9:57–58)

Irrespective of whether Dewey is read as a secular or as (with qualifications) a religious thinker, his proposal to enhance humankind's growth through what he saw as the religious qualities and values in experience is to be applauded. The integration of science and religion he aims at is difficult, perhaps impossible, to achieve, but both scientific and religious thinkers may benefit from his reconciliatory efforts. No radical atheism in the style of Daniel Dennett or Richard Dawkins can ever promote the—even scientific—"common faith of mankind" Dewey propounded.[97] Nor can, of course, religious enthusiasts' potentially antiscientific ideas. The Deweyan middle ground—just like the pragmatist middle ground in many other philosophical problems—is hard to occupy, but it might itself be seen as an ideal we may indefinitely seek to actualize.

THREE

RORTY VERSUS PUTNAM:
NEOPRAGMATIST PHILOSOPHY OF RELIGION

In this chapter, I move from classical pragmatism—the Jamesian and Deweyan considerations I have explored in the previous two chapters—to what has come to be called *neopragmatism*, and to its actual and potential contributions to the philosophy of religion. Neopragmatism, however, is not a unified philosophical school of thought. Since the 1980s, some leading (mostly American) philosophers have been described by this term, emphasizing their background in classical pragmatism. It is widely agreed that the two most important neopragmatists are Richard Rorty and Hilary Putnam; other key figures include Joseph Margolis, Nicholas Rescher, and Susan Haack. The latter two have, in particular, sought to advance Peirce's pragmatism, while the most famous neopragmatists have turned to James and Dewey instead. Moreover, some authors distinguish neopragmatism from "new pragmatism," suggesting that the latter need not be based on "old" pragmatism, despite thematic similarities.[1] It is often a problem whether the label "neopragmatist" should be attached to a particular thinker; occasionally, the word is used exclusively to refer to Rortyan pragmatism, while some use it broadly to cover different philosophical views influenced by the pragmatist tradition.

Classical pragmatism strived to reconnect philosophical theorizing with human practice. The pragmatic maxim, formulated by Peirce and James, advises us to consider what conceivable practical results our conception of an object may involve; our conception of such results *is* then our conception of that object. Neopragmatists share this general pragmatic approach to philosophical and scientific problems. However, a neopragmatist is clearly not merely someone who today studies classical pragmatism. Neopragmatists generally seek to apply pragmatist insights into contemporary problems, including the one concerning the relations between science and religion. This is what Rorty has done in his own way as well.

Like the classical pragmatists, neopragmatists have promoted in significant ways the science-religion dialogue. While few neopragmatists are primarily philosophers of religion, neopragmatism as a philosophical framework is applicable to the problem of understanding religion and its relations to science. This chapter therefore focuses on Rorty's and, to some extent, Putnam's neopragmatisms, especially as they emerge as approaches to the relation between science and religion. Some other neopragmatist thinkers and ideas relevant to this topic will only briefly be introduced toward the end of the chapter. The Rorty versus Putnam contrast is, however, crucial for understanding neopragmatism, also because it is an opposition between secular and religiously engaged pragmatisms.[2]

Rorty: Pragmatist Philosophy as Cultural Politics

Rorty's version of neopragmatism is clearly the best known among philosophers and nonphilosophers alike. In his book *Philosophy and the Mirror of Nature* (1979), Rorty redescribed the history of Western philosophy in insightful ways, arguing that the problems of skepticism and the external world are "optional" and need not be taken seriously. Neither the mind nor language is a "mirror of nature" purporting to accurately represent external reality. Language—statements, vocabularies, and what Wittgenstein called "language-games"—is a human invention, a collection of tools people may, pragmatically, use for various purposes. No vocabulary (neither scientific nor religious, for instance) is more intimately in touch with the way the world is "in itself" than any other; no linguistic framework is "Nature's own." This is of profound significance for the science-religion dialogue. Language is used quite differently for different purposes; its goal is not to represent the way things are but to satisfy human needs and interests. Its main goal, then, is to help us "cope" with the world.

In later works, Rorty urges that pragmatists should enter a "post-Philosophical culture," giving up "Philosophy with a capital 'P'," that *solidarity* is prior to objectivity, and *democracy* to knowledge, that truth is not a goal of inquiry, that we should embrace an *antirepresentationalist* pragmatism, giving up the illusion of accurate representation, along with an *ironism* suspicious of any "final vocabularies," and that "cultural politics" should replace traditional philosophical inquiry.[3]

Rorty was a radically secular thinker until the 1990s.[4] His criticism of the metaphysical and epistemological tradition of Western philosophy is closely connected with his secularism: he has identified assumptions that have played the role that was in more traditional worldviews reserved to God. Such is, for instance, the "absolute," "independent" reality, the world *an sich*. According to Rorty, as human beings and civilization grow more mature, such assumptions are given up. We should not think of ourselves as being "responsible" or "answerable" to any nonhuman power, divine or not. Accordingly, we should not base our inquiries on the assumption that we are aiming at truth as accurate representation of independent reality. Thus, secularism is a key to Rorty's critique of Western philosophy; he has—to the dismay of scientific realists and naturalists—continuously argued that philosophers have failed to promote such a truly secular attitude.

Rorty's *ethnocentrism* (captured in the slogan, "we have to start from where we are") is, however, close to *cultural relativism* (though Rorty explicitly denies being a relativist), leaving room for the autonomy of both scientific and religious descriptions of experience. Science is no more closely connected with the way the world is than religion—or any other human practice—is. People living within a religious *ethnos* have to start from where *they* are. Accordingly, Rorty does not maintain, as many atheists do, that scientific progress has made, or will make, religions irrational, unjustified, etc. He holds that modern people ("we Western liberals") would do better without religious vocabularies, just as they would do better without racist or sexist ones—or without the vocabulary of scientific realism and truth-seeking inquiry. Scientific realism and religious fundamentalism, Rorty argues, are "products of the same urge," because attempting to convince people that they ought to develop an "absolute conception of reality" and attempting to convince them that they ought to "live 'for God only'" are "of a piece"; both are "attempts to make one's own private way of giving meaning to one's life—a way which romanticizes one's relation to something starkly and magnificently nonhuman, something Ultimately True and Real—obligatory for the general public."[5]

Philosophy cannot adjudicate between the disputes of science and religion, because it possesses no ahistorical "God's-Eye View." Secularism—or "anti-clericalism"—is therefore not primarily a philosophical but rather a cultural-political issue. However, the problem, according to many critics, is that if Rorty's ethnocentrism leads to relativism, his neopragmatism lacks the normative resources of saying that this is what *ought to* be maintained. We will, in what follows, repeatedly return to this problem, which might simply be labeled "the problem of normative force."

Rorty's attitude to religion slightly changed during his last years. It would be mistaken to call him anything else than secular in his late writings; yet, he authored several essays on religion in the 1990s and 2000s.[6] I will next discuss the significance for the philosophy of religion of Rorty's view on *hope*, as well as his suggestion that the question of religion is ultimately a question of cultural politics rather than philosophy.

Beliefs, including religious and metaphysical ones, are for pragmatists habits of action, inseparable from our practice-embedded being-in-the-world (to employ Heidegger's phrase), in which various hopes, fears, and other attitudes are inextricably present. We could hardly acquire *any* beliefs in the pragmatist sense, unless we encountered reality in a context colored by hope, being oriented toward future actions which (we hope) may change the world. In a Peircean context, Elizabeth Cooke has argued that we need to hope that our questions are genuinely answerable for us to be able to inquire at all.[7] Critics view Rorty's treatment of hope—for many, a paradigmatic neopragmatist picture of hope—as an unfortunate trivialization of this concept. After all, Rorty's "philosophy of social hope" is part of his strictly antimetaphysical pragmatism: inquiry does not deal with the way the world is, but is a matter of conversation, replacing contingent vocabularies by other (equally contingent and replaceable) vocabularies.

In the three-essay set entitled, "Hope in Place of Knowledge: A Version of Pragmatism," Rorty proposes that hope should replace knowledge as our central goal and key philosophical concept.[8] This is essential to the future-oriented approach of pragmatism, both classical and "neo." Because pragmatists "do not believe that there is a way things really are," they suggest replacing the reality-appearance distinction by the one "between descriptions of the world and of ourselves which are less useful and those which are more useful."[9] Here the concept of hope becomes urgent, because "useful" means "useful to create a better future."[10] Moreover, it is Rorty's own metalevel hope that hope would, hopefully sooner rather than later, replace the pursuit of knowledge as a key human project.

Neither realism nor theism leaves room for the right kind of hope, in Rorty's view. Citing Dewey's 1903 claim that Ralph Waldo Emerson should be seen as "the Philosopher of Democracy," Rorty says: "Hope—the ability to believe that the future will be unspecifiably different from, and unspecifiably freer than, the past—is the condition of growth. That sort of hope was all that Dewey himself offered us."[11] He also speaks about "romantic hope" as a "willingness to substitute imagination for certainty, and curiosity for pride," connecting this to the Deweyan rejection of the distinction between contemplation and action, and to the more general pragmatist rejection of the dichotomy between theoretical and practical approaches to reality.[12] He further notes that, with the romantics, history "began to replace God, Reason and Nature as the source of human hope."[13]

Religion offers "hope for redemption through entering into a new relation to a supremely powerful nonhuman person," while philosophy offers hope for redemption through "acquiring a set of beliefs that represent things in the one way they truly are."[14] Philosophers' "Love of Truth," the urge to get something (knowledge, mind, morality, or something else) "right," is the secular version of traditional religious hopes.[15]

These hopes should be abandoned, because in a "literary culture," both philosophy and religion are "optional literary genres."[16] Again, the problem is the one we already raised above: how can Rorty *argue* for these hopes being wrong or misguided? How does his preferred view get its normative force?

Through his pragmatic hope, Rorty joins Gianni Vattimo's—and to some extent Dewey's (see chapter 2)—efforts to reinterpret the Christian tradition in terms of secularization, attempting to save religion from "onto-theological" metaphysical assumptions and doctrines: "To save religion from onto-theology you need to regard the desire for universal intersubjective agreement as just one human need among many others."[17] Rortyan hope is, then, thoroughly secularized: "My sense of the holy, insofar as I have one, is bound up with the hope that someday, any millennium now, my remote descendants will live in a global civilization in which love is pretty much the only law."[18] It remains unclear, however, whether this admirable hope should be called "religious" in any sense; this lack of clarity is analogous to Dewey's ambiguities with the notion of God.

Nevertheless, many pragmatists undoubtedly applaud Rorty's emphasis on hope. In James's pragmatic examination of metaphysical problems, there is also an implicit current of hope running through the discussion (see chapters 1 and 4). Pragmatism, for James, "shifts the emphasis and looks forward into facts themselves," asking, "What is this world going to be? What is life eventually to make of itself?" Metaphysical puzzles are not viewed as conflicts between complete, finished views. Rather, they are individual attempts to come to terms with different considerations reason may offer in favor of one or another way of interpreting experience. For instance, the theory of the free will (contrasted to determinism), is "a general cosmological theory of *promise*" and thus "a doctrine of *relief*."[19] Turning toward the future is as essential here as in Rorty's neopragmatism, and therefore hope also is.

However, Jamesian pragmatists may hold that hope should *not* be disconnected from metaphysical pursuits, as it is in Rorty's pragmatism. They may understand hope as a pragmatic way of approaching metaphysics, as an irreducibly ethical attitude to the study of metaphysical puzzles. A "Jamesian" neopragmatist attempts to make both metaphysics and ethics more relevant by reconnecting both with the hope for a better future. Such a metaphysically pregnant hope, which may, according to Cooke, even play a "transcendental" role,[20] being constitutive of any humanly possible inquiry or even thought, is "social hope," too, but not exactly in the Rortyan sense. Arguably, if such a social hope is genuine, then it is in touch with the way the world is, from the perspective of the social practices engaged in, transformed, and redescribed by those embracing it. Rorty's dichotomy between hope and knowledge is one of the dualisms he—as many critics have pointed out—is unpragmatically committed to, despite his pragmatic urge to destroy dichotomies.

Thus, according to Rorty's critics, his neopragmatism fails to sufficiently account for the role played by hope in inquiry, religious "inquiries" included, although his emphasis on this concept is certainly highly relevant to neopragmatist philosophy of religion. Furthermore, Rorty's way of locating religion exclusively in the "private" sphere of individuals' lives, instead of the "public" sphere of common concerns, is also, for many critics, an utterly unpragmatist one—even though it may have the admirable ethical and political motivation of promoting liberal and tolerant ideas.[21] Pragmatists have since Peirce, James, and Dewey pictured the human individual as an individual-in-a-community, with no sharp separation between private and public issues. If religion is merely private, then, arguably, no genuine religious traditions—and, hence, no religious experiences either, if those experiences are "tradition-laden"—can arise. On the other hand, perhaps that is desirable from the perspective of Rortyan secularism. Yet, it is hard to understand how a thinker inspired as much by Dewey as Rorty is can seriously suggest that religion ought to be viewed as a merely private affair. Dewey's *A Common Faith* (1934), examined in the previous chapter, is a key pragmatist text celebrating the profoundly communal nature of religious experience, albeit extending (like Rorty) the religious qualities of experience beyond traditional dogmatic, supernaturalistic religions and the often antidemocratic social structures they have been associated with.

Rorty's perspective on religion is resolutely antimetaphysical. Religion, like everything else, should be emancipated from foundationalist, essentialist, ahistorical pursuits. Here he follows Dewey but goes much further. "Literary intellectuals" and "ironists," according to Rorty, should not only transform culture into a "post-Philosophical" one; they should also bring religious experiences, needs, and interests into a "postmetaphysical" era. Very little remains from traditional theism in such a "religion after metaphysics." Very little, then, remains from the traditional science versus religion contrast.

Rorty's atheism, secularism, or anticlericalism can hardly be said to constitute a normatively defended or argued position, let alone a philosophical theory. In his last writings, Rorty emphasized the cultural-political status of his suggestions concerning religious (and other) ways of using language. Philosophical criticism of religion is, for Rorty, a matter of cultural politics, not of metaphysics or epistemology. It is a matter of what kind of vocabularies should be maintained in "our" culture (and of how to define "our" culture, or who "we" are). The metalevel issue of whether cultural politics should "replace ontology," as it in Rorty's view should, is itself a matter of cultural politics, which is "the only game in town."[22] The critical question is whether this view is coherent. Can Rorty consistently maintain that we should not argue for atheism, or any other philosophical view? Once more we encounter here the problem of normative force.

According to Rorty, "the question of whether or not to talk about the existence of immaterial and infinite beings is not one of transcendental philosophy but rather one to be turned over to cultural politics."[23] Debating over concrete political questions related to religious ways of life, such as whether female Muslim students should be allowed to wear veils on campus, is "more useful to human happiness" than debating over the existence of such beings.[24] Furthermore, Rorty "drops" the idea that theology employs special kind of "symbolic forms," along with "the idea that God requires to be talked about in a special way because he is a special kind of being."[25]

For Rorty, as already emphasized, religion is a private matter: "our religion is our own business—something we need not even discuss with others, much less try to justify to them, unless we feel like doing so."[26] He claims, controversially, that this is what "most intellectuals" today hold. Again the critic who wonders how Rorty gets the normative resources to render his position plausible may point out that people, at least reflective people, have an intellectual duty to justify their views about religion, or at least a duty to discuss those views as critically and rationally as possible with others. This is not to say that people ought to engage in evidentialist philosophy of religion, or in the religion versus science debate. Yet, political issues surrounding religion can hardly be debated if religion is thoroughly privatized, moved beyond the public use of reason.

Rorty's account of religion as private is illuminated through his curious comments on *polytheism*. Echoing James and Nietzsche, Rorty characterizes polytheism as the view that there is "no actual or possible object of knowledge that would permit [one] to commensurate and rank all human needs."[27] This is comparable to Rorty's ironism about "final vocabularies." Yet, for a truly religious person, such an account may sacrifice the seriousness and profundity of one's commitment. Religion, for such a person, is not a matter of choice, like the choice of clothes or a personal style.

Rorty's most sustained account of a pragmatist philosophy of religion can be found in his essay, "Pragmatism as Romantic Polytheism."[28] He offers five theses he believes the pragmatist ought to subscribe to:

1. Antirepresentationalism: beliefs are habits of action.
2. Romantic utilitarianism: there is no competition between science and religion; nor should one draw contrasts between cognitive and noncognitive or serious and nonserious matters or ways of speaking.
3. The distinction between projects of social cooperation and projects of individual self-development (largely paralleling the one between public and private matters) is important.
4. There is no "love of Truth": "It is never an objection to a religious belief that there is no evidence for it. The only possible objection to it can be that it intrudes an individual project into a social and cooperative project, and thereby offends against the teachings of *On Liberty*."
5. Religious fundamentalism is morally irresponsible, betraying the ideals of human fraternity and democracy.[29]

This philosophy of religion is not identical to the classical pragmatists'. James, according to Rorty, *should* have said something like this: "[W]e are free to describe the universe in many different ways. Describing it as the

drifting of cosmic atoms is useful for the social project of working together to control our environment and improve man's estate. But that
description leaves us entirely free to say, for example, that the Heavens
proclaim the glory of God."[30] James should *not* have talked about the
literal and objective truth of religious beliefs but should have been satisfied with what he said in "The Will to Believe": "we have a right to believe
what we like when we are, so to speak, on our own time. But we abandon
this right when we are engaged in, for example, a scientific or a political
project."[31] However, the problem here is whether reflective people, say,
academics or intellectuals, shouldn't *always* be "on their own time," autonomous and independent. Rorty may not, then, be able to encourage
intellectual *responsibility* through his private versus public dichotomy.
When contrasting "one's own time" to public, cooperative projects, he is,
arguably, unpragmatic. The critic may point out that one should, even
when cooperating with others in shared projects, *be oneself*, taking responsibility for one's commitments.

Rorty prefers Dewey's philosophy of religion to James's, because Dewey
"was much less prone to a sense of guilt than was James."[32] However, this
sense of guilt may be what ultimately makes religion a deep issue in James,
in a way it never is—from a Jamesian perspective—serious enough in
Dewey. Rorty recognizes the role played by the concept of guilt in James's
pragmatism, but he overlooks the fact that this concept (or related ones,
such as sin and evil) may be needed to make religion serious for James.
If, "in a democratic society, everybody gets to worship his or her personal
symbol of ultimate concern,"[33] democratic worship may lack the kind of
depth associated with religious ways of life. If everyone started to worship, say, money as a personal symbol of ultimate concern, this would
hardly be a religious activity.

Rorty's neopragmatist perspective on religion may thus have difficulties
in maintaining the seriousness of (especially Jamesian) pragmatist philosophy of religion in which guilt plays a strong role.[34] Thus, it may have
difficulties in accounting for the fact that religious faith is, for many,
truly an "ultimate concern." Another worry that we have encountered—
indeed, a worry repeatedly arising in Rorty's neopragmatism—is that
Rorty may have sacrificed the normative resources of critical philosophy
of religion by reducing the problems of faith to mere cultural-political

clashes of vocabularies. Such reductionism is not part of the classical pragmatists' heritage. Rorty is *not* guilty of the "end of philosophy" line of thought sometimes associated with his neopragmatism, because he does maintain in an important, though primarily cultural-political, role for philosophy; yet, it remains unclear whether there is any critical, normatively structured way to discuss religion (e.g., in dialogue with science) seriously and argumentatively within Rortyan neopragmatism. In this regard, it seems to me that the "classical" pragmatist philosophies of religion offered by James and Dewey are overwhelmingly superior to their most famous neopragmatist successor.

Putnam: Synthesizing Pragmatism and Realism

Hilary Putnam's work on realism opens up another key version of neopragmatism. Indeed, neopragmatism has largely emerged from a critical dialogue between Putnam and Rorty on realism and truth. Both have subscribed to pragmatism, citing classics like James and Dewey; yet, they disagreed with each other about the significance of this tradition. I will offer some brief comments on Putnam's philosophy of religion in order to set Rorty's above-discussed views in their proper dialogical context.

Putnam has progressed from a scientific (metaphysical) realism through what he used to call "internal realism" toward a commonsense realism, or "cultivated" naive realism, which he claims to find in the philosophy of the later Wittgenstein.[35] In his critique of metaphysical realism, Putnam draws on the views of Kant, the classical pragmatists (especially James and Dewey), and Wittgenstein. However, instead of detailed interpretations of these thinkers, he creates and recreates his own conception of realism and truth, including realism about religion, drawing inspiration from their ideas.

For Putnam, *metaphysical realism* is the conjunction of three theses:

1. There is a way the world is in itself, mind- and language-independently; i.e., the world consists of a fixed set of mind-independent objects and properties.
2. The world can, in principle, be described in a complete, unique, absolutely true representation (presumably an ideal scientific theory).

3. Truth is a nonepistemic notion, correspondence between linguistic items (statements, beliefs, or theories) and objects or states of affairs existing in the mind-independent world.

Putnam's *internal realism* is, essentially, the denial of these theses.[36] Claiming that the world can be correctly described from multiple perspectives, reflecting our interests and purposes, internal realism is a version of the *pluralism* one finds in pragmatists like James and Dewey (see especially chapter 4). The internal realist joins Rorty in urging that no description of the world, not even the most advanced scientific one, is the world's own. Descriptions available to us are grounded in human purposes and practices. Ontology, truth, and reference are internal to conceptual schemes serving different purposes. The upshot of this *conceptual relativity* is that we live in a human world; there is no "ready-made" world. It is, in Putnam's view, flatly scientistic—and hence culturally harmful, or even dangerous to the dignity of human persons—to view science as the superior language-game describing absolute reality.

In the 1980s, Putnam characterized truth as idealized epistemic justification, rational acceptability, or warranted assertability, regarding truth (as conceived by the internal realist) as an epistemic notion contrasted to the nonepistemic correspondence concept of truth of metaphysical realism. More recently he has noted that his epistemic theory of truth (and internal realism) were misguided attempts to replace the unintelligible picture of metaphysical realism by a rival picture. We should, instead of succumbing to either metaphysical or internal realism, adopt a commonsensical "natural realism."[37]

The metaphysical realist's theses cannot, Putnam holds, simply be denied: we cannot affirm their negations, because the negation of an unintelligible statement is equally unintelligible as the original one. The metaphysical realist does *not*, according to Putnam, reach out for something (i.e., an absolute conception of the world) which is a meaningful goal and which we fail to achieve; our inability to describe the world absolutely is no failure, because the very idea of such a description collapses into unintelligibility—as does the internal realist's view, if construed as the negation of such an idea. This change in Putnam's neopragmatism took place in the mid-1990s. It has a pragmatist background, insofar as he finds James's natural realism, along with Wittgenstein's focus on the "ordinary," among his sources.

The relevance of these reflections on realism to the philosophy of religion is obvious. Religious statements or (in Rortyan terms) vocabularies should not be conceived of along the lines of metaphysical realism any more than scientific or commonsense ones should. If any realism is acceptable, it must be "pragmatic." Moreover, both scientific, commonsense, and religious (and other) perspectives on reality may contain some "truth," and so do our moral worldviews; Putnam accepts no gulf between facts and values.[38]

Putnam's views on realism, especially internal realism, have been severely criticized both by realists affirming the reality of a mind-independent world and by more radical (Rortyan) neopragmatists who want to set the issues of realism and truth aside as fruitless pseudoproblems. It has been argued, among other things, that metaphysical realism is not an "all or nothing" affair: one can endorse one or two among the theses 1–3 above, without endorsing them all.[39] Putnam, however, has stressed that it is unclear whether those theses make sense in the absence of one another. Moreover, even though Putnam rejects the internal realism he initially propounded, he continues to think that the metaphysical (scientific) realist's attempt to find a privileged (scientific) standpoint for describing reality in itself, independently of practice-laden perspectives, hopelessly fails. His attacks on strong realism have turned into general attacks on the reductionist, scientistic dream of representing ultimate reality in terms of physical theory. Thus his work on this topic has deep significance for the philosophy of religion. If scientism is rejected and no scientific perspective is treated as "absolute," then religious perspectives are also allowed to enter critical, rational discussions. The pragmatist point here, echoing James, is that both scientific and religious perspectives must be evaluated pragmatically, in terms of how well they satisfy human purposes.

It remains undecided whether Putnam's rejection of metaphysical realism can be combined with a pragmatic (commonsense) realism affirming the objectivity and independence of the world or whether it leads to a conception of the world as dependent on human practices. Putnam has been interpreted as a relativist or even an idealist, but he has reminded his critics that he never regarded the facts obtaining in the world as dependent on how we use language (in any normal sense of "dependent"). Still, there is no privileged (scientific) perspective available for any absolute description of those facts. One option is to interpret Putnam's view as "empirical realism" in Kant's sense. The world is, according to such a (re)interpretation, constituted by purpose-oriented practices roughly in the manner in which the empirical world is a human construction, without being illusory or fictitious, according to Kant's transcendental idealism.

Putnam's views, in general, are thus a mixture of Kantian, pragmatist, and Wittgensteinian insights—and this holds for his neopragmatist philosophy of religion, in particular. There is a sense in which reality, and truths about it, are human constructions, but this does not entail a Protagorean relativism of individuals or cultures as "measures of what there is." It is always from a purposive, practice-embedded point of view that we say whatever we say about the world we take to be real; following Wittgenstein, Putnam emphasizes the *context-sensitivity* of meaning, justification, and rationality.[40] It is only in particular contexts of philosophical bewilderment that, for instance, we are required to justify our beliefs about objective worldly facts. As there are several relevant contexts of investigation and justification, this view is close to pragmatic pluralism. In a religious or theological context—a context serving specific purposes—certain statements may be (held as) true, or rationally justified, even though they are not justified in a scientific context serving different purposes. Religious contexts do not require us to justify our views in the same way as scientific contexts do.

Putnam has never been a radical secularist in Rorty's manner, though it was only late in his philosophical development—not before the 1990s—that he began to reflect on his religious views philosophically.[41] His neopragmatist treatment of the science versus religion controversy integrates pragmatist (Jamesian-Deweyan) and Wittgensteinian insights. Together with Wittgensteinian philosophers of religion, Putnam argues that an evidentialist approach seriously mischaracterizes religious faith. Religion is not a scientific theory intended to explain observable events; it is misleading to either support or criticize it on the basis of evidence (or lack thereof). Rather, religion is tied to deeply rooted forms of life within which we find significance for existence. Even if religious ideas can be said to be "empirically tested," they must be understood differently from scientific theories. Religious views are tested "in the laboratory of life,"[42] not in a scientific research laboratory.

Some atheists maintain that "modern science has answered, or at least sketched a satisfactory answer to, *all* the problems with which metaphysics was traditionally concerned, and the answer simply leaves no room for religion . . . except as a historically and culturally important kind of *escapism.*"[43] However, from Putnam's pragmatist and Wittgensteinian perspective, the religious way of looking at reality is *not* "simply another scientific hypothesis, to be examined by the criteria of predictive accuracy, simplicity, and conservation of previous (scientific) belief."[44] Religious statements can be neither refuted nor confirmed by evidence. The materialist, reductionist, scientistic critic of religion fails to understand what religion—the religious form(s) of life—is.[45] The religious fundamentalist commits the same mistake.

Religious responses to life are, for Putnam, varied, but the "potentiality" for making religious language one's own is "a basic human potentiality," and it takes "something experiential and not merely intellectual to awaken that possibility in a human being."[46] Religion should not be overintellectualized—as James argued a century earlier. Putnam, however, reserves a role for intellectual discussion of religion in a way different from Rorty's reduction of philosophy (of religion) to cultural politics. Putnam summarizes his account of how to philosophize about religion into three principles: The principle of experiment: "Ideas must be tested in practice." The principle of fallibilism: "No human being and no body of human opinion is infallible." The principle of communication: "Truth is by its very nature public. Whatever your existential commitments may be, if you claim truth for them, you must be willing to discuss them."[47] Following these principles is to be prepared to test religious views "in the laboratory of life." While Putnam is sympathetic to Wittgensteinianism, he attacks the thinkers he calls "pseudo-Wittgensteinian 'language game theologians'" for giving up the possibility of reasonably criticizing religious beliefs.[48]

How a rational critique of religion ought to be conducted on a prag-matic basis is, however, not obvious from Putnam's writings. There is an element of existentialism and even mysticism in his position. He draws inspiration from negative theology, particularly Maimonides,[49] and ul-timately regards religious ways of life as individuals' deep personal commitments—to some extent resembling Rorty's privatized religion. Characteristically, Putnam finds James's perspective on religion superior to Dewey's, though—in contrast to Rorty.[50] Yet, Putnam's mystical ten-dencies might also be compared to Dewey's notion of "natural piety," the awe we (may) feel when encountering the vast totality of nature and real-izing our tiny role in its scheme of things (cf. chapter 2).

As another difference to Rorty, Putnam does consider religious ideas and commitments deep, profound, and ultimately significant. "There sim-ply is no uncommitted place to stand with respect to the religious dimen-sions of human life," he writes.[51] Claiming to be "religious" is therefore an "awesome responsibility."[52] The issue is existential in the sense of going deep into the very being of a human being: *what it is to believe that God is personal and loves individuals depends on who one is all the way down and how one lives all the way down.*"[53] How one uses the word *God* can only be explained with reference to who one deeply is, and how one leads one's personal life.[54]

The basic difference between the two leading neopragmatists' views seems to be that Rorty opposes (traditional) religious ideas, whereas Putnam is a "believer," a "practicing Jew." He even finds religious sig-nificance, though no sound philosophical theorizing, in the traditional proofs of God's existence.[55] While in Rorty's case it is unclear whether, and how, the suggested cultural-political replacement of religious (e.g., Christian) vocabularies by secular ones could be normatively supported, in Putnam's case the problem of normative force is slightly different. The problem now is whether his respect for individual, personal ways of liv-ing religious lives leaves room for any public discussion of reasons for preferring one such (form of) life to another. Putnam may in the end arrive at religious mysticism replacing rational argumentation by blind faith. This is another way of losing normative force, quite different from Rorty's.

There is also another problem in Putnam's thought about religion and God. While his desire to approach religion as a "way of life" avoiding all kinds of fanaticism and fundamentalism, as a way of truly encountering one's life and that of the other human beings around oneself, and especially as a way of extending ethical responsibility to humankind as a whole, Putnam seems to reduce God to something like a human construct—thus coming close to the kind of problems we discussed in the previous chapter in relation to Deweyan pragmatic religious naturalism. This is what he says in a recent interview based on his 2008 book, *Jewish Philosophy as a Guide to Life*:

> I appreciate the God of negative theology, but I'm a religious person, and the available God, the God I imagine, is a human construct. . . . In my spirituality, I visualize God as a person. It's not that I believe God is a person. . . . Okay, do you believe God has a mind? No, of course not. To see that God is a half-truth. We construct God in response to demands we don't make. I don't have a philosophical theory of metaphysics to account for that. All these religious existentialists have a sense of encounters, the spiritual encounter which is life-transforming.[56]

One easily thinks here about the famous Wittgensteinian statement that my attitude to another person is an attitude toward a soul, which does not mean that I would have the "opinion" that the other "has" a soul.[57] However, the problem here, as I see it, is not that Putnam resorts to the vocabulary of "construction"; rather, the problem is that he wants to avoid metaphysics at all costs. The pragmatist, in the sense of pragmatism I have been developing here (and will continue to develop in the upcoming chapters), should not be afraid of metaphysics. On the contrary, the pragmatist should be happy to embrace a metaphysical picture of "transcendental" construction of religious reality, pragmatically rearticulated. In any case, Putnam is certainly correct to require that this human construction of divinity *must* include an ethical dimension: "How hard it is to acknowledge other human beings. The love of God means nothing; the vertical dimension means nothing without the horizontal dimension. It's not love of God if it doesn't lead to the commandment to love your neighbor."[58]

Neopragmatism, Philosophical Anthropology,
and "Problems of Religion"

Our discussion of neopragmatist philosophy of religion would be seriously incomplete if it failed to address the future of the field. Thus, I want to supplement my discussion of Rorty and Putnam by briefly reviewing the work of a younger-generation neopragmatist philosopher of religion, Ulf Zackariasson, who has during the past decade very interestingly examined religion in the light of what he calls "pragmatic philosophical anthropology."[59] Unlike Rorty and Putnam, Zackariasson is primarily a philosopher of religion; indeed, his 2002 book is one of the relatively few comprehensive treatments of the philosophy of religion from the perspective of pragmatism.[60] The study challenges the basic conceptions of religion at work in mainstream Anglo-American analytic philosophy of religion, proposing nothing less than a reorientation in how we should think philosophically about religion. This reorientation is largely based on a philosophical anthropology adopted from the pragmatist tradition.

Zackariasson's main purpose is itself characterized pragmatically: he wants to answer the question of whether we can "develop a conception of religion that will enable us to deal more fruitfully with the problems of religion"[61]—more fruitfully, that is, than analytic philosophy of religion has been able to. The "problems of religion" he is interested in are numerous, and they come in three groups: first, there are problems that individuals face when they find themselves surrounded by several incompatible religious traditions (and secular alternatives); secondly, at an interreligious level, one may ask whether another religious tradition can be criticized and on what kind of criteria; and thirdly, one may examine the status of values and beliefs that can be derived from religious and other views of life.[62] Insofar as pragmatism may help us in dealing with these and other problems of religion, it undoubtedly turns out to possess significant pragmatic value. Accordingly, Zackariasson subjects pragmatism itself to pragmatic scrutiny, seeking to show that it *is* a pragmatically significant approach to religious issues, grounding a philosophy of religion that is superior to the mainstream alternatives.

As Zackariasson uses "pragmatism" to refer to classical pragmatism, particularly to the philosophies of Peirce, James, Dewey, and Mead, he does not pay attention to the ways in which pragmatism figures in, for example, Putnam's philosophy of religion. However, following Joseph Margolis and Richard Bernstein, he admits that pragmatists are united not by a common essence but (only) by family resemblances in a Wittgensteinian sense. Even so, he characterizes pragmatism in terms of "a shared philosophical method" and a shared philosophical anthropology, that is, a "similar orientation in the way they approach human phenomena and the human subject."[63] This orientation, he goes on to claim, is different from the one we find in contemporary analytic philosophy of religion.

I have some minor doubts here: is it correct to say that pragmatists' philosophical anthropology is "significantly different from the one shared by most contemporary philosophers"?[64] This seems too strong, given pragmatists' affinities with, say, phenomenology. In any event, Zackariasson offers a number of lucid formulations of the basic insights of pragmatist philosophical anthropology: "The being that is capable of thought and purposive action is an agent situated in a world with some regularities on which to base intelligent action, a world that is also full of contingency, making the attainment of equilibrium something we must struggle for"; and further: "human beings are biologically and socially constituted organisms concerned about upholding a state of equilibrium between themselves and the environment."[65] These ideas are then interestingly connected with Charles Taylor's work on transcendental arguments, reinterpreted as referring to a pragmatic transcendental condition of human life as we know it.

The resulting picture is a pragmatically relativized conception of transcendental argumentation rooted in philosophical anthropologies. I agree that this outlook provides a promising overall picture of the philosophical resources pragmatism has in dealing with human problems. But I am still slightly suspicious of Zackariasson's claim that the classical pragmatists *shared* a philosophical anthropology, as there are, for instance, important differences between Peirce and James. Zackariasson comments upon James, Dewey, and Mead at length, but he largely neglects Peirce (as, admittedly, I also must do in this book). His readings of such key pragmatist themes as James on religious experience, Dewey on inquiry and habituality, or Mead on meaning and the mind are, in my view, sound but not particularly novel—nor, of course, need they be, as these discussions are included in his volume because they are primarily used for systematic, metaphilosophical purposes. The goal of the work is a reconstruction of contemporary philosophy of religion rather than any essentially new historical interpretation of pragmatism.

In particular, I find Zackariasson's Deweyan discussions of "philosophy as criticism" very illuminating, and I share his view that when criticizing a conception of religion we also criticize the philosophical anthropology associated with that conception.[66] Thus, as a metaphilosophical "inquiry into philosophical practice" Zackariasson's work is impressive. It should not be read as a mere exercise in the philosophy of religion (although of course it is that, too); it is, more broadly, a critical pragmatic study of a certain kind of pragmatic conception of philosophy, based upon a pragmatic conception of human nature. Furthermore, Zackariasson's treatments of, among other things, the interpretative character of anthropological inquiry, of philosophical anthropologies as "interpretative frameworks" within which (only) transcendental arguments may have a legitimate use, of "metaphilosophical pragmatism" as an attitude urging us to "evaluate philosophical anthropologies with an eye to the consequences they have for how well we can handle problematic situations we have to deal with,"[67] and of the reasons why a pragmatic conception of religion need not be reductionist are extremely promising—and in several ways I have in this book come close to many of these themes.[68]

From a pragmatist perspective, however, I see one major problem in Zackariasson's approach. He relies on a relatively sharp distinction between philosophical problems and practical problems, classifying the "problems of religion" as belonging mainly to the latter category.[69] This I find rather unpragmatic. For pragmatists, the philosophical *is* practical, and the practical may always contain philosophical dimensions. By separating between the two, Zackariasson defines his views in somewhat unpragmatic terms that he otherwise successfully avoids. Our "extraphilosophical" problems may, he claims, serve as the "common ground" we need in order to be able to go on arguing with each other about religion (or about anything). Even so, our philosophical practice may, and does, transform the extraphilosophical problems that seem to ground it. So, at least, a pragmatist might, and in my view should, argue. There may simply be no clear separation between the philosophical and the extraphilosophical—and this is, I maintain, something that pragmatists, in particular, should appreciate. The pragmatists' rejection of any principled dichotomy between the theoretical and the practical also yields a similar rejection of a sharp boundary between the philosophical and the extraphilosophical.

Furthermore, in a section entitled "Some Philosophical Topics Pragmatically Considered," nicely alluding to James, Zackariasson sets out to show that his pragmatism does not amount to antirealism in metaphysics and semantics but rather steps outside the realism versus antirealism dispute as traditionally conceived.[70] Here he makes things a bit too easy, for instance by distinguishing between the notions of *construction* and *constitution*: our environment, he tells us, is not "constructed" by our practices, although it is "constituted" in them.[71] A critic might argue that this is just a terminological innovation. The underlying philosophical idea might have been explicated by comparing the "transcendental" constitution of the world within human practices that pragmatism—at least Zackariasson's favorite kind of pragmatism engaging in pragmatic transcendental arguments based on philosophical anthropologies— employs to, for example, the somewhat similar conception of the constitution of the objects of experience that one finds in the phenomenological tradition.

Zackariasson rightly draws attention to Putnam's doctrine of conceptual relativity and the role of conceptualization in human practices; it is right here that the question of transcendental constitution (or construction) of the (empirical) world arises. Thus, *pace* Zackariasson (and Putnam and Rorty), I do not think that the pragmatist can entirely avoid the realism issue, any more than Kant and his followers could (either in the philosophy of religion or in other areas), even though I would be the first to admit that this issue is in pragmatism treated in a more complex and perhaps more innovative manner than in standard defenses of either realism or antirealism.

Zackariasson perceptively finds William Alston's Christian philosophy *relativistic*.[72] Religious claims can, in reformed epistemology, be only practice-internally validated. As has often been argued, Wittgensteinian philosophers of religion cannot escape the problem of relativism, either.

Nor can Zackariasson himself completely escape it—nor any pragmatist, for that matter. When Zackariasson says that "the resources for criticism and reform of a religious practice are not limited to criteria internal to that practice" and that "we have good reasons for taking a critical stance to it when we face situations where we detect problems with our present view of life,"[73] he should note that "taking a critical stance" is itself part of our more inclusive practice. How, then, can we respond to those who do not find *that* practice a defensible one, or a good habit of action, at all? I believe the relativism issue is with us to stay. This is something that both pragmatists and Wittgensteinians, in philosophy of religion and elsewhere, should admit—without succumbing to any naive "anything goes" view. Any philosophy invoking "practices," "forms of life," or other normatively structured frameworks enabling rational thought or inquiry must seriously face the challenge of relativism (see also chapters 1 and 4).

Zackariasson's discussions are perhaps not as rich in interpretations of classical pragmatists as one might expect from a study on pragmatism, but this lack is well compensated by the penetrating comparisons he provides between pragmatism and analytic philosophy of religion, without forgetting other contemporary thinkers that do not directly fall into either of these camps, such as Charles Taylor, Alasdair MacIntyre, and Martha Nussbaum. I very much sympathize with Zackariasson's willingness to put pragmatism into work, to use it in a reconstruction of our philosophical practice of dealing with religion in such a way that pragmatic philosophizing contributes to "human flourishing." Sometimes Zackariasson is too modest, however. Instead of saying that he does not discuss the question of how a metaphilosophical pragmatic argument can "justify a pragmatic philosophical anthropology,"[74] he might have noted that his book as a whole takes significant steps toward providing such a pragmatic justification. This is not to say that his own positive contribution to pragmatist philosophy of religion, presented mainly in terms of the notion of *reflective equilibrium*, containing a defense of the possibility of judging (religious) emotional responses as appropriate or inappropriate, and culminating in the affirmation of the possibility of normatively criticizing views of life, is fully satisfactory. But his discussion is throughout balanced and pragmatically open to suggestions from various rival standpoints. Its open and fallibilist spirit represents a truly pragmatic attitude at its best.

Therefore, Zackariasson succeeds—at least better than the leading neopragmatists we have examined earlier in this chapter—in his main effort, namely, the attempt to sketch a philosophical picture of the possibility of criticizing and reforming religious practices and views of life and of normatively discussing religious problems that is not blind to the pragmatic "goods of religion" religious people may enjoy in their lives. Such goods may, as any pragmatist ought to admit, have a role to play in our debates over the justifiability of religious ways of living and thinking. Disagreements over these goods will undoubtedly persist as long as there are reflective religious believers and nonbelievers, as Zackariasson admits. In any case, Zackariasson's work is an excellent demonstration of the ways in which a pragmatist may approach those disagreements, and its philosophical significance far exceeds the narrow scope of pragmatism scholarship (or even philosophy of religion).

In addition to the 2002 book, Zackariasson's numerous articles also make very interesting contributions. For example, he insightfully compares James's account of moral considerations regarding what we can say about God to Wittgensteinian "grammatical remarks," noting that the Jamesian pragmatic view is, possibly, superior because "pragmatic grammatical remarks have a significantly *forward-looking* character."[75] This forward-looking nature of pragmatist examinations of religion—of pragmatist attempts to deal with, or respond to, what Zackariasson calls "problems of religion"—is also central in his critical analysis of the "adequacy debate" regarding the adequacy of philosophical views on religion from the point of believers. Here Zackariasson partly continues from the dissertation, characterizing philosophy of religion as "a series of responses to problems which involve religious practices," while constructively focusing on the debate between D. Z. Phillips and his critics, in particular.[76]

The possibility of moral critique of religion is central here—and again Zackariasson finds his resources for such critique from the pragmatist tradition, including James. As "moral considerations enter . . . into the very formation of religious practices," he notes that "moral critique of religious practices is a natural part of the way religious practices function."[77]

Such moral critique is thus not something completely external to those practices themselves; when philosophers engage in such critique, they again respond to "problems of religion." One of the most important virtues of pragmatism in this regard is its ability to avoid strict, essentialist boundaries between religion itself and its philosophical interpretations and critiques. The ability of pragmatism to respond to problems of religion better than many other orientations results from pragmatists' pursuit of philosophy "with a human face."

As also noted in the introduction to this book, one of the problems that religious practices raise in contemporary societies is the place of religion in politics and other public discourses—the roles that religion might, or should not, play in "the public sphere." Zackariasson also engages with this issue in several writings.[78] Therefore, it seems to me that neopragmatist philosophy of religion has a lot to learn from Zackariasson's contributions. His new book (still uncompleted) on religion in the public sphere, analyzed from the pragmatist point of view, will undoubtedly be a significant work.

Final Reflections

As Zackariasson's example makes clear, neopragmatism has over the past few decades spread from the United States, the homeland of pragmatism, to Europe and other countries. For example, Dirk-Martin Grube, a philosopher-theologian working in the Netherlands, has also explored pragmatist themes in the philosophy of religion, especially the methodology of seeking a pragmatically balanced "reflective equilibrium," while Eberhard Herrmann, a philosophical-theological thinker based in Sweden, defends a "pragmatic realism" regarding religious belief indebted to Putnam.[79] European scholarly communities and networks such as the Central European Pragmatist Forum and the Nordic Pragmatism Network, as well as several centers of pragmatist inquiry in Germany, attract philosophers and other researchers working on the science-religion dialogue. Thus, while the leading neopragmatists have been American, inheriting and critically developing the essentially American tradition of pragmatism (albeit with its European, particularly Kantian and Hegelian, roots), this American way of thinking about religion is increasingly firmly established in Europe and elsewhere, too. The cultural contexts for the science versus religion debate are, obviously, quite different in these different countries. In particular, neopragmatist inquiry may in fact be *better* suited to a European setting in which the issue of, say, evolution versus creationism is not at all relevant in the way it is in the United States.

The bearing of Putnam's and Rorty's neopragmatisms on the philosophy of religion still needs to be examined. The interpretation and appropriation of their positions in this regard has barely begun, and this chapter has hardly been able to offer more than an overview with some critical remarks connecting these approaches to the main themes of this book. Moreover, pragmatist philosophers of religion may, and should, work in close cooperation with other related currents, such as religious naturalism and process philosophy (including process theology). In some cases, it may be difficult to determine whether a particular thinker or position should be labeled "neopragmatist" or just, say, "naturalist." Pragmatism is an open-ended tradition with flexible boundaries. It may be a sign of its vitality that it has been able to accommodate both religious and secular viewpoints, attracting thinkers from both camps. In this sense, Rorty's elaborations of neopragmatism, in philosophy of religion and elsewhere, are more than welcome, even though the pragmatist philosopher of religion definitely need not agree with his most problematic proposals, such as the sharp private versus public dichotomy that seems rather unpragmatistic—against the background of Dewey's communally oriented philosophy of religion, in particular.[80] In contrast, both Putnam and Zackariasson offer healthier neopragmatist contributions to the philosophy of religion.

FOUR

THE JAMESIAN PRAGMATIC METHOD
IN THE PHILOSOPHY OF RELIGION

In the introduction, I started from the observation that contemporary philosophy of religion is in a relatively confusing state, as the different approaches often disagree even about the very nature and methods of the philosophy of religion. I also pointed out that the status of pragmatist philosophy of religion in this situation is ambivalent: generally speaking, pragmatists seek a middle path between extreme realism and antirealism, as well as evidentialism and fideism. How exactly this is done, however, must be studied in detail; one key pragmatist thinker such a study should focus on is, obviously, William James. In chapter 1 I touched upon Jamesian pragmatism in the philosophy of religion (and in chapters 2 and 3 I reviewed some Deweyan and neopragmatist ideas). In this chapter I will take a more detailed look at how the Jamesian pragmatic method functions in this area of philosophy, especially when it is connected with another central element of James's thought, pluralism.

In this chapter I will reemphasize not only the Kantian reconstrual of James (and pragmatism generally) defended earlier in this volume but also the more metalevel view, also hinted at but not yet substantially argued for, that a healthy understanding of religious thought presupposes a pragmatist (practice-oriented) standpoint that is inherently *pluralistic*. In contrast, the mainstream positions in the philosophy of religion are *monistic*, privileging some particular essentialist conception of the "true" nature of religious language, belief, and other relevant notions. A possible exception is Wittgensteinian philosophy of religion, with its focus on the plurality of language games; yet, this tradition has its dogmatic features, too. In any event, for pragmatists, there is no single, absolute, overarching perspective from which religious issues ought to be viewed but a plurality of relevant philosophical standpoints, reflecting the plurality of our practices of life. I hope to elaborate on this important idea as the chapter unfolds.

I will proceed as follows. After introductory remarks on James's pluralism in its plural meanings, I will outline Jamesian pluralism in some more detail as an ethical and a metaphysical (or meta-metaphysical) position. I will then show how Jamesian pragmatism goes beyond the evidentialism versus fideism debate and will then further suggest, in a parallel fashion, that it also goes beyond the realism versus antirealism debate (as standardly conceived in contemporary philosophy of religion). Pluralism is the key pragmatist principle to be used to overcome both debates.

Thus, I will continue to develop the argument, already begun in chapter 1, that the problems of realism versus antirealism and evidentialism versus fideism, among others, receive new interpretations when examined from a pragmatically pluralist perspective. Pragmatist philosophy of religion, committed to the normative task of critically evaluating, and not just explaining and understanding, religious beliefs and practices,[1] may crucially contribute to the science versus religion dialogue, which vitally needs a comprehensive and tolerant account of both scientific and religious practices and their diverging conceptions of rationality (cf. my introduction to this book). A lot has gone wrong in this dialogue, as is witnessed by the controversies over teaching evolution in schools in the United States, the increasing conflicts between radical, fundamentalist Islam and the rest of the world, the equally increasing hostility toward even moderate Islam in various countries, and other unfortunate developments. Pragmatism—in my view, particularly Jamesian pragmatism—is well equipped to advance a much more deeply understanding approach to the issues of science versus religion, offering us pluralism and tolerance but no uncritical relativism. This is achieved through a practice-oriented reconsideration of religion as ultimately based on ethics.

Pragmatic Pluralism

According to William James, the problem of *monism versus pluralism* is the deepest and "most pregnant" in philosophy.[2] In Lecture IV of *Pragmatism*, James applies the pragmatic method to the problem of "the one and the many." The pragmatist must inquire into the multitude of ways in which the world can be taken to be "one" (or "many"). First, the world is one subject of discourse. Second, there are continuities ("hanging together") in the world. Third, there are "lines of influence" of various kinds—including James's fourth point, causal unity. More importantly, James's fifth point identifies "generic unity" in the world: things belong to different classes of *genera*, existing "in kinds."[3] James's sixth and seventh dimensions of "oneness" are the unity of purpose and aesthetic unity. The eighth and philosophically perhaps the most controversial dimension is, finally, the notion of "the one knower"—that is, the Hegelian monistic idealists' Absolute, which James sets out to critically examine at some length. James argues, famously, that the pragmatist prefers the pluralistic and empiricist approach to the monistic and rationalistic postulation of the Absolute—a popular metaphysical postulate in the late nineteenth and early twentieth century—whose only pragmatically acceptable cash value, according to James, is the occasional "moral holiday" it might grant us. The debate with monistic idealists', including particularly F. H. Bradley's, views was one of the most important controversies James engaged in toward the end of his philosophical career. This is how he concludes the discussion of the one and the many in *Pragmatism*:

> "The world is one," therefore, just so far as we experience it to be concatenated, one by as many definite conjunctions as appear. But then also *not* one by just as many definite *dis*junctions as we find. The oneness and the manyness of it thus obtain in respects which can be separately named. It is neither a universe pure and simple nor a multiverse pure and simple. And its various manners of being one suggest,

for their accurate ascertainment, so many distinct programs of scientific work. Thus the pragmatic question "What is the oneness known-as? What practical difference will it make?" saves us from all feverish excitement over it as a principle of sublimity and carries us forward into the stream of experience with a cool head.[4]

Monism and pluralism must, hence, be treated pragmatically: no rationalistic metaphysics dogmatically set up in advance of our piecemeal inquiries into the different ways in which the world can be said to be "one" or "many" can do the job of settling the issue. Applying the pragmatic method, James arrives at what may be characterized as the ethical superiority of pluralism over monism:

> Pluralism . . . has no need of this dogmatic rigoristic temper [of monism]. Provided you grant *some* separation among things, some tremor of independence, some free play of parts on one another, some real novelty or chance, however minute, she is amply satisfied, and will allow you any amount, however great, of real union. How much of union there may be is a question that she thinks can only be decided empirically. The amount may be enormous, colossal; but absolute monism is shattered if, along with all the union, there has to be granted the slightest modicum, the most incipient nascency, or the most residual trace, of a separation that is not "overcome." Pragmatism, pending the final empirical ascertainment of just what the balance of union and disunion among things may be, must obviously range herself upon the pluralistic side.[5]

We must not fail to see that there are a number of different pluralisms at work in James's pragmatism. In one important sense, pluralism amounts to a *metaphysical* theory (set against the Absolute), according to which there are, instead of one single "knower," "bits and pieces" of "pure experience" pretty much everywhere; it is therefore inseparable from James's radical empiricism, according to which pure experience is the "neutral stuff" (beyond the subject-object dichotomy) out of which the world is "made."[6] I agree that James's theory can be read in this way, and his metaphysical opposition to the monistic idealists' Absolute is a key element of his pragmatism, especially *A Pluralistic Universe* (1909). According to pluralism, as characterized in that late book, "the substance of reality may never get totally collected" and "some of it may remain outside of the largest combination of it ever made."[7] Multiplicity is pragmatically preferable to all-inclusiveness—both scientifically and ethically.

However, just as James argues in *Pragmatism* that the world can be "one" or "many" in a variety of different ways, there are other ways of being a pluralist. I will in this chapter emphasize an alternative to purely metaphysical construals of pluralism: perhaps pluralism, for James, is not primarily a metaphysical doctrine (presupposing radical empiricism) but a *metaphilosophical* one, insisting on the possibility of a plurality of different "correct" metaphysical positions, and thus coming closer to the general argument of *Pragmatism*, as well as the later defense of "internal realism" and "conceptual relativity" (or even explicitly "pragmatic pluralism") by Putnam and other neopragmatists.[8] This metaphilosophical pluralism can also be called *meta-metaphysical*, as it is concerned with the very nature and the correct (pragmatic) methodology of ontology or metaphysics, replacing the assumption of there being a single absolute conception of reality (or, as Putnam often puts it, the idea of a "God's-Eye View") by the notion of several acceptable ontologies, each serving different pragmatic purposes. The Jamesian view, spelled out in Lecture VII of *Pragmatism*, in particular, that objects do not exist "ready-made" but only relative to our purposes or categorization can also be compared, in addition to Putnam's ideas, to Nelson Goodman's controversial theory of "worldmaking."[9] This position comes in an important respect very close to Kantian *transcendental idealism*, which is also opposed to strong realism: the world is not knowable *an sich*; any humanly knowable or experienceable structure it may have is imposed on it by us.[10] Yet, in addition to James's general distaste for the Kantian transcendental vocabulary and methodology, there is a crucial difference to Kant: pluralism. There are, instead of just one transcendental structure of experience, many ontological structures, each based on human practices and their inherent purposes, or the needs they serve. For instance, science and religion—to take the obvious case—may be argued to serve different human purposes and hence categorize reality differently.[11]

In fact, it is hard to see how the purely metaphysical doctrine of radically empiricist pluralism, closely analogous to the view labeled "neutral monism," defended at some point by Ernst Mach and Bertrand Russell, among others, could be seriously regarded as "pluralistic" at all. *Could* such a monism—a form of substance monism[12]—really be a form of pluralism? Shouldn't we, rather, maintain the possibility for such monism(s) only within a pluralism of different metaphysical alternatives that all need to be pragmatically examined and evaluated within a more inclusive pluralism? Arguably, James's metaphysical pluralism (radical empiricism), *qua* substance monism, is incompatible with his meta-metaphysical pluralism, which seeks to argue against such monistic ontologies that would seem to presuppose a God's-Eye View on the world. James's Kantianism, I like to think (though conclusive textual evidence is very hard to find), ultimately prevails over the empiricism he inherited from the British empiricist classics like David Hume. In order to be pragmatic pluralists in the meta-metaphysical sense, we should drop the metaphysical overtones of radical empiricism.

There is, then, a plurality of pluralisms. There are both metaphysical and (at the metalevel) conceptual, methodological, and metaphilosophical versions of pluralism. I am obviously aware of the fact that I am departing from James's own usage of these terms when I advance the metaphilosophical (meta-metaphysical) version of pluralism rather than the others. Yet, I am developing a *Jamesian* pragmatist philosophy of religion instead of seeking to faithfully describe his actual views. What is more, there is also a crucially important *ethical* (and even political) aspect to Jamesian pluralism, to which I will now turn, in order to be able to (later) emphasize the entanglement of metaphysical and ethical issues in Jamesian pragmatism. In due course I will, then, focus on the relevance of James's pluralism(s) to the philosophy of religion generally.

Ethical Pluralism, Individualism, and Otherness

James's clear refusal to follow utilitarianism (or any other straightforward versions of consequentialism) all the way down in his seemingly fairly consequentialist ethical thought presumably resulted from his respect for the irreducible value of *other individuals*—of different voices and perspectives represented by concrete people, groups, and cultures.[13] Antireductionistically, James (along with other pragmatists) maintained that genuine individuality is possible only in a community, while neither the individual nor the community can be reduced to the other. What

James's philosophical pluralism means in ethics is that there is, and can be, no single, absolute, overarching moral theory. Rather, we must let individual voices, including those that may be very unfamiliar to us, be heard in the moral conversation of humankind. In particular, as James memorably put it, we must not be "deaf to the cries of the wounded": these, even more than other voices, are among those that we always need to listen to. James firmly opposed imperialisms of all kinds, metaphysical and political alike—that is, all attempts to suppress or dominate over the individual.

The modal phrases in the above sentences present us with personal, individual "cans" and "musts." These moral possibilities and necessities are just that: moral. However, one may argue that the "must" to hear other voices is, in James, itself grounded in a kind of perspectival empiricism: James himself did hear a number of different "voices." Arguably—though this is a biographical matter not to be settled here—he truly listened to what other people had to tell him about their experiences, or at least tried to do so. Even so, one might also ask whether James himself is something like an "absolutist" about his perspectivalism, or a realist about the many voices there are to be heard, that is, a realist and absolutist about there being a "must" to hear those voices.

Pluralism, then, is a complex idea in James. It is, as we have already seen, both a metaphysical (or meta-metaphysical) and an ethico-political idea (or, perhaps better, an *ideal* never fully realized). While James argued, in *A Pluralistic Universe*, that reality cannot be metaphysically reduced to any monistic scheme, advancing "piecemeal" approaches instead, it is equally important to realize that in ethics and politics we can never reach an "absolute" conception of what is universally best for human beings and societies, either. Different suggestions, opinions, experiential perspectives, and interests must each have their say.[14] As James maintains in his 1898 lecture, "Human Immortality," encouraging his readers to acknowledge their (our) "half-brutish prehistoric brothers": "'Tis you who are dead, stone-dead and blind and senseless, in your way of looking on. You open your eyes upon a scene of which you miss the whole significance. Each of these grotesque or even repulsive aliens is animated by an inner joy of living as hot or hotter than that which you feel beating in your private breast."[15] What we should do in thinking about ethics and politics, according to James, is simply open our eyes, look at the world surrounding us and all the others who inhabit (or inhabited) it with us, and achieve "an imaginative understanding of the inner experience" of those others.[16] This imaginative understanding is to be distinguished from theoretical knowledge. We do not primarily *know* that there are other experiencing beings (or "other minds"); rather, we find ourselves embracing an "attitude towards a soul" to others, to *acknowledging* them ethically.[17]

Pluralism, in addition to being meta-metaphysical in the sense indicated above is a metaphilosophical principle for James even in a broader way: a crucial aspect of the need of acknowledging others, possibly very different from myself, is the need to acknowledge the value of different philosophical approaches (again, possibly very different from my own). We must understand that others may have quite different "philosophical temperaments" from our own,[18] and we are responsible for our own philosophical temperament at least to the extent that it does not dogmatically repress those of others. It has been pointed out, plausibly, that a certain kind of individualism lies at the heart of James's philosophical work, unifying a number of his views.[19] We must take seriously the diverging ways in which individual human beings—an open-ended plurality of them—experience the world. Pluralism and individualism go tightly together here: we must tolerate, or "acknowledge," other individuals' plural perspectives on reality, perspectives that cannot be reduced to a single absolute perspective. It is easy to see that this pluralism—or perspectivalism, as it also might be called—is as much ethical as it is metaphysical and epistemic.

This metalevel position has significant consequences for the ways James understood the nature and tasks of (moral) philosophy. Sergio Franzese persuasively argues in one of the few book-length studies on James's moral philosophy that, even in his famous 1891 paper, "The Moral Philosopher and the Moral Life,"[20] James does not offer any particular moral theory but critically examines the very project of theorizing about morality. James is a "philosophical anthropologist" instead of a moral philosopher narrowly conceived. Offering a close reading of "The Moral Philosopher and the Moral Life" and other texts, seeking to correct the widespread misunderstanding that James in that paper puts forward just another ethical theory, Franzese maintains, plausibly, that James's essay is "not the sketch of a system of moral philosophy, but . . . a critical analysis of the conditions of possibility of moral philosophy," an inquiry into "the constitutive attitudes and activity of moral philosophers."[21] I find this an accurate statement of James's project. James, however, is not only a philosophical anthropologist but engages in something that may, in Kantian terms, be called the *metaphysics of morality*. He *seems* to propose a subjectivist ethical theory basing moral obligation in individual interests, but he actually attacks *any* "totalizing ethical system," because such systems destroy individuals' "real possibilities."[22] No single principle, not even subjectivism or (merely theoretically construed) moral individualism, can ground actual moral life in all its perspectival variety. It is along these lines that James finds moral philosophy possible "only as a critical science which takes each moral ideal as an hypothesis and each moral choice as an experiment."[23] In the 1891 paper, James indeed argues that "there is no such thing possible as an ethical philosophy dogmatically made up in advance" and that "there can be no final truth in ethics . . . until the last man has had his experience and had his say."[24] This is, quite obviously, an expression of metaethical fallibilism, but it is much more.[25]

Accordingly, the fundamental flaw of utilitarian moral theory, from a Jamesian perspective, is *not* that the consequences of actions should not be taken seriously in ethics but, at a metalevel that it *is* a moral theory in the first place, sacrificing the concrete, pluralistic richness of ethical perspectives to an allegedly neutral and universal—monistic—principle. It is for these reasons that a certain kind of fundamental *tolerance*, deeply connected with pluralism and individualism, plays a crucial role in James's moral vision. In order to live ethically, we truly ought to take others' individual perspectives on life into account. In this sense, James's views—especially his criticism of the "blindness" in human beings which blocks us from recognizing genuine otherness—can be compared to the ethics of acknowledging the other, familiar from the work by philosophers as different as Emmanuel Levinas and Stanley Cavell.[26]

Another commentator, José Medina, has even suggested that a conception of political *solidarity* can be based on James's ideas.[27] James emphasized not only pluralism and individualism but also the closely connected conception of the ineliminable *relationality* of all individuals: nothing can exist in a self-sustained manner, but individuals possess their identities only by belonging to networks of mutual interdependence. While James's arguments for the reality of relations are mainly derived from his radical empiricism, the above-mentioned doctrine that what ultimately exists is "pure experience" (which includes not just experienced or experienceable objects and events but also relations), this metaphysical position is, once again, set in an ethical context. Although James's pluralism and relationalism are general metaphysical views according to which "nothing can be understood in and by itself, but rather in relation to other things, in a network of relations," they are irreducibly ethical (and even political) positions, as they apply with full force to the reality of the self: "to have a sense of self is to have a sense of the dependences that compose one's life."[28] We are, Medina reminds us, "diverse and heterogeneous beings who are shaped and reshaped through diverse and heterogeneous networks of interpersonal relations"; the Jamesian self *is* a bundle of such relations.[29] There is, then, no self at all independently of its relations.

Even James's controversial, even notorious, pragmatic account of *truth*, according to which truth is what "works"—the theory developed in the sixth lecture of *Pragmatism*, in particular—should, according to Medina, be understood in this context. True beliefs are those that are "good to live by", and when maintaining a belief we are responsible for its consequences in our lives and those of others.[30] In this way, the pragmatic "theory" of truth is connected not just with agreeable consequences but with solidarity and justice.[31] Among pragmatist thinkers, Dewey was of course more strongly oriented to issues in democracy, solidarity, and social justice (see chapter 2), but it is vital to note that James's pragmatism was concerned with these topics, too, albeit less directly and explicitly. It would be highly misleading to suppose that Dewey was the only one among the classical pragmatists with a strong sense of social and ethical mission. On the contrary, James's conception of truth, applicable to religion, is ethical and political to the core, although this is not at all explicit in his remarks on truth.

Beyond Evidentialism and Fideism

James's core philosophical principle, his version of the pragmatic method, can itself be understood as the "meta-metaphysical" principle that the conceivable ethical aspects and implications of different metaphysical views, ideas, and issues ought to be taken seriously when evaluating the content of those views, ideas, and issues, as well as their acceptability. When employing the pragmatic method, the Jamesian pragmatist examines, for example, metaphysical problems from an ethical perspective. James shows us what this means in the case of such traditional controversies as those concerning the notion of substance, free will versus determinism, theism versus atheism (or materialism), and monism versus pluralism.[32] The metaphysical truth of pluralism is itself ethically grounded. Pluralism, we may say, is a pragmatic constraint on, or even a necessary precondition of, metaphysical inquiry, when the latter is understood in a pragmatist sense. No pragmatically adequate investigation of the ways the world must be taken (by us) to be can ignore the plurality of ethically relevant purposes, perspectives, or contexts of conceptualization and categorization that Jamesian pluralism emphasizes. In metaphysics as much as ethics, there are different "voices" to be heard, very different ways people (need to) take the world to be.

While James's pragmatic willingness to examine metaphysical problems by taking into account their ethical dimensions should generally be seen as a key element of his moral thought, this willingness is nowhere as clear as it is in the case of religious metaphysics. Again, we should, James maintains, tolerate—and not just tolerate but respect—individuals' different religious ways of experiencing reality. Pluralism thus once more prevails. Franzese, commenting on James's overall project, notes that "everything must be thought and directed in the perspective of the moral question," which implicitly inspires and organizes all of James's work.[33] Our actions tend "toward morally ordering the world"; hence, James's anthropology culminates in the insight that "the moral problem is the ultimate and fundamental problem of a being who needs to choose in order to exist"[34]—sounding somewhat like Jean-Paul Sartre's existentialism, whose affinities with James have been emphasized by Putnam, among others.[35] Even religion must be approached from this ethical perspective. Indeed, as I suggested in chapter 1, James may be interpreted as arguing for the reality of God (or gods—he is not always particularly clear about this) on moral grounds. The "religious hypothesis" is needed for us to be able to lead "strenuous moral life." It seems that we have to believe, or must at least reserve ourselves the right to believe, that God exists, in order to be able to take morality seriously and to avoid falling into moral nihilism. This argument can be compared to the way in which Kant defended theism as a "postulate of practical reason" (see further comments on this below). Yet, for the Jamesian pluralist, God's reality may be religiously experienced or theologically explored in a plurality of different ways. Moreover, there is always some hesitation and ambivalence in James's attitude to theism, especially in his late thought after the *Varieties*—as has been pointed out by David Lamberth among others—but this again brings him closer to Kant, who was ambivalent in a somewhat similar way: there can be no rational proof of the existence of God, yet religious faith is an ethical need for us.

While ethics and religious faith are thus closely tied together in James, just as they are in Kant, and while a religious commitment may serve as an energizing source of strenuous moral life, it would be misleading to simply view ethics as dependent on religion. Rather, James's pragmatic method advises us to locate the true significance of our religious (or nonreligious) or metaphysical commitments in their ethical aspects. Accordingly, just as much as moral life may depend on religious faith, that faith may (perhaps only) be justified in ethical terms—analogously to Kant's "postulate" of God's reality. However, only a *finite* God can, according to James, be defended along these pragmatic lines. James's picture of the divinity is, hence, very different from more standard metaphysical theisms, including even Kant's (in which God's existence is an issue subordinated to the practical use of reason but the God thus reached is, presumably, infinitely powerful). The conception of God as a supremely powerful Absolute was ethically unsatisfactory for James; above all, it conflicted with his pluralistic individualism.[36] James therefore heavily debated both monism and pluralism and the related issue concerning the infinity versus finitude of divine reality with the monistic idealists (e.g., Hegelians) of his times.

James, as Franzese puts it, includes God in "the anthropological dimension," suggesting that this notion answers the human need for eternity and meaningfulness in life.[37] Theism encourages us to see our action as ultimately purposeful, in contrast to materialism, determinism, and absolute idealism, which "crush this prospective hope"; thus, the moral acceptability of religious beliefs must be measured by the extent to which they prompt us to "energetic action."[38] However, this is not sufficient to make his anthropological approach to the problem of God precise. In particular, the basic issue of *realism* remains unsettled: does James maintain that God is a human construction based on ethical needs and purposes? What would that even mean? While we need to return to these questions below, it is clear that, for James it is primarily in ethical terms that we must assess our metaphysical commitments, religious or otherwise. Even the investigations of individual religious experiences in the *Varieties*[39] are based on the ethical interest toward others' inner perspectives, and are thus related to the tolerant pluralism James defended especially in his late writings, a pluralism itself ethically superior to its monistic rivals.

Equipped with Jamesian pluralism as an ethico-metaphysical principle, we may attempt to reconceptualize the theism versus atheism and evidentialism versus fideism issues in an explicitly ethical manner. Both evidentialism and fideism, arguably, turn out to be insufficiently ethical responses to the problem of theism versus atheism. This is because they are ultimately monistic responses, failing to take ethically seriously the individual experiences—different "voices"—and their enormously rich contexts, replacing such thickness of experience by straightforward philosophical theories of the justification of religious beliefs. It is, in short, not only philosophically narrow-minded but unethical to leave out of sight the ethical aspects of such a major metaphysical problem as the issue of God's reality (cf. chapter 1). Theism *may*, according to both Kant and James, be rationally acceptable in terms of practical reason (though we must not forget their shared ambivalence, as pointed out above), or more generally from the standpoint of the vital human needs and interests embedded in our practices of life. From a Jamesian point of view (and arguably from the Kantian point of view as well), the religious believer's faith in God need not be made scientifically acceptable, or warranted in terms of "neutral" criteria of reason, because it is ultimately not a matter of science or evidence; what is important is to make it ethically acceptable in the face of evil and suffering that we, believers and unbelievers, experience in the world we live in. Yet, this is *not* to agree with fideism that there can be no rational critical discussion of matters of faith at all. On the contrary, it is to critically rethink the conditions for the possibility of such discussion (and its limits).

Although this is not James's own way of putting the matter, I would like to reaffirm a point I made in chapter 1: the proposal to defend the reality of God by pragmatic means presupposes something like transcendental idealism (in the loose sense characterized above); the world is not absolutely independent of us but is responsive to our ethical (or more generally valuational) needs and interests, or "in the making" through an open-ended plurality of such needs and interests. We structure reality in terms of what our moral agency requires; there is no prestructured, "ready-made" world that we could meaningfully engage with, as for us there is no "God's-Eye View"—even to God's reality. The world we find ourselves living in is structured by us—not merely by our "cognitive faculty," as in Kant, but also by our various practical interests and purposes.[40] Pluralism, once again, is the key difference to Kantian constructivist metaphysics here: the world is ontologically "structured" from a plurality of different perspectives. Yet, this structuring is at least analogous to the dependence of empirical reality on the structure imposed by the transcendental subject in Kantian transcendental philosophy (transcendental idealism). In order to carry this through, we also need a pluralistic reconstruction of the transcendental subject itself, presumably in terms of social practices. The world-structuring transcendental subject(ivity) is itself perspectival, not an "all-enveloping noetic unity,"[41] but an open-ended set of practice-engagements based on individuals' needs and purposes. (A further question, not to be taken up here, concerns the structuring of this subjectivity itself: *who* is responsible for the—again ethically relevant—task of reconceptualizing transcendental subjectivity into this new shape?)[42]

Moreover, *is* this world-structuring process really metaphysical, or should we simply confine ourselves to an ethical, "merely pragmatic," account of Jamesian pragmatism? Is there "really" a God, or are we just entitled to act "as if" there were one? *Why* should the world be "responsive" to our ethical needs, after all? We should now look more closely into the way James argues for the reality of God, as a manifestation of his pragmatic method at work.

In terms of the evidentialism versus fideism opposition (as explained in the introduction to this book), James is a middle-ground thinker, pluralistically avoiding both of these monistic extremes. I will now explain more fully how his pragmatic way of justifying theism is neither evidentialist nor fideist but a genuinely third option. The leading idea here is James's Kantian-like subordination of the metaphysics of theism to ethics, already preliminarily explored in chapter 1.

I return to the observation that James may be interpreted as a pragmatically theistic metaphysician pretty much along Kantian lines, if we understand his "pragmatic method" not as a method of simply getting rid of metaphysical pseudoissues (in which case this method would be little more than an early version of the logical positivists' verificationist theory of meaning) but as a method of making explicit the pragmatic core of metaphysical disputes that would otherwise remain obscure and interminable. From a Jamesian pragmatist point of view, as much as from the Kantian one, ethics and metaphysics are deeply intertwined.[43] Religion, or theism, is pragmatically legitimated as a postulate needed for morality, for our ethical life and practices. This is the practical relevance of Kant's idea of the primacy of practical reason inherited by James.

The problem here was already discussed in chapter 1: can theism (or the "theological postulate") be practically (pragmatically) legitimated a priori, by reason's capacities only (as in Kant), or just empirically or psychologically, as an attitude "energizing" moral life, because we are the kind of beings we are (as in James)? My suggestion here is simply that, as Kantian transcendental (critical) philosophy more generally synthesizes the precritically opposed epistemological doctrines of empiricism and rationalism, we may reconcile Kantian (transcendental) and Jamesian (pragmatist, empirical, psychological) ways of justifying theism ethically. The theism issue cannot be resolved in total absence of ethical considerations. And to take those considerations into account is, again, to emphasize the metaphysical relevance of different thinkers' plural individual situations—of different "voices" and individuals' "over-beliefs," including James's own, as presented in the *Varieties*.[44]

Analogously to Kant's moral proof of God, I attempted in chapter 1 the following reconstruction of what might be seen as the Jamesian argument for theism (which is very different from any standard evidentialist argument, yet irreducible to fideistic antiargumentativeness):

1. Human moral pursuits (that is, "morally strenuous living" or the "morally strenuous mood" of life) are possible, in a full, serious, and "energized" sense, *only if* (we believe that) God exists.
2. Human moral pursuits are possible (because actual).
3. Therefore, (we should believe that) God exists.

Here premise (2) is not indubitable, if we take seriously the scientific, materialist view of the world according to which there is merely the "dead," physical universe without any "higher" or "spiritual" elements. The Jamesian pragmatist cannot take the reality of the moral point of view for granted: morality *may* turn out to be an illusion. We can never be absolutely sure that there is a place for morality in our lives.[45] However, it is because of the uncertain situation in which we must face the world—because we cannot take for granted that there is a place for (genuine) morality in our lives—that we *are* entitled in adopt the theistic belief, in "willing to believe," which then, *ex post facto*, will (if anything will) be able to render our lives morally significant, after all.

It is along these lines that we should, I believe, read James's defense of theism in the third lecture of *Pragmatism* (as argued in chapter 1). Whether or not we are entitled to interpret James's arguments as quasi-transcendental in a Kantian sense, it is clear that theism, for him, plays a role in overcoming the absurdity of human existence; *here*, in this ethical function, lies its metaphysical value, pragmatically considered, though obviously its success in overcoming moral (and metaphysical) nihilism and absurdity is never guaranteed. In both cases, the Kantian and the Jamesian, what we arrive at through the pragmatic ethical transcendental argument is a form of moral theology. This is part of the fallibilist realization that complete or absolute success is never guaranteed. God's possible existence is based on the needs and interests of our moral life. Furthermore, as already indicated above, in order for such a grounding of a metaphysical thesis in ethical premises to be possible, (pragmatic) transcendental idealism must be presupposed. The metaphysical reality of God cannot, we have seen, be settled independently of ethical considerations. This rethinking of the relation between ethics and metaphysics goes far beyond the "ethics of belief" as commonly understood. Insofar as God's help may be needed for the moral struggle for the world's "salvation," we are ethically justified in adopting the metaphysical beliefs of theism. But even more strongly, we may have a *duty* to believe in God's reality, *if* that is the only way to make sense of such a struggle, or the only way for us (or any given individual) to join it.

Avoiding both evidentialism and fideism, once again aiming at a middle path, a genuinely religious person whose theoretical and practical perspectives on life cannot be neatly distinguished from one another may consider theism an ethico-metaphysical truth guiding her/his entire life. This kind of "living truth" of theism might be something that is concretized in one's *habits* of religious life, requiring *trust* instead of the kind of intellectual evidence that scientific beliefs require.[46] This central role played by trust might also lead us to examine James's pragmatism as a philosophy of *hope*—which is indeed what James says theism (or spiritualism) is, in comparison with atheism (or materialism), in the pragmatic consideration of these doctrines in terms of the future they "promise."[47] Pluralism, moreover, promises to bring trust and "intimacy"—instead of "foreignness"—to our relation to the universe, enabling us to feel "at home" in the world.[48] These obviously ethically relevant habits of hope and trust, enhancing feelings of intimacy rather than uncanniness, may be among the key practical "results" of theistic belief. Such belief must itself, when pragmatically analyzed, be subjected to pluralistic treatment: there is no single metaphysically correct way of being a theist—no single absolute way God is, or can be, real for the one who believes "rightly"—but there is an antidogmatic plurality of pragmatically defensible ways of living ethical life energized by faith in God (and also a plurality of ways of avoiding such faith). The danger to be avoided, always, is dogmatism.

Beyond Realism and Antirealism

Having suggested that James's pragmatism goes crucially beyond the evidentialism versus fideism debate, I will now move on to consider the other debate characteristic of recent philosophy of religion—realism versus antirealism—already mentioned in the introduction. Again, it turns out that Jamesian pragmatism offers a genuinely third option, which, ones more, is rooted in Kantian ideas. This time I will discuss the issue by commenting on one recent commentator.

In his essay, "Pragmatism, Realism, and Religion," Michael R. Slater defends James against a number of widespread misunderstandings.[49] Yet, I find his treatment of James problematic enough to require critical comments that will further highlight the kind of Jamesian application of the pragmatic method in the philosophy of religion already defended above. As Slater focuses on the issue of realism in James's pragmatism, and since this issue has been central in Kantian and post-Kantian transcendental philosophy as well, it is worthwhile to consider in more detail what kind of a realist James—or the contemporary Jamesian philosopher of religion—is, or might be.

Slater seeks to show that James's pragmatism not only is compatible with realism (including religious realism) but is even a species of *metaphysical realism*. James, we are told, "combines a 'humanist' account of truth with a commitment to metaphysical realism," while also defending "a pragmatic version of the correspondence theory of truth."[50] I agree about the latter point—provided that the correspondence theory is not understood as being necessarily connected with metaphysical realism. That is, far from being a naïve subjectivist or relativist, James clearly starts from the commonsense idea that truth involves some sort of agreement between our "ideas" (beliefs, statements, theories, and so on) and reality, seeking to specify this notion of agreement pragmatically, in concrete experiential terms.[51] Slater offers sufficient textual evidence for this reading. However, the claim that James is a metaphysical realist, even in a general sense, is inaccurate.

Much of what is at issue here depends on what exactly we should mean by "metaphysical realism." Slater's definition of this notion follows the one given in a recent philosophy dictionary: according to the metaphysical realist, "there is a world of mind-independent objects."[52] Slater thus rejects Putnam's threefold characterization of metaphysical realism as the commitment to the following theses:

1. The world consists of a definite set of mind- and scheme-independent objects and properties.
2. The world can in principle be described by means of a single complete true theory, that is, there is an "absolute conception of the world," formulated from an ideal "God's-Eye View."
3. Truth is a nonepistemic correspondence relation between our statements (or whatever the ultimate truth-bearers are) and the mind-independent entities and facts of the world.[53]

Now, while there certainly is a sense in which James does accept the realist view that there is a mind-independent world, and the related account of truth as agreement with such a world, he can hardly be taken to endorse even the relatively broad notion of metaphysical realism understood as the commitment to there being "a world of mind-independent *objects*" (my emphasis). This is because James finds the very notion of an object dependent on human purposes. This is especially clear in the seventh lecture of *Pragmatism*, where he argues that reality is something we (help to) create, to which we inevitably make an "addition"—something "still in the making"—and that anything we may call a *thing* is "carved out" by us in and through our purposive practices.[54]

Moreover, even James's theory of truth, albeit starting from the idea of "agreement" (as Slater correctly shows), is not a version of the correspondence theory, insofar as the latter is viewed (as it is by most metaphysical realists) as an essentially nonepistemic account of truth. That is, metaphysical realists and correspondence theoreticians would not accept the Jamesian epistemic characterization of correspondence (agreement) in terms of confirmation and experiential satisfaction[55] as a characterization of the proper sort of correspondence required by a realist theory of truth. Furthermore, a metaphysically realist philosopher like D. M. Armstrong, defending not just correspondence but an asymmetrical, metaphysically cross-categorical "truthmaking" relation from the world to true propositions,[56] would hardly view such a metaphysically benign version of correspondence sufficiently realistic.

A much more helpful description of the Jamesian conception of truth could be achieved by emphasizing the fact that James, unlike metaphysical realists, refuses to draw a principled distinction between the *meaning* of truth and the *criteria* of truth. Even strong metaphysical realists may regard the latter as epistemic, but for James the very meaning of truth is epistemic all the way down, and inseparable from our pragmatic criteria of arriving at truths. Metaphysical realists can hardly accept this as a correspondence theory of truth proper, but James deliberately—and in my view with good reason—blurs the distinction between meaning and criteria, pragmatically proposing that the meaning of truth largely lies in the epistemic criteria we employ for arriving at the truth. There is no pragmatic meaning of truth available *in abstracto*; what the concept of truth means for us is inseparable from the plurality of epistemic practices we engage in in order to reach truths. This applies to religious truth-seeking, too (assuming that there is such a thing).

According to Slater, while truth is an "*event*" and "happens to an idea or statement," as James often says, "what ultimately *makes* our beliefs and statements about reality successful is their agreement with reality."[57] This is correct, but then again agreement itself is understood in terms of satisfaction, of concrete "leadings" from one bit of experience to another. It should be made more precise that the kind of success relevant here is epistemic. Moreover, the "making" involved here is a kind of truthmaking, insofar as truth itself amounts to success, but it is very different from, say, Armstrong's metaphysically realistic notion of truthmaking.[58] Slater admits that James takes truth to be an epistemic concept, but "epistemic *precisely on account of its relation to reality*."[59] A metaphysically realist correspondence or truth-making theoretician, such as Armstrong, would have none of this. The "relation to reality" that truths have must be nonepistemic in order to be sufficiently realistic.

Slater, moreover, is one of the very few commentators on James who perceive that there are "transcendental arguments that are basic to his pragmatism," one of them being the realistic bunch of arguments seeking to show that "if beliefs or statements about reality are to be either meaningful or true, there must first be a reality to which they refer," and that "in order for a belief or statement about some reality to be true it must also *agree* with that reality."[60] The existence of a mind-independent reality is argued to be a necessary condition for the possibility of truth.[61]

Slater points out that James had difficulties in balancing his realist and "humanist" ideas,[62] even at times "undercutting his commitment to realism" by suggesting that "reality is somehow altered or reconstructed through our cognitive interactions with it."[63] This is a revealing formulation, because in my view it is right here that James arrives at what is essential in his "realism," namely, its subordination to (what I have called) his *transcendental pragmatism*.[64] We need not read James as claiming that we alter or reconstruct reality in any causal, factual, or empirical sense through our cognitive interactions with it; these alterations and reconstructions—or the dependence of reality on us and our cognitive powers—are, rather, in Kantian terms "transcendental." It is only in the sense in which the spatio-temporal framework and the categories, such as causality, are established by us, or imposed by us on the world we are able to experience, according to Kant, that reality is, for James, dependent on us or altered by us in cognition. Our "worldmaking," to borrow a term of Goodman's more recent neopragmatism which is in some ways analogical to James's pragmatism,[65] is transcendental, not factual— although neither James nor Goodman is willing to put the matter in precisely these terms. Nevertheless, just as Kant was able to defend empirical realism within, and indeed held that it is made possible by, his transcendental idealism, James is able to endorse a form of empirical (though not metaphysical) realism within his transcendental pragmatism. I agree, then, with Slater when he argues that we need both realism and humanism about truth.[66] But it is important to see that the kind of realism that we may maintain compatibly with humanism is empirical realism, and the kind of humanism we may maintain compatibly with realism is transcendental humanism (or transcendental pragmatism). This can be seen as a specification of the deep analogy between Kant and James that I already defended in chapter 1.

Similar Kantian or quasi-Kantian reflections apply to what James has to say about religion and "religious reality." Our postulation of "an unseen religious order"[67] is transcendentally dependent on our religious life. Slater perceptively notes the analogy between Kant and James that was already emphasized above:

In a move similar to Kant's in the *Critique of Practical Reason*, James argues that while the basis of morality is autonomous from religion, our desire to lead "morally strenuous" lives and to offer an account of moral objectivity cannot plausibly be satisfied unless we postulate God's existence. James's view, in brief, is that we cannot fully awaken our moral capacities and sustain them at their highest level without believing that our moral obligations are ultimately grounded in a moral standard that transcends any merely human standard.[68]

Once again, this is both correct and incorrect. For Kant, or for James, morality cannot be based on a religious standard, because morality, in order to be genuine morality at all, must be autonomous. However, leading a truly moral life, or trying to make sense of such a life, may lead us to postulate divine powers. Slater's important discussion of James's "way of simultaneously acknowledging both the autonomy of morality and the necessity of religious commitment for realizing certain moral goods" could be significantly enriched, if he explicitly phrased his reading of James in terms of Kant's notion of the postulates of practical reason, and if he connected *this* with his accurate observation that there are transcendental arguments in James.[69]

Hence, I wonder whether James might again be read as arguing transcendentally when suggesting (according to Slater) that "there are moral goods that can only be gained (if at all) by supplementing our worldview with metaphysical and religious beliefs,"[70] and whether this might even amount to a pragmatic-transcendental argument ultimately grounding metaphysical and religious postulations upon ethical premises. Moreover, analogously to what was already suggested above, a transcendental account of religious realism as subordinated to transcendental pragmatism—the plurality of our religious lives and moral outlooks—would strengthen the reading of James as a religious realist by setting his peculiar kind of realism in its proper context. Note, however, that religion would then be grounded in ethics (*not* the other way round); Slater puts the cart before the horse when he claims (in the quote above) James to have maintained that "our moral obligations are ultimately grounded in a moral standard that transcends any merely human standard." Such religious standards—if we may thus call them—are available to us only on the basis of prior ethical standards, which are inescapably human.

James, as has repeatedly been emphasized in this chapter, is not just a pragmatist but also (among other things) a pluralist. As Slater also notes, "James's pragmatism entails a commitment to *pluralism* at both the theoretical and practical levels."[71] This pluralism is both religious—respecting individuals' (as well as nations' and historical epochs') particular "overbeliefs"—and ethical, emphasizing tolerance toward different ways of life.[72] Slater needs to defend a combination of realist and pluralist pragmatism in order to "account for the potential reality of some of the objects of religious belief, experience, and devotion . . . while rejecting the narrow exclusivism characteristic of many realist approaches to religion."[73] This is obviously a pragmatically desirable goal. Indeed, for the purposes of religious ethics and the philosophy of religion more generally, this is one of the main reasons for taking James seriously in contemporary discussions and for getting his realism right; my discussion of James's pluralism earlier in this chapter comes, then, close to Slater's views in this regard.

One should, however, once again ask what exactly James's pluralism amounts to. In the introductory remarks above, we saw that pluralism, as developed in *A Pluralistic Universe* and other late works, amounts to a radically empiricist metaphysical theory according to which there is a plurality—bits and pieces—of "pure experience." But we also noted an important alternative reading, according to which pluralism, for James, is not primarily a metaphysical doctrine but a metaphilosophical (or "metametaphysical") one, emphasizing the possibility of a plurality of different "correct" metaphysical positions maintained from different practice-embedded perspectives. There is, then, as we have seen, a plurality of pluralisms. There are both metaphysical and (at a metalevel) conceptual, methodological, and metaphilosophical versions of pluralism, as well as an ethical, social, and political aspect to James's treatment of pluralism. My fear is that Slater's emphasis on James's alleged metaphysical realism may in the end commit him to a monistic rather than pluralistic picture of James. That is, a pragmatic pluralism, in its different dimensions, can be much better accommodated within the kind of reading I have proposed, in contrast to Slater's metaphysically realist reading. Pluralism itself may not be a transcendental doctrine but it may require transcendental pragmatism in order to be fully developed—in its plural outlooks.

There is also—for pragmatist readers of James, at least—a plurality of correct readings of James, each good or pragmatically useful, for its own purposes. I have in this section tried to show that Slater's picture of James, while correcting many of the catastrophic inaccuracies of James scholarship, is too much a picture of a metaphysical realist to represent either the real James or the James that deserves to be defended as a contributor to contemporary discussions in the field. Furthermore, while my own "transcendental James" may not be the real James, either, I do believe that a rereading of James as a kind of transcendental pragmatist illuminates the troubles he had with realism and idealism, while also providing us with ample conceptual resources for making sense of his unique combination of realism, pluralism, and humanism. I obviously agree with Slater that "there is much in James . . . that is philosophically interesting and defensible, and much that might variously strengthen or challenge our prevailing philosophical assumptions."[74] I have only suggested that the best of James, and even the best of his (religious) realism, can be brought out by (re)interpreting him as a transcendental pragmatist instead of a metaphysical realist. This strategy is actually in accord with Slater's pluralistic proposal to "take James in piecemeal fashion rather than taking him wholesale."[75] This metalevel interpretive pluralism is, presumably, the only acceptable methodology for the pragmatist interpreter of James, who is as fallibilist in her/his interpretations of other philosophers, including her/his favorite ones, as in any other beliefs.

Finally—to conclude my dispute with Slater—while I am very sympathetic to his general discussion of the relation between ethics and faith in James, I am not quite certain that even his overall claim that "the dependence of morality on some form of religious faith is *the* dominant ethical theme in James's . . . writings" is correct.[76] James might admit, with Kant, that morality is autonomous and that moral requirements bind us irrespectively of our religious commitments, while continuing to argue that religion gives us the (only?) genuine motive for moral life—which is to say that there is no extraethical motive after all, as religion itself, pragmatically understood, is (as I am, in a way, arguing throughout this volume) "deep" in us, quite as deep as morality itself is.[77] There is no religious grounding available for morality; ethics cannot depend on religion. Yet, ethical life may be inextricably intertwined with religion, which in the end symbolizes the seriousness of the ethical perspective itself.[78]

Final Reflections

One goal of this relatively lengthy argument has been to illuminate from a Jamesian pragmatist perspective some fundamental conceptual, primarily metaphilosophical, issues concerning the status of theism (and the theism versus atheism dispute)—as well as the metalevel contrasts, evidentialism versus fideism and realism versus antirealism. The relations between metaphysics and ethics have been particularly emphasized. Indirectly, I hope I have been able to offer reasons for adopting a Jamesian pragmatic method for a pluralistic reexamination of such major issues in the philosophy of religion.

Moreover, the metaphysics of theism James defends by means of his ethical argument must be clearly distinguished from the equally unpragmatic monistic metaphysics of atheism (materialism) and absolute idealism. The latter's postulation of the Absolute, while it may give us "moral holidays," is as problematic ethically as the former's mechanistic, purely physical, deterministic "block universe." Faith in God can only, if at all, be "justified" within the moral lives we are (and must be) committed to; such a justification is itself pluralistic, relativizing the reasons for postulating divine reality to individual believers' life situations and contexts of existential considerations. Evidentialist justification, which avoids this contextualization, is, by contrast, essentially monistic and thereby not just epistemically but ethically problematic. We also have to take seriously the *moral task* of justification of our lives before we can even start arguing for, or against, theism. This is to accept the primacy of the ethical point of view we are continuously challenged to occupy—and hence the autonomy of morality in relation to everything else, including religion—but it is this primacy itself that renders that point of view deeply metaphysical. It is in this sense that we might speak about the *codependence* (mutual dependence) or perhaps *coconstitutivity* of metaphysics and ethics in Jamesian philosophy of religion, and Jamesian pragmatist philosophy more generally. Moreover, in order to avoid construing ethics and religion as completely separate from each other (in James), we might also regard them as coconstitutive, at least in the sense that (as has been argued repeatedly) religion can receive its only justification from morality while, conversely, moral life and its commitments may receive their depth and seriousness from a religious interpretation, or from the possibility of viewing moral duty *as if* it were commanded by God.

I have repeatedly pointed out that pragmatic pluralism must be taken to a "metalevel"—both in metaphysics and in the philosophy of religion. Instead of ending up with radical relativism, as too straightforward forms of pragmatism may threaten to (cf. chapters 1 and 3), the present discussion has, I hope, taken important steps toward a truly pragmatic pluralism in the philosophy of religion. In conclusion, then, I want to suggest that James's pluralism is the true heir of the *pragmatic method*, especially in its applications to the philosophy of religion (and, extrapolating from this case study, more generally as well). Charles S. Peirce characterized the pragmatic method, the pragmatist maxim, as a method of "making our ideas clear."[79] He required that we should consider the conceivable practical results the objects of our ideas (beliefs, theories, concepts, or conceptions) might have in the course of experience. James transformed this originally scientific method of conceptual clarification into a more *weltanschaulich* relevant method of making our ideas pragmatically relevant in terms of human experience at large. Here, in the case of religion, it is crucially important to take into account not just the diverse religious experiences that individuals have had and may have, but also the diversity and plurality of conceptual, theological, and philosophical approaches to those experiences, that is, the richness of philosophical and theological traditions through which people have tried to understand and organize their religious lives and problems. What this means is that no single philosophy of religion, not even James's own pluralism or pragmatism, can offer us an overarching, privileged perspective on the deeply problematic phenomenon of religion. We really do need a plurality of perspectives, as I have argued already in the introduction and chapter 1. This antireductionism is the true message of Jamesian pragmatism: we must be prepared to employ conceptual frameworks and philosophico-theological interpretations of religion different from, and even in tension with, pragmatism, in order to fully account for the pragmatically relevant differences in people's religious options and problems. We need a truly pluralistic pragmatism in the philosophy of religion. We need *genuine acknowledgment of otherness*—both different religious outlooks and different theological or philosophical (metatheological) approaches. This is what we can get, if we apply the pragmatic method in its Jamesian formulation. Yet, we must also acknowledge our human limitations and finitude: very often we are not capable of the kind of acknowledgment, let alone mutual recognition, that we ought to cultivate in our relations to our fellow human beings.

Thus, even the pragmatist should not be blind to the genuine pragmatic value of nonpragmatist ideas. While, for instance, we may follow James in arguing that the monistic idealists' Absolute is ethically unacceptable and that metaphysical and religious pluralism makes better sense of a melioristic moral struggle for a better world, we should also keep our eyes open to the possible ethical virtues of such monistic postulations. We should not dogmatically reject them without pragmatically considering them, or perhaps even experimenting with them in our religious or nonreligious lives. Furthermore, the antiessentialist and antifoundationalist pragmatist can hardly just say that pragmatism itself is "essentially" pluralistic (although I may have come close to saying precisely that in the above discussion of Jamesian pragmatic pluralism). Also more monistic versions of pragmatism (e.g., Peirce's?) need to be acknowledged, as they also play a pragmatically valuable role in advancing certain human purposes—for example, scientific, if not religious, metaphysical, or ethical. Our pluralism, then, should be connected with our acknowledgment of the ethical grounds of metaphysics:[80] pluralism is an expression of acknowledging the inevitable dependence of metaphysical inquiry on the inquirers' concrete individual, ethically loaded perspectives (including their individual "philosophical temperaments"). Individuals may, for instance, weigh in their different ways the different criteria that can be used for determining the acceptability of metaphysical views, and there cannot be any absolute or universal algorithm for this weighing. Accepting this pluralism is to be a pragmatist, in the Jamesian sense, to be prepared to put metaphysical and theological ideas into action by evaluating them ethically in individuals' lives—social lives of course included. This, in short, is to employ the pragmatic method in one's metaphysical and religious considerations.

The problem is, then, how to distinguish such pluralistic applications of pragmatism and the pragmatic method from relativism, from the shallow doctrine that "anything goes"—regarding religion or anything else. Which "voices" should be heard, and which ones (e.g., pseudoreligious ideas postulating mysterious causal connections between religious activities, such as prayer, and divine reality) should, albeit upon careful consideration, be silenced? What does it mean, after all, that we "hear" (or fail to hear) a philosophical voice? These questions constitute a fundamental problem that pragmatists simply have to live with. This problem must eventually be connected with the issue of *reflexivity*. When listening to *other* (metaphysical, philosophical, religious) voices in addition to pluralism, don't we have to say that pluralism itself is just one (or, rather, many!) of the many different correct philosophical views? Yes, I suppose we do have to accept this, at least in a sense. However, pluralism does not entail a shallow "anything goes" relativism; or, better, any relativism we might be pragmatically entitled to embrace is itself only relatively and contextually acceptable. Above all, reflexivity means responsibility. Even if no "voice" (even pluralism itself) is absolute and infallible in human affairs, we can intelligently inquire into the pragmatic acceptability of *any* particular perspective. Many perspectives will undoubtedly easily, through a proper pragmatist examination, be found unsatisfactory, ethically unacceptable, or even pseudoreligious (cf. chapters 5 and 6).

Moreover, as the remarks above on James's relations to the problem of realism and to the Kantian issues of transcendental philosophy make clear, James himself was no shallow relativist at all, even though he is sometimes taken to be one.[81] He was, in the pragmatic sense of the term, as fully a "realist" as anyone—especially when it comes to acknowledging the full reality and religious significance of human suffering, mortality, and evil (cf. chapter 5). Therefore I am confident that his pragmatism can be employed as strongly as any other philosophical approach in a campaign in favor of pluralism, yet against radical relativism. More generally, pragmatism, we may learn from James, is not an antimetaphysical approach (as is often supposed, also by pragmatists themselves); in contrast, it is *metaphysically serious*. It is metaphysically serious because it is ethically serious. The pragmatic method should lead us to "know reality" in a more concrete, experiential, and practice-embedded sense, bringing us in an engaged contact with the world we live in. This contact requires ethics, and an ethical interest lies at its center. There is no nonethical way to "know reality" at all. On the other hand, saying this is not yet to say much about the *content* of the ethical grounds of metaphysics and theology. When arguing, from a Jamesian perspective, that we have to examine the pragmatic core of our metaphysical and religious convictions ethically (and that such a pragmatic core is nevertheless "metaphysically serious"), we must be continuously prepared to reflect on the kind of ethical perspective we are occupying. Ethics can never be just given to us; through our ethical evaluation of our religious (or nonreligious) commitments, we are also evaluating our ethical perspective itself, including its ability to contribute to our overall self-critical reflection on our lives.

Part of the reality we need to "know" pragmatically, in and through our lives with other human beings, is the reality of evil and suffering. The reality of evil, already taken up in passing several times in this chapter and the previous ones (especially chapter 1), is a crucial part of the world the pragmatist needs to understand, acknowledge, and actively deal with. Chapter 5 is devoted to that topic.

FIVE

THE PROBLEM OF EVIL AND
THE LIMITS OF PHILOSOPHY

There has been a recent revival, especially after 9/11, of philosophical interest in the concept of evil in its various dimensions. Without attempting to summarize this already comprehensive discussion,[1] I want to start this chapter by drawing attention to some basic contrasts, tensions, and oppositions that need to be taken up when examining the concept of evil. There is, first, the familiar distinction to be drawn between *natural* and *moral* evil (typically epitomized in two names: Lisbon and Auschwitz). *Religious* and *nonreligious* approaches to the problem of evil constitute another important contrast: Is evil something "merely human" or something non- or inhuman (or, possibly, superhuman) and therefore only religiously or theologically accountable?[2] Thirdly, the *theodicism* versus *antitheodicism* opposition arises from questions such as the following: Is a theodicy needed? Or are theodicies even possible? Does evil (or do related phenomena, such as unnecessary suffering) have a purpose, meaning, function, or justification?

The last of these three contrasts is my main focus in this chapter. I will examine the theodicism versus antitheodicism opposition not only from a pragmatist perspective but also transcendentally—once again analogously to Kant's transcendental examination of the necessary conditions for, and limits of, the possibility of human experience—by drawing attention to the *limits of philosophical reflection* or even more broadly to the *limits of language*, that is, of language—philosophical or nonphilosophical—appropriate for speaking about evil. This opposition, I will argue, is more fundamental than the standard one between religious and nonreligious approaches. What we will be particularly concerned with here is *moral* appropriateness: how should we speak, and possibly philosophically theorize about, evil and suffering, in order to adequately appreciate the victims of (moral) evil and suffering, in particular, acknowledging their moral integrity, dignity, and status as persons? What kind of moral practices of approaching evil should we develop and maintain in our ethical or religious lives? These are particularly important questions for pragmatist philosophers today, because by considering this kind of problems we may pragmatically evaluate the "goods" that religious life and thought may bring to human existence, as well as the many ways in which religious life may go seriously wrong. Examining the problem of evil through such questions concerning moral appropriateness can thus be seen as applications of the pragmatic method to this particular topic.

The classical pragmatist most central to my concerns is again James. This chapter, however, is not primarily a chapter *on* James or even on Jamesian pragmatism; it is, rather, an exploration of a certain kind of understanding of the problem of evil which provides a context in which James's approach to this issue becomes particularly relevant. I will have something more explicit to say on James toward the end of the chapter (revisiting some of the issues already touched upon in chapter 4). First, however, I will prepare the ground for a philosophical appreciation of his way of facing the reality of evil, tragedy, and suffering as experiential facts of human life.[3]

In addition to the three tensions listed, there is a metalevel contrast to be drawn between those views according to which evil is a relevant and philosophically acceptable concept and those that find it useless, unacceptable, or irrelevant.[4] My pragmatic-transcendental examination will offer some reasons for adopting the former view. However, the crucial issue is *how* to construe the philosophically relevant notion of evil.

It is important to note that both theodicist and antitheodicist views can be religious or nonreligious. There are, then, secular theodicies. Accordingly, I am using the concept of theodicism in a very broad sense, covering any view, religious or nonreligious, that requires a justification of evil or suggests that evil is in some sense meaningful.[5] In particular, a fundamental question for philosophers of religion here is whether *any* theodicist approach to the problem of evil can be "genuinely religious." Conversely (and slightly paradoxically), it might even be argued that antitheodicist approaches, even when nonreligious, are the *only* "genuinely religious" options we have in the discourse on evil, that is, theodicies, even when explicitly religiously formulated, are not and cannot be genuinely religious.[6] That is, a religious person avoiding pseudoreligious superstition should avoid justifying evil.

I propose the following table, with the question mark indicating the basic task of this chapter, to which I hope a pragmatist approach might contribute.

	Theodicism	**Antitheodicism**
Religious	Leibniz, Swinburne	Dostoevsky, Phillips (Wittgensteinians)
Nonreligious	Hegel, Marx	?

The Challenge

I will not go through the familiar terrain of logical versus epistemic (evidential) versions of the problem of evil, nor of the evidentialist background assumptions of mainstream philosophy of religion today. Instead, suffice it to say that I am quite convinced—not only by Jamesian pragmatism (cf. chapter 4) but also by Wittgensteinian philosophy of religion and related approaches—that evidentialism, at least in its standard forms, is hopeless, failing to capture anything like the genuinely religious attitude to evil and suffering.[7] The theistic view that there is God is simply not a hypothesis to be tested against "evidence," including the empirically undeniable reality of evil (the piece of evidence regarded by atheists as the most significant defeater of religious beliefs). The problem of evil does not function as an "atheological" argument in the straightforward sense imagined by atheist critics of religion.[8] This is because a religious attitude to the evil around us is *not* the scientific attitude of testing hypotheses.

This, however, does not make things easy neither for the believer nor the nonbeliever. The major challenge, marked by the question mark in the table above, is to develop—supplementing what may be seen as Dostoevskyan or Wittgensteinian ideas in the philosophy of religion—a *nonreligious form of antitheodicism*, in which the understanding of the deep obscenity and sheer ethical unacceptability of "explaining away" evil (or quasi-justifying it) is analogous to the understanding of theodicies as superstitious or even blasphemous in the religious or theological context. This is, at a more general level, one way of criticizing sharp religious versus nonreligious dichotomies: (anti)theodicism has (quasi-)secular analogies, and one's antitheodicist commitment may be far more important, both ethically and religiously, than one's explicit religious or theological commitments, or one's qualifications as a believer in terms of institutionalized religion. Accordingly, a nonreligious antitheodicism should be understood as highly, even crucially, relevant to the philosophy of religion, especially when pragmatically developed. Extending antitheodicism beyond religious thought proper may, somewhat paradoxically, be an important contribution to our philosophical understanding of religiosity.

When studying some of the recent literature on evil, we may, while starting from a secular philosophical perspective, appreciate the ways in which this notion has "depth" and "intractability" which, however, should neither be reduced to its religious dimensions (but rather adjusted to a largely secular modern world) nor banalized in terms of religious fundamentalism typical of, say, the dichotomous rhetoric of good and evil that George W. Bush and many others monstrously resorted to in the "war on terror" succeeding 9/11.[9] Religion is more deeply in us—rooted in our conceptions of moral obligation, of responding to other human beings and finding one's way in the world—than we often want to, or even can, acknowledge.[10]

The problem concerning the limits of language, connected with the limits of ethically appropriate philosophical reflection, emerges as a crucial issue as soon as the depth of the concept of evil is emphasized in this quasi-religious manner. How to appropriately speak about evil? Is this ultimately the task of something else than rational scientific or philosophical discourse? But then again, can there be poetry or literature or philosophy, or even any significant, responsible inquiry into the human condition, after Auschwitz? Taking this question seriously presupposes taking seriously the quasi-religious depth of evil. One key idea I want to propose in what follows is that the transcendental (yet pragmatically approachable) issue concerning the limits of language is a problem both in religious and theological approaches and in secular ones. Both have to deal with the "intractability" or "inscrutability" of evil.[11] Yet, even when it takes us to the limits of language, or beyond, evil is an important and legitimate philosophical concept, though presumably not a scientific or explanatory one (I will get back to this point below). We may not be able to explain human actions by referring to the idea of evil, but we might need that notion in order to describe them in their true colors—even if we by engaging in such descriptions (in viewing evil as "deep") in a sense transgress the boundaries of legitimate discourse.

Our major challenge, then, is to be able to seriously—"existentially"—acknowledge the deep, even quasi-religious intractability of evil, its being a challenge to our world comprehension (or the very comprehensibility of the world) itself,[12] while avoiding mystifying assumptions of there being something like "Satanic greatness" in evil. Regarding the latter idea, Hannah Arendt's very important contrast between the banality of Nazi evil and the mystifying tendencies to see Satanic greatness in it ought to be kept in mind: a typical Nazi figure like Adolf Eichmann is not "great" in any way; he is a strikingly ordinary character while committing horrendous actions.[13] One way of reformulating the search for a nonreligious antitheodicist approach is to say that we are looking for a way to integrate the insight into the intractability of evil with the recognition that evil is often banal, lacking profundity. (Evil is, thus, deep in a certain way while not being deep in another way.) This challenge may itself be deep enough to be of interest to philosophers of religion, too, even if the main task is to provide a perspective on evil independent of any theological assumptions.

However, before developing antitheodicism further and indicating its connections with Jamesian pragmatism, I should briefly review the evidentialist discourse on evil I am criticizing in this chapter. I can only pick one example from contemporary discussions of these issues. I have chosen to comment on Peter van Inwagen's theory of evil, as spelled out in his 2006 book on the topic, because it is one of the most impressive recent analytic achievements of theodicism.

In his carefully argued book *The Problem of Evil*, based on the Gifford Lectures he delivered in 2003, van Inwagen emphasizes that he is *not* offering a theodicy but only a "defense." A theodicy and a defense need not differ in content; both are stories according to which both God and evil exist, but a theodicy is put forward as "the real truth of the matter," whereas a defense is, according to its author, a story that "may or may not be true" but is argued to be consistent and epistemically possible.[14] In my terminology, a "defense" of this kind may still belong, and typically belongs, to the "theodicist" tradition: the one who offers a defense—a story trying to make sense of God's allowing there to be evil—is still engaged in the process of justifying God's (possible) actions and reasons for them, even if she/he does not claim that the story told is true. The mere appeal to the epistemically possible is justificatory in nature. Moreover, the problem of evil for van Inwagen basically means the problem of reconciling God's existence with the fact that there are "bad things" in the world.[15] He refuses to recognize any depth in the concept of evil itself, as distinguished from (mere) badness. Furthermore, he notes that his task is "a purely intellectual one," a theoretical examination of the problem of evil understood as "the problem that the real existence of bad things raises for theists."[16] Thus, van Inwagen simply denies the intractability or inscrutability of evil emphasized by thinkers like Bernstein and Neiman.

It is obviously very important for a philosopher to be explicit about the limitations of her/his approach and methodology. In this sense, I think van Inwagen's project is exemplary: he is very honest about what he is doing and what he is not doing (at least more explicit in this regard than many other mainstream analytic philosophers of religion). On the other hand, if my proposals in this chapter are on the right track, the kind of thing he sets out to do is *not* what philosophers of religion ought to do.

Van Inwagen is not particularly sensitive to the religious and existential depth of the problem of evil, and of the corresponding religiously profound concept of evil. Not only does he set aside the Kantian-Arendtian concept of "radical evil"; he also rejects the idea that there is some "overarching problem of evil" in the sense proposed by Susan Neiman.[17] This is what he says:

> I am only a simple-minded analytical philosopher.... As I see matters, the problem of evil is what it has always been, a problem about God and evil. There is no larger, overarching problem of evil that manifests itself as a theological problem in one historical period and as a problem belonging to post-religious thought in another. I don't know how to argue for this conclusion, because I wouldn't know how enter into anything I would call an argument with someone who would even consider denying it.[18]

At this point, it seems to me, van Inwagen reveals the fundamentally *ahistorical* nature of his philosophical position, including his methodology. One of the key messages of not only this chapter on the problem of evil but of this entire book on pragmatist philosophy of religion is that, when viewing religious ideas as responses to human problems naturally emerging within our practices, we are dealing with historically developing and reinterpretable matters. While evil itself may be a persistent feature of human life in this world, a fundamental experience that will be with us to stay, our interpretations of and responses to evil may take very different forms during the history of human thought. Theodicist responses, I am trying to argue, are unacceptable *for us*, in the particular historical situation we are now in, within the kind of practices we have developed.

In addition to developing a highly theoretical philosophical approach to the problem of evil and thereby manifesting insensitivity toward any attempts to historicize the problem, or the relevant notion of evil, van Inwagen is even more strikingly insensitive toward the ethical need to avoid overly intellectualized accounts of this problem. He suggests that "for all logic can tell us, God might have reasons for allowing evil to exist that, in his mind, outweigh the desirability of the nonexistence of evil,"[19] and that God may have foreseen that "free will is a sufficiently great good that its existence outweighs the evils that have resulted."[20] He also adds that in the end it might happen that "every evil done by the wicked to the innocent will have been avenged, and every tear will have been wiped away,"[21] and goes on to speculate that, just as "there can be cases in which it is morally permissible for an agent to permit an evil that agent could have prevented, despite the fact that no good is achieved by doing so," this is "the moral structure of the situation in which God finds himself when he contemplates the world of horrors that is the consequence of humanity's separation from him."[22] Here van Inwagen engages in a theoretical speculation that might not only be considered insulting and even obscene by victims of evil but that may also be argued to be philosophically defective because of its failure to *engage*, existentially and comfortingly, with human beings' problems—their experience of evil—at all.

God's having *reasons* to allow evil—reasons that may outweigh some other considerations—makes God a calculating monster.[23] It is not primarily the argumentative structure carefully canvassed by van Inwagen that the antitheodicist should be opposed to; it is, much more fundamentally, the picture he offers of the divinity and human beings' relations to both God and history that we should find simply ethically unacceptable. Van Inwagen does point out that his account does explain why God might allow, and might have a reason to allow, evils happening to people "without any reason," because "being separated from God" means to be "the playthings of chance."[24] *Therefore* people, including children, suffer and die horribly "*for no reason at all*."[25] Yet, God has, according to van Inwagen's defense, reasons—and even good, ethically sound reasons—to allow *this* to be the case.

Just as van Inwagen says he finds it difficult to argue with those who claim to be able to grasp something like a comprehensive problem of evil, I find it very difficult to provide any argumentative response to van Inwagen's "defense" at this point. (This is also partly because I do not regard the problem of evil as an atheological argument in the first place.) I find it simply ethically disastrous—and, when it comes to one's theological picture of the divinity, possibly even blasphemous—to suggest that God might have good reasons for allowing the world to be a place in which innocent children are, say, led to gas chambers. If one's philosophical approach leads one to say things like that, then there is something wrong with that philosophical approach. One should not only recognize the "limits of argumentation"—the fact that we should not always follow the intellectually most sophisticated argument, wherever it leads[26]—but one should more generally be continuously aware of the ethical context in which one's philosophizing takes place.

Part of this ethical context, for a Jamesian pragmatist at least, is that philosophy should, in dealing with (as Dewey put it) "problems of men," offer *comfort* to the suffering.[27] Now, van Inwagen is again conscious of the limitations of his approach (and this is obviously to his merit). He says quite explicitly that he is not, in offering his defense, attempting to even hypothetically comfort anyone.[28] It is precisely for this reason that we should reject his "defense" with the words James directed at Leibnizian theodicies, that is, as "a cold literary exercise, whose cheerful substance even hell-fire does not warm."[29] A philosophical reflection on the problem of evil should avoid the God's-Eye View adopted by van Inwagen and should sincerely acknowledge our human limits in dealing with this problem, maintaining sensitivity not only to the victims of evil but also to everyone needing comfort in the (historically developing) situation of having to live within such limits. My challenge in this chapter is to develop an antitheodicist philosophy of religion, based on pragmatism along the lines of the previous chapters, that will be more sensitive to the human dimensions of the problem of evil than van Inwagen's purely theoretical approach.

Transcendental Limits of Language

One obvious reason for van Inwagen's failure to adequately deal with the concept of evil is, arguably, his basic philosophical point of departure, evidentialist analytic philosophy of religion, which is diametrically opposed to both Kantian and pragmatist approaches to these issues. Van Inwagen not only fails to deal with the historical and practice-laden character of the problem of evil; he also fails to respect the human limits—particularly ethical limits—that enable us to seriously discuss the notion of evil in the first place. Therefore, in order to properly discuss the transcendental dimensions of the problem of the limits of language, some remarks ought to be made on Kant's conception of *radical evil*. Kant, of course, was a crucial figure in shifting attention from natural evil to moral evil—to evil as a concept concerning human action instead of natural forces.[30]

From the Kantian perspective, evil is, primarily, something that concerns the *moral subject*: radical evil is not just the empirical tendency to prioritize happiness, well-being, or personal needs and interests in contrast to the moral law, but the subject's *free choice* of maxims prioritizing happiness to the moral law. We are *responsible* for this choice and this prioritization, and therefore we are "radically" (at the root) evil. Our tendency to freely prioritize maxims contrary to the moral law is, like our acting out of pure respect for the moral law, ultimately inexplicable and incomprehensible.[31]

This very important idea receives its modern expression in Wittgensteinian conceptions of moral subjectivity. The Wittgensteinian perspective in contemporary moral philosophy also takes seriously the transcendental issue concerning the limits of (moral) language—whether the starting point is the early or the later Wittgenstein—and thereby also the issue concerning the ethical standpoint(s) from which philosophy itself starts.

According to the early Wittgenstein, good and evil are features or predicates of the (transcendental, metaphysical) subject, not anything "in" the world, let alone objects of any kind.[32] Just like Kant's theory of radical evil, Wittgenstein's view turns attention to the moral subject itself. This insight, while not preserved as such in Wittgenstein's later thought, still plays a transformed role there. For the later Wittgenstein and philosophers following him, the question is how to appropriately speak about morally good and evil. That is, how should *we*—viewing ourselves as the subjects committed to the ethical project of adequately understanding and responding to the evil we find in our world[33]—philosophically or generally rationally discuss evil? For instance, according to D. Z. Phillips, we morally speaking *cannot*, say, call the Holocaust "naughty" any more than we can (aesthetically speaking) meaningfully call the Grand Canyon or some other majestic natural formation "pretty" or "nice"; when doing so, we in a sense breach the limits of ethically—or aesthetically—possible language use.[34]

In a sense, if we take Wittgenstein's insights far enough, evil cannot be predicated of any object but only of the subject, the first person, *me*—which amounts to a kind of transcendentally solipsistic account of evil.[35] This is one case of the limits of language (or, in late-Wittgensteinian jargon, of language games) morally possible for us. The crucial issue is *my* relation to the world, reflected in my use of language. Indeed, Wittgensteinian philosophers, including Phillips, have vigorously, and in my view with justification, attacked more mainstream philosophers of religion engaging in theodicies (or "defenses"), such as Swinburne and van Inwagen, who could be said to approach the problem of evil from a "God's-Eye View" instead of a finite human, personal point of view manifested in both Wittgensteinian moral philosophy and Jamesian pragmatism (despite their many differences).[36] Given this task of carefully critically reflecting on *our own* ethical language use, we may return to our basic questions. After theodicies, is there any longer any role for the concept of evil to play in rational discourse? *Can* we theorize or speak about evil in *any* appropriate way, or is it as hopeless as our attempts to attach any accurate linguistic labels to the Holocaust (for instance, "naughty" or "bad" won't do, but neither will "Satanic," and we may be unable to find *any* description appropriate—we may find ourselves simply lacking words—other than "evil"). There are different possible reactions here.

For example, Phillip Cole maintains that we should reject the very notion of evil in serious philosophical or intellectual discussions. Unlike most other theorists of evil, Cole actually argues against the reality of evil, specifically against our being able to *explain* human actions in terms of this notion—in any nonmythological way—and thus suggests that we had better give up the very concept of evil in philosophical discourse. Nevertheless, he notes that the fundamental question of "the meaning of humanity" lies behind our attempts to understand the meaning(s) of evil.[37]

John Kekes seems to take a view opposite to Cole's: evil is a concept that can and in some cases ought to be used to denote certain actions, events, and even people; there are criteria that can be set for singling out evil actions from nonevil ones.[38] Susan Neiman, furthermore, finds evil highly central in the history of philosophy; it is a key issue regarding the question of the meaning and intelligibility of the world (to be revisited below).[39] Peter Dews, in turn, argues (and I have to some extent followed his argument in my remarks above) that there is a certain kind of "depth" in evil, yet depth that should be accounted for without the traditional religious overtones associated with this notion.[40] Richard Bernstein, as has already been mentioned, urges that we need continuous rethinking of the notion of evil, that we need to acknowledge its profound "intractability", and that we should be wary of "abusing" it (e.g., for short-sighted political purposes).[41] And there are many other interesting reactions that cannot be taken up here.[42] In any case, as different as these approaches are from each other, most of them are superior to the theodicist "defense" that van Inwagen and other evidentialist philosophers of religion are seeking in their purely theoretical exercises (see the previous section).

Understanding Evil

On the basis of the above discussion, and hoping to clarify the ways in which evil is and is not a threat to meaning and comprehensibility, I want to reemphasize a distinction familiar from the philosophy of the human sciences, namely, the one between *explanation* and *understanding*. Evil is, presumably, not an explanatory concept; here we should agree with Cole. Yet, some human actions must be *described* (and hence interpreted and understood) as evil—lacking any better or more appropriate descriptions, lacking any other morally appropriate way of describing those actions. Hence, the denial that evil functions as an explanatory concept does not entail the denial of its interpretive value.[43] For instance, attaching the label "evil" to the perpetrators of the Holocaust, or at least to their actions, seems to be the only moral option available; employing this notion enables us—not to explain why the Holocaust took place but—to attempt to understand more deeply the nature of the evil engaged in by the perpetrators, including its "banality" in Hannah Arendt's sense.

In some cases understanding an individual action or event in a correct or appropriate (morally appropriate!) manner may, then, presuppose that we describe, conceptualize, and categorize it under the description (vocabulary, discourse) of evil. This means that we place it in a certain ethical, historical, political and perhaps also theological context that makes it intelligible as the special kind of action or event it is. A description of something or someone as evil may even be something that we morally speaking owe to the victims of that action or that person (which is obviously something very different from explaining those actions or the agents' reasons for performing them, let alone "explaining them away" as evil). After such a description or understanding of an action as evil (in a special context) has been provided, the action *can* also be explained, possibly in quite different ways, for instance, intentionally by employing something like the practical syllogism,[44] say, by referring to Adolf Eichmann's attempts to promote his career and his beliefs about the necessary means for achieving such goals, or causally by referring to pathologies or other merely causal and natural, hence unintentional, facts and processes (e.g., psychopathic murderers' actions).[45]

However, while we certainly *can* understand evil actions, often extremely well, evil also takes us to the very limit of understanding. As Susan Neiman has argued in her profound book *Evil in Modern Philosophy* (2002), evil is a challenge to *comprehensibility in general*, not just to understanding individual actions, events, or people. Let us pursue this challenge in some more detail by connecting the challenge of comprehensibility (understanding) with the pursuit of what may be called meaningful life, a pursuit that goes to the heart of Jamesian pragmatism in the philosophy of religion.[46]

How *could* human life in this miserable world be experienced and understood as meaningful? More precisely, given the unbelievable sufferings of our fellow human beings, and given our own unavoidable guilt in the face of that suffering,[47] how could our experiences of meaningfulness, or the significance we perhaps claim to construct by living through our lives, be anything but illusory? The cosmos does not seem to care for our aspirations at all; in particular, it could not care less for our search for meaning and comprehension. Is the concept of meaning(fullness) even coherently applicable to, say, the life of someone who truly, nonself-deceptively recognizes that some of her/his fellow humans have gone through the Holocaust (not to talk about the victims themselves)? Can the process of constructing meaning in and through life even get started in such a person's life? It is, after all, *meaningless* evil and suffering that is usually presented as a fundamental challenge for the value of human life (and for theism), and hardly anyone can deny that the world as we know it is full of meaningless evil and suffering.[48] This is one way of saying that the cosmos, as we limited humans experience it, seems to be fundamentally absurd, meaningless, incomprehensible.

The search for meaning in life, including the attempts to overcome absurdity and to understand and live with (apparently meaningless) evil, is, we should once again observe, both metaphysical and ethical. As Neiman puts it, "we ask about the point of making theoretical sense of the world when we cannot make sense of misery and terror."[49] Do we have to "deny philosophy"—accepting the limits of not just philosophical but presumably any rational or intellectual discourse in contrast to, say, religious discourse—if we take evil seriously, admitting that it cannot, and perhaps even ethically should not, be theoretically analyzed?[50] These worries go to the heart of the problem of justifying any kind of theoretical, intellectual, or contemplative attitude to life—an attitude that seems to underlie the very issue of the meaning of/in life, as well as theodicist attempts to find evil meaningful. Yet, it is not merely the theoretical attempt to understand life's meaning and value that is threatened by evil. The fact (if it is a fact) that "the world contains neither justice nor meaning" is a threat both to our acting in the world and to our understanding it.[51] Philosophy, according to Neiman, begins—and threatens to stop—with questions about "what the structure of the world must be like for us to think and act within it" (rather than beginning with purely theoretical skeptical issues that largely seem to define our philosophical tradition).[52] Just like the problem of evil inseparably entangled with it, the problem of finding meaning in life is "fundamentally a problem about the intelligibility of the world as a whole," a problem presupposing a tight link between ethics and metaphysics.[53] It is twentieth-century evil, in particular, often captured in the single word *Auschwitz*, that seems not only to render evil itself ultimately "intractable" and unintelligible but also to undermine "the possibility of intellectual response itself," challenging all rational efforts to understand the world and our life in it.[54]

Referring to *The Brothers Karamazov*, Neiman writes (and I tend to agree with her here):

Dostoevsky underlined the idea that the problem of evil is not just one more mystery. It is so central to our lives that if reason stumbles there, it must give way to faith. If you cannot understand why children are tortured, nothing else you understand really matters. But the very attempt to understand it requires at least accepting it as part of the world that must be investigated. Some hold even this much acceptance to be unacceptable. Thus the rejection of theodicy becomes the rejection of comprehension itself.[55]

The problem of evil—not as a mere theological puzzle but as a deep human problem—is, then, a real test case for any views that may be defended regarding the issue of meaning. If no meaning can be found in a world of evil and suffering—in a world in which children are led to gas chambers—then the only *ethically* acceptable reaction *might* be to give up the intellectual, rational search for meaning altogether (including philosophical discourse) and to adopt religious faith instead. This recognition of the limits of philosophical inquiry might, moreover, be the only decent way to live with one's inescapable guilt and shame of being human, with one's being, helplessly, part of a world in which children are tortured. But, again, such a move, which we might conceive as the Jamesian "sick soul's" response to the evil and suffering in the world,[56] could also be ethically (and perhaps even religiously?) challenged. One might, and perhaps even should, insist on the continuous need for rational, philosophical discussion, even about evil.

Our deepest questions seem to be left unanswered. It is still not at all clear what the adequate philosophical or intellectual response to evil could and should be. The possibility remains, however, that someone might find *this* frustrating situation itself meaningful. That is, the fact that no final answers, substantial or methodological, to our worries about evil and meaningfulness have been or ever can be given, might be taken to be among the key potential sources of meaning in our lives. These might be fragile and definitely less than fully consoling sources of meaning, but they might be sources nonetheless.

The kind of conception of evil as a challenge to comprehensibility itself sketched here might, furthermore, be argued to need metaphysical backing in terms of, for example, Peirce's "real generals" (scholastic realism).[57] The same can, I believe, be said about Kant's famous theory of evil as a tendency (*Hang*) to certain kinds of prioritizations of maxims: it is not any individual action by itself but the *general tendency* to adopt certain kinds of maxims instead of others that is relevant. Evil, when connected with the issue of the very comprehensibility of the world we live in, is inevitably anchored in *modal* concepts, and in the ways in which certain concepts necessarily structure our moral lives and our ways of attempting to understand those lives.[58]

Evil, then, is "general" not particular; our task of understanding needs to be "modalized." We are not just attempting to understand individual phenomena—actions and agents—but generalities in which they are involved.[59] It is from this generality that the issue of the comprehensibility of the world as such also emerges, and is challenged by evil. As a generality, evil is never exhausted by its actual instances. It is a human potentiality, a "real possibility" for each of us, even when things seem to be going well.

Jamesian Pragmatism and Evil

Even though we have been led to a metaphysical construal of evil as a general potentiality, it is extremely important to reemphasize the need to resist any kind of mystification. Evil as such is certainly *not* incomprehensible: we do know and understand a lot about events we can only describe as evil, such as the Holocaust, and describing some events, actions, or people as evil may be a necessary requirement (providing the relevant context) for properly understanding and eventually even explaining them (bearing in mind that the notion of evil itself is not an explanatory concept, as suggested above). Yet, as has been suggested, evil—even individual (though possibly very complex) events, such as the Holocaust—may make the world in general incomprehensible. In a world like this, nothing ultimately matters; nothing we comprehend, understand, or know matters or even can matter (as we saw Susan Neiman arguing above). The problem of evil, in the strictly antitheodicist sense considered in this chapter, is not a problem of unexplainability or incomprehensibility as such—not the problem of our being unable to explain some *particular* events—but an existential (or existentialist) problem of *general* meaninglessness.

World and life lack significance, when seen under the aspect of evil—as the "sick soul" sees them through her/his fundamental melancholy.[60] This is a version of the idea, which we owe to Theodor Adorno, that there can be "no poetry after Auschwitz" that I find compelling.

Yet, as briefly proposed above, we might find meaning in this meaninglessness itself. This idea corresponds with Albert Camus's famous notion of "human revolt" (*l'homme revolte*).[61] Here, however, James's pragmatism—which is in fact not very far from the existentialist tones of Camus or, say, Jean-Paul Sartre (see also chapter 4)—could, perhaps slightly surprisingly, once again be relevant to our concerns. James writes in the same intellectual and spiritual setting Neiman and others operate in, that is, a context in which evil is a challenge to our attempt to find life meaningful at all (a context, I noted above, very different from the theoretical context typical of van Inwagen and other mainstream evidentalist philosophers of religion). Acknowledging evil and absurdity, as well as the quasi-transcendental limits of philosophical theorization and reflection, yet affirming an active, melioristic attitude (against an unavoidably tragic background), can be seen as a Jamesian contribution to the present discussion. According to James, as I read him, we should not philosophically theorize in a theodicist manner about the potential justification or meaning of evil and suffering. We should, rather, acknowledge evil and its victims by not attempting to explain it away; and we should simply fight against evil instead of accepting it by justifying it.

In his posthumously published work, *Some Problems of Philosophy*, James contrasted pluralism and monism in terms of the problem of evil as follows:

> Evil, for pluralism, presents only the practical problem of how to get rid of it. For monism the puzzle is theoretical: How—if Perfection be the source, should there be Imperfection? If the world as known to the Absolute be perfect, why should it be known otherwise, in myriads of inferior finite editions also? The perfect edition surely was enough. How do the breakage and dispersion and ignorance get in?[62]

Accordingly, the theoretical approach of monists (e.g., Hegelian idealists) leads to the theodicy problem, while the practical approach of the pluralists (including James himself) starts from the acknowledgment that evil is real—not to be explained away or justified—and focuses on the task of "how to get rid of it." In *Pragmatism*, James argued against "the airy and shallow optimism of current religious philosophy" that what suffering human beings experience "*is* Reality": "But while Professors Royce and Bradley and a whole host of quileless thoroughfed thinkers are unveiling Reality and the Absolute and explaining away evil and pain, this is the condition of the only beings known to us anywhere in the universe, with a developed consciousness of what the universe is."[63] A Leibnizian theodicy, in particular, postulating a "harmony" of the universe, amounts to—to quote again James's memorable phrase—"a cold literary exercise, whose cheerful substance even hell-fire does not warm"; hence, the idealist and optimist philosophers James argues against are, he says, "dealing in shades, while those who live and feel know truth."[64]

James's *Pragmatism* actually opens the project of advancing a melioristic philosophy with a discussion of the reality of evil. And in the final pages James returns to evil, suffering, loss, and tragedy:

> In particular *this* query has always come home to me: May not the claims of tender-mindedness go too far? May not the notion of a world already saved *in toto* anyhow, be too saccharine to stand? May not religious optimism be too idyllic? Must *all* be saved? Is *no* price to be paid in the work of salvation? Is the last word sweet? Is all 'yes, yes' in the universe? Doesn't the fact of 'no' stand at the very core of life? Doesn't the very 'seriousness' that we attribute to life mean that ineluctable noes and losses form a part of it, that there are genuine sacrifices somewhere, and that something permanently drastic and bitter always remains at the bottom of its cup?
>
> I cannot speak officially as a pragmatist here; all I can say is that my own pragmatism offers no objection to my taking sides with this more moralistic view, and giving up the claim of total reconciliation. . . . It is then perfectly possible to accept sincerely a drastic kind of a universe from which the element of 'seriousness' is not to be expelled. Whoso does so is, it seems to me, a genuine pragmatist.[65]

It is this very same moral seriousness that I have found essential to emphasize in the contemporary discourse on evil. Our moral life with other human beings in this world full of suffering is inevitably tragic. Given our human finitude, we will never be able to fully overcome evil and suffering; yet we must, melioristically, try. James, therefore, is a highly important figure in the philosophical context I have sketched in this chapter. His pragmatism is not only generally relevant as a critical middle path solution to several controversies in contemporary philosophy of religion (as argued in chapters 1 and 4, in particular) but also *a* promising move toward the kind of antitheodicism I have argued we vitally need.

Yet, even the notion of tragedy might lead us astray here in something like a theodicist manner. Tragedies, though not themselves theodicies, are meaningful and deep in a sense in which real-world evil events and processes such as the Holocaust often are not.[66] In addition to James, we might also be reminded of a thought found in Ralph Waldo Emerson. Reflecting on the loss of his son, he notes that grief "does not touch me: some thing which I fancied was a part of me, which could not be torn away without tearing me, nor enlarged without enriching me, falls off from me, and leaves no scar. . . . I grieve that grief can teach me nothing, nor carry me one step into real nature."[67] Evil is even more evil because of its inability to teach us how to avoid it, and because of its trivializing our efforts to understand the world in general, even when it (the evil around us) is itself understandable and a possible object of scientific explorations. This is a very important aspect of the existential challenge to comprehensibility and meaningfulness I have tried to understand in this chapter.

Living with Evil?

It is particularly interesting to observe that Jamesian pragmatism is in many ways superior to the various forms of neopragmatism available in philosophy today. I will now briefly explain why. We need to live with evil, and at the same time we have to fight against it, perhaps somewhat like the way we fight against disease we have to live with, too. This task is, as has already emerged in my discussion, both ethical and metaphysical. However, its metaphysical aspect—which might include a religious or theological aspect as well—is often missing from contemporary pragmatist proposals. I will demonstrate this very important contrast between Jamesian pragmatism and some of its more recent heirs by quoting Richard Rorty's well-known characterization of what he used to call "post-Philosophical culture." In the Rortyan utopia, "when the secret police come, when the torturers violate the innocent, there is nothing to be said to them of the form 'There is something within you which you are betraying. Though you embody the practices of a totalitarian society which will endure forever, there is something beyond those practices which condemns you.' "[68]

Rorty admits that this thought is "hard to live with," as in the post-Philosophical culture we finally realize that we are "alone, merely finite, with no links to something Beyond."[69] This is part of Rorty's general project of "de-divinization," of thoroughgoing atheism applied not just to religion but to all other areas of culture, including philosophy in particular.[70] When the secret police arrives, there is nothing transhistorical (and nothing to be found *in* human history, for that matter), or nothing deep in the human mind (or soul), that would condemn their torturous practices. Insofar as it is an essential feature of totalitarianism that individuals *qua* individuals are made superfluous,[71] the totalitarian practices aiming at such destruction of individuality are simply among the many practices and "vocabularies" we may engage in or employ, none of which is objectively correct from a super-perspective beyond those practices and vocabularies.

There is, moreover, nothing over and above the contingent historical clashes of practices and vocabularies—clashes that are, in the end, merely causal, instead of being rational or normative. Any candidate for such trans- or ahistorical transcendence would be guilty of an unpragmatic metaphysics that the Rortyan liberal ironist—however strongly committed to preserving liberal and democratic values—sets aside as a remnant of the theological past of humanity. Thoroughgoing atheism is thus connected with radical antimetaphysics. Appeals to truth, humanity, history, conscience, personhood, or guilt are just quasi-secular counterparts of appeals to God, and they are therefore of no use when the secret police comes. Nothing metaphysical (or theological) is.

While I share the view that *theodicist* metaphysics must be resisted, I believe a Jamesian pragmatist should be challenged to encounter this Rortyan line of thought and to thereby also examine the possibility of a pragmatist metaphysics—or, better, a pragmatist metalevel attitude to metaphysics—that takes seriously the need to actually *live with* the metaphysical pictures (or their antimetaphysical criticisms) emerging in the course of our lives and practices, pictures that may be needed to encounter the reality of evil. Religious metaphysics can also play a role in such pragmatist explorations, as James maintained.

As already mentioned, Rorty admits his post-Philosophical utopia is hard to live with. As Kraut points out, a philosophical strategy undermining our ability to condemn torturers fails to conserve our ordinary practices in a way that a pragmatist strategy might be expected to do.[72] I agree: a pragmatist position is seriously defective, if it prevents us from truly living with the views it advances. From a pragmatist perspective, metaphysical views (ideas, theories, positions) should be evaluated in terms of their ability to help us live—especially, to help us live ethically. This conception of pragmatist metaphysics is, arguably, central in James's pragmatism, in particular; in this sense, metaphysics, as pragmatically conceived, has an ethical core, or ethical grounds (insofar as we are able to understand the notion of "grounds" here in a nonfoundationalist fashion).[73] A pragmatist metaphysics must—and this is an ethical "must"—be able to oppose totalitarian attempts to make human beings superfluous as individuals. It must, however, be employed as a resource in fighting evil, not as a theodicist justification of a "yes, yes" attitude to the world (see the quote from James in the previous section).

From the perspective of Jamesian pragmatism and its account of the ethical grounds of metaphysics, we may thus formulate an *ethical norm* for any pragmatically adequate or acceptable metaphysical (or antimetaphysical) theorizing and reflection: we *are* entitled to, or even pragmatically—ethically—required to, commit ourselves to such a metaphysical view of humanity, history, soul, and so on (or virtually anything that Rorty finds a mere counterpart of theological ideas) that will enable us to fight evil, that is, to respond to the secret police, to condemn the torturer—or, recalling the critique of van Inwagen, to offer comfort to the victim.[74]

Insofar as it makes sense to construct ethical norms constraining pragmatically acceptable metaphysical theorizing or reflection, as I suggest, we may say that *any* metaphysics—or, in particular, any antimetaphysics, including neopragmatist, ironist, or liberal antimetaphysics of the Rortyan kind—must be able to meet the "response to the secret police" test. Otherwise, we would fail to meet our duty to recognize, or acknowledge, the suffering of those who *were* (or *are*) visited by the secret police. As James frequently pointed out, we must not be "deaf to the cries of the wounded." We must be able to hear the rich plurality of individual voices of suffering human beings, against totalitarian attempts to make them superfluous, and we must also use whatever metaphysical or theological means we have at our disposal to condemn their torturers and to console the victims. This is what it means to take seriously others' perspectives on the world—especially those of the victims and sufferers of evil—and this is, it seems to me, James's fundamental premise, a premise that makes his project fundamentally opposite to both Rorty's and, say, van Inwagen's (despite those philosophers' enormous differences).

While our fundamental human task, according to the pragmatists (both classical and more recent), should focus on ameliorating human life, this life is led *with* metaphysics and not properly ameliorated by completely detaching it from metaphysics. The metaphysical problems James discusses in the third and fourth lectures of *Pragmatism*, such as theism versus materialism, freedom versus determinism, and monism versus pluralism, are discussed precisely from the ethical perspective of making them relevant in human life. A pragmatist approach to metaphysics is, hence, set in a normative context allowing or enabling (or even encouraging) us to find adequate responses to those—including the secret police—attacking humanity, and to those who suffer from such attacks. These responses, though they may in the end have to be metaphysical or even religious, must above all be responses we can live with, and possibly even die for. Pragmatist metaphysics cannot rely on any religious or other "spiritual" convictions—here I of course agree with Rorty (and, *pace* Rorty, with Kant)—but it may arrive at metaphysico-theological ideas as a result of a careful pragmatic consideration of what kind of responses we are really able to live with in an ethically responsible way, as has been suggested in earlier chapters. The secular version of antitheodicism I have pursued in this chapter may also have to be metaphysical in the pragmatist sense sketched here.

Richard Bernstein calls Rorty's position *deep humanism*, capturing its key idea in the recognition that we can appeal to no "outside authority" such as God, Truth, or Reality—that is, that there is *"nothing that we can rely on but ourselves and our fellow human beings."*[75] This somewhat "tough-minded" (to use a Jamesian term) "self-reliance" (to use an Emersonian term also employed by Rorty himself)[76] is indeed a key idea in pragmatism, which has given up dogmatic, infallibilist beliefs in authorities and is willing to reinterpret our fundamental philosophical notions such as truth and reality from a thoroughly human perspective. Yet, in some cases our "deep humanism" should let us transcend not only our context, vocabulary, or *ethnos*,[77] but also everything merely human. Our reliance on our fellow human beings requires us to take seriously their "voices," especially the "cries of the wounded"—voices and cries that occasionally (e.g., when the secret police knocks on the door) reach out for something beyond the merely human.

Moreover, a commitment to (or a reaching out for) something *transcendent* may in some cases be a (quasi-)*transcendental* precondition for our ability to engage in some "deeply human" practices, for instance, religion.[78] A truly deep humanism must also allow for the "tender-minded" aspects of our reliance on ourselves and others, aspects that at least in some important cases may amount to steps toward transcendence. I doubt that Rorty's "deep humanism" can sufficiently acknowledge this. Again, James's pragmatist philosophy of religion comes to the rescue at this point: we may reach out for transcendence simply on the basis of our natural human needs and interests, from within human practices and their ethical concerns, especially the need to cope with evil. In short, while according to Rorty we are not responsible to anything else but other human beings, this very responsibility may in some cases require that we take seriously the idea of being responsible to something *other* than just other human beings. This is, or comes close to, a recognition of the possibility of a pragmatically rearticulated transcendence.

As ethical norms (I have argued) govern all metaphysical reflection, including our reflection on how to respond to evil, all the way from the start, beginning with the need to respond to the secret police—that is, the need to react morally and politically to the evil around us—our conception of ethical normativity itself should not be based on any *prior* metaphysical account of, say, the emergence of normativity from a purely factual, naturalistically explainable base. Such a metaphysics of emergence is acceptable as far as it goes, that is, when we are engaged in a purely metaphysical project and bracketing its ethical grounding, but its limitations must be acknowledged. It must itself already conform to the ethical (pragmatic) norm presented above. Moreover, it is *unethical*—and therefore, again, pragmatically unacceptable—to ground normativity on an allegedly nonnormative metaphysical basis.[79] Pragmatist metaphysics, or antimetaphysics, must respect the prior ethical conditions for the possibility of engaging in any serious metaphysics at all. This, again, amounts to respecting a certain kind of *limit* of philosophical theorizing.

Accordingly, the present inquiry is *not* concerned with "placement problems" (that is, how to "place" values and normativity in the world in terms of, for example, nonreductive pragmatic naturalism).[80] We have, rather, been led, through the problem of evil, to take up the opposite task of articulating ethical norms of metaphysics, including the metaphysics of normativity and values themselves. I am, thus, in the business of providing "norms of being" that the pragmatist philosopher of religion must take very seriously.[81] *Any* fact in the human world challenges us ethically. Any situation we are in may make *us* evil. Again, we should perceive an analogy to Kant: just as Kant's categories are normative requirements for objects (objecthood), we are here seeking to identify ethically normative pragmatic requirements for humanly possible metaphysical postulations.

By way of conclusion, let me note that even the general discussion of pragmatist metaphysics and normativity, which often has a strongly melioristic tone, should be intimately connected with "negative" moral concepts such as evil, although that connection usually remains only implicit in explorations of pragmatist metaphysics. An ethically adequate metaphysical reflection must reserve a key place for these notions. The philosophical pragmatist simply cannot avoid exploring the concept of evil (and related concepts, such as guilt, shame, suffering, etc.). Indeed, as we have seen, for James evil is a much more central concept than might initially appear, if one just takes a superficial look at his melioristic pragmatism. Evil—and especially the need to avoid the unethical theodicies postulated by the absolute, monistic idealisms of his times—plays a key role in *Pragmatism* and elsewhere, as was observed in the previous section.[82] Thus, while pragmatist metaphysics seeks consolation, ways of living with evil and suffering, not just any kind of religious, theological, or metaphysical consolation is ethically acceptable. We must, for ethical reasons, resist theodicies, both in their religious and secular versions; my criticism of Rorty should not be misunderstood as an apology for an optimistic metaphysics grounded in an "all is well" picture of the universe.

The theodicist claim that "all is well"—that there is in the end no evil, or that whatever evil there is is ultimately explained away or justified within a monistic theistic scheme—is in fact the other side of the coin of the Rortyan de-divinization discussed above. These are just two ways of avoiding a full engagement with the problem. Neither can respond to the secret police. Theodicism does not take the task of responding seriously, because "all is well"—nothing really needs to be done in the "yes, yes" world (to use James's memorable phrase again)—while the Rortyan ironist surrenders without being able to respond at all. Philosophers of religion seeking to offer a "defense" such as van Inwagen's are here firmly in the theodicist camp. Pragmatist metaphysics, in contrast, requires an active response—perhaps primarily to the victims, assuming that in many cases the perpetrators of evil are beyond rational response—based on the continuous struggle against evil and for a better world, a response that has to be sought again and again, even if it will never be final and may have to resort to religious and transcendent vocabularies that are eventually hard to reconcile with rational, argumentative philosophical discourse. Such a response *may* amount to the acknowledgment of the impossibility of comprehension.[83] In any case, it *must* include a recognition of the limits of (mere) philosophy.

Final Reflections

Evil, then, is still important as a philosophical (and theological) concept, but it must not be abused by breaking the limits of morally appropriate language use. This is an ethical "must," emerging *from within* ethics, not from any imagined neutral standpoint beyond ethics. The abuse of evil, such as the rhetoric of war against evil engaged in by people like G. W. Bush after 9/11, fails to respect the limits and the (transcendental) intractability we have examined above.[84] There are limits that ought to be respected if we wish our attitude to evil to be ethically serious and, perhaps, religiously genuine (see also the conclusion to this book).

Moreover, the notion of evil is abused when the fundamental issue of the intractability of evil—of evil as a challenge to the comprehensibility of the world (and life) in general—is not taken seriously. This *is* taken very seriously by James. To fail to take these issues seriously is in fact to engage in theodicist thinking, broadly conceived. The very point of a theodicy is to guarantee meaning and coherence in the world, specifically in the concept of God in the case of religious theodicies. The fundamental challenge of evil is the lack of such meaning and coherence. Acknowledging our inability to find ourselves in a fully comprehensible world is an ethical duty we have to the victims of the varieties of evil which we can to some extent examine and understand but whose full significance to our being-in-the-world can ultimately only be captured by the notion of the absurd. Our ability to invoke such existential or even existentialist vocabulary in our project of living with the incomprehensibility of the world is therefore fundamentally antitheodicist. Pragmatists, in particular, should put such abilities into full use. It is also very well compatible with the generally fallibilist approach of pragmatist inquiry to refuse simple theodicist attempts to find fundamental order and coherence in the world.

At the same time, a self-reflexively critical pragmatic word of warning is in order. The defense of antitheodicism in this chapter should *not* be taken to imply that we could with good conscience just be deaf to some suffering people's need to find explanations, causes, and even reasons for their suffering. In some cases, theodicies *may* be consoling, although I have resisted the theoretical conclusion that they would generally be consoling—or even, in most cases, ethically or religiously acceptable. The theodicism versus antitheodicism distinction may itself have to be contextualized and "softened," to the extent that theodicies, too, may have limited acceptability in some human situations. After all, pragmatists should, while making philosophical distinctions, never rely on essentialistic dichotomies or dualisms; the distinction between theodicist and antitheodicist approaches to evil that I have emphasized in this chapter is no exception. In the end there may be more continuities between these approaches than I have been able to recognize in my criticism of theodicies.

Moreover, as pragmatists, along with Wittgensteinians, clearly ought to acknowledge, our language use has its contexts that are necessary for the emergence of any meanings that are possible for us. There are significant moral aspects to that emergence of meaning. Facing an individual who suffers, or has been a victim of evil, but who nevertheless founds comfort in the theodicist belief that her/his suffering had some (either secular or divine) reason and purpose, we should definitely not launch our antitheodicist attack, at least not immediately. That would simply be cruel, and one need not be Rortyan in order to subscribe to the slogan that Rorty often repeats, that is, that being cruel is the worst thing we can do. Hence, the specific ways in which philosophical ideas may or may not be comforting must, once again, be set in contexts of discourse and practice. It is one thing to reject theodicies in the context of a philosophical publication or conference; it is quite another thing to reject, say, a dying person's desperate attempt to stick to a theodicy and find purpose in her struggle (even though we would be willing to philosophically reject that attempt as illusory). There may be contextually relevant uses of the language of theodicy that even the antitheodicist pragmatist philosopher of religion must acknowledge. Yet, theodicism, in the sense that religious belief *ought to* include a theodicy, must, I have argued, be firmly rejected.

On the other hand, the pragmatist should not draw a sharp boundary between philosophical positions and everyday life, either. Still, there are cases where we can hardly avoid drawing such a boundary. We may, in order to avoid cruelty, have to accept theodicies in some situations while philosophically generally rejecting them. In this sense, the pragmatist's situation, when it comes to seeking a morally appropriate response to evil, may in the end be tragic. It is hard for us to avoid abusing evil.

In the end, it might even be suggested that we cannot but abuse the notion of evil, if we apply it to *others*.[85] It is, perhaps, only ethically applicable *to me* (as a transcendental subject along the lines of Wittgenstein's *Tractatus* and its transcendentally solipsistic account of the relation between the subject and the world). In this sense, the concept of evil plays a role analogous to the notion of guilt.[86] On the other hand, it might also be suggested, following Arendt, that we do need the moral and political courage of applying the concept of evil to others, too—especially to the kind of historically influential wrong-doers like Eichmann, about whom we do have to be able to say that they are, or were, evil. But then again, it is we ourselves who must say this. We cannot delegate our moral responsibility for such attributions to anyone else. Whomever or whatever we designate by the concept of evil, *we* are responsible for such world categorizations, and categorizations of people. We are also ethically responsible, especially to the victims of evil, for our philosophical elaborations and theorizations; we should not be ethically indifferent to the ways we, and others, speak about the problem of evil. What we do, or fail to do, with our notion of evil—or with any other ethical notions at our disposal—is certainly not beyond good and evil.

This is also a deeply Jamesian point. While I have insisted on the need to acknowledge the reality of evil, as part of our need to acknowledge its victims as human individuals, evil is *not* acknowledged as an element of a "ready-made," categorization-independent world. It is *our* categorization, dependent on the (moral, metaphysical) perspective of the subject—whether social or individual. *We* shape the world into what it is for us, into something that we may find either good or evil, or both.[87] Our categorizations are engagements with the world that we continuously reconstruct. This is, perhaps, the pragmatist version of the Wittgensteinian idea of good and evil being applicable only to the transcendental subject. It is a metaphysical picture of subjectivity (and the world) we are able to live with.

CONCLUSION

In the previous chapters I have argued for the pragmatic need to adopt, antireductionistically and antiessentialistically, *different perspectives* on issues in the philosophy of religion: Kantian (the postulates of practical reason); Jamesian (the ethical grounding of metaphysics and theology); Deweyan (naturalism, the emancipation of "the religious" from supernaturalism); neopragmatist (integrating these perspectives with Wittgensteinian influences); and others. I have not attempted to interpret these positions in any historical detail; I have, by "philosophizing historically,"[1] examined their relevance to pragmatist philosophy of religion today. Moreover, Jamesian pluralism, I have suggested, is *a* (not *the*) *metaperspective* urging us to accommodate all these (and other) historically contextualized voices in our on-going attempts to understand religion and religiosity better. These voices deserve to be carefully listened to in contemporary philosophical reflections on these matters.

Summarizing My Arguments

The findings of the previous chapters can be summarized as follows. First, I have argued for a certain kind of *Kantian pragmatism*, seeking to integrate the pragmatic and the transcendental—as well as, on the basis of this integration, the ethical and the metaphysical (both generally and in relation to the philosophy of religion, in particular). Secondly, I have suggested that pragmatist philosophers of religion should follow Dewey in embracing *nonreductive naturalism*, against any dogmatic supernaturalisms (but also against militantly atheist attempts to judge all religious views irrational). Thirdly, especially in my discussions of neopragmatist philosophy of religion, I have emphasized the need to take *normativity* seriously. Philosophy of religion is a matter of normative assessment of our philosophical attempts to deal with religious issues (or "problems of religion," as Zackariasson puts it; cf. chapter 3).

Fourthly, my defense of pragmatist philosophy of religion has been a defense of a way of thinking about religion *beyond dichotomies*. The key dichotomies I have rejected are the ones between evidentialism and fideism and between realism and antirealism, both of which have shaped contemporary approaches to the philosophy of religion in unfruitful ways. I have proposed an *Aufhebung*—a critical overcoming—of these dichotomies on the basis of Jamesian pragmatism, in particular. Finally, and perhaps most importantly, I have also tried to show why pragmatist philosophy of religion must not only go beyond these dichotomies but beyond any *theodicist* picture of "justifying evil." The problem of evil has thus turned out to be a true test case for the pragmatist position developed in more general philosophy of religion.

After lengthy inquiries into these pragmatist ways of examining religion, it is time to consider some more metalevel issues. One question not yet considered in this volume is the old one concerning the very nature of religion. What *is* religion? I did not begin with this question, because I do not think that pragmatist inquiry can start with any definitions purporting to provide the essence of the phenomenon inquired into. I am not providing a definition to conclude with, either. But I want to return to the question and I hope to be able to illuminate it by way of conclusion.

Religion and Pseudoreligion

It is a commonplace that defining *religion* is a very difficult, if not hopeless, task. Scholars of comparative religion, for example, seldom propose any explicit definitions; nor do philosophers of religion. I am not going to propose anything like that, either. My aims are once again located at the metalevel: what I am interested in is the very possibility of drawing the, or even *a*, boundary between religion and nonreligion, particularly between religion and what I call "pseudoreligion" (or what may as well be called "superstition," and what may also sometimes come close to "hypocrisy").[2]

I want to examine whether attempts to draw such a boundary are committed to *essentialism*, namely, to a view according to which certain essential "religion-making" properties are required for a given activity or way of thinking to be religious, or to be accurately describable as religious. If such an essentialist view were true, an explicit definition of religion would be a meaningful goal, and its possibility would be a necessary presupposition of any normative discussion of religion and religiosity. If, however, no essentialism is invoked, or if essentialism is rejected as a hopelessly outdated form of metaphysics, then the question arises whether any religion versus pseudoreligion (or religion versus superstition) boundary can be drawn at all. This issue takes an especially interesting shape in the Wittgensteinian tradition in the philosophy of religion. On the one hand, it seems that Wittgensteinians like D. Z. Phillips confine their task to the mere *description* of religious ways of using language—the rules of religious "language-games," as one might put it, keeping in mind that Wittgenstein himself never explicitly applied his concept of a language game to religion. On the other hand, such philosophers are often busily commenting on the "right" or "correct" (and conversely, "wrong" and "incorrect") ways of using religious language. This latter *normative* task, the attempt to *lay down* rules for *genuinely* religious language-use, seems to be a crucial part of their philosophizing about religion, even if they explicitly commit themselves to a mere description of language games, that is, to merely observing that such-and-such rules are *de facto* involved in such-and-such communities, practices, or forms of life. Analogously, pragmatist philosophers of religion, seeking to understand religious practices in Dewey's socially oriented manner, or individual religious experiences along the lines explored by James, may arrive at normative statements about the ways such practices *ought to* be engaged in, or about the kind of experiences a genuinely religious person may or may not enjoy. We have seen examples of this above: the genuinely religious person, according to Dewey, is a naturalist rather than a super-naturalist; she/he is, according to James, a pluralist rather than a monist; she/he avoids any theodicist assumptions, and so forth.

Now, insofar as pragmatists (or Wittgensteinians) engage in norma-tive discussion of religion, are they committing themselves to essential-ism? If they are, don't they end up with self-reflective incoherence, given these philosophical orientations' hostility to essentialist assumptions? And if they are not, how does their position in the end differ from a full-blown *relativism* according to which no religion versus pseudoreligion is possible, except in the context of some particular religious tradition or standpoint?[3]

A comprehensive treatment of these problems would require us to study in some detail a number of specific religious or theological concepts and conceptions in relation to which the distinction between correct and in-correct, or properly (genuinely) religious and pseudoreligious, ways of speaking and thinking can be applied. Such concepts include, for exam-ple, prayer, death and immortality, evil, the concept of faith itself, and the relation between religion, on the one side, and such human practices or social institutions as science and morality, on the other. Some of these issues have already been discussed in some detail in the chapters above; others have only been or will be mentioned in passing. In particular, the analogies between the contrasts between religion and pseudoreligion, on the one hand, and genuine morality and its distortions, on the other, should be emphasized (as should be clear on the basis of our treatment of the problem of evil in chapter 5). These issues are not identical, but their similarity is illuminating.

I should note, moreover, that my investigation of the religion versus pseudoreligion division in these concluding remarks will be focused on religious thinking and language use, instead of religious or religiously inspired actions (though of course words are deeds, too, and anyone in-spired by either the pragmatists or the later Wittgenstein must in one way or another tie meaning to action). A terrorist might pray solemnly, in some sense highly religiously, and then go on to blow up hundreds of innocent people, with the prayer still on her/his lips. Such behavior should obviously be classified as pseudoreligious. However, this chapter is concerned with the questions of whether, and how, our more narrowly linguistic, conceptual, and/or argumentative life can manifest both religious and pseudoreligious aspects.

It is useful to briefly introduce the issue I am going to explore through examples. Just as the Wittgensteinian method in the philosophy of religion advises us to look at particular language games, instead of offering a universal theory of what religion is, the pragmatic method is also meant to be applied to specific cases. It is from the perspective of such an apparently antiessentialist inquiry that the threat of essentialism arises.

We may ask, then, what kind of talk or thinking about, say, the following six topics should be considered genuinely religious, as distinguished from pseudoreligious or superstitious:[4]

> *Prayer.* Here the contrast is between religion and magic: the religious prayer is not a magical attempt to make God do something one wants Him to do but an expression of one's sincere trust in God, whatever happens, along the lines of the famous phrase, "thy will be done." A magical attitude to prayer yields superstition *par excellence.*
>
> *Death, mortality, and immortality.* Here a distinction can be drawn between, for example, the Christian hope for survival or resurrection and the kind of fundamentalist certainty about one's salvation that various sects, Christian and non-Christian, preach.
>
> *Evil and suffering.* Here, as I argued in chapter 5, a truly religious person does not aim at a theodicy justifying God's ways to humans but, perhaps rather, simply stops questioning and trusts God, whatever His will brings about in the world.
>
> *Faith.* The genuinely religious believer, again, trusts God, rather than seeking epistemic certainty about God's existence. Religious faith built upon such trust is more fundamental than any evidence one might come up with (or lack), either for or against theism.
>
> *Religion and morality.* A major issue is the contrast between tolerance and fundamentalist, hypocritical moralizing, for example, on

homosexuality and other sex/gender issues or other socio-politically relevant matters. Tolerance, obviously, should be understood as the genuinely religious alternative here, based on the requirement to love one's neighbor.

Religion and science. The truly religious believer is, once again, an antifundamentalist, refusing to accept either fundamentalist pseudosciences, such as creationism, or the typical atheist criticism that scientific progress abolishes the credibility of religious beliefs.[5]

In cases such as these, we *should* (or at least would like to) be able to say that certain fundamentalist ways of thinking are not only pseudoscientific (as creationism surely is) but also pseudoreligious, yielding superstition instead of genuine religion. The cases can also be combined, and they often are. For instance, we would, I think, be prepared to regard as pseudoreligious someone who prayed in order to manipulate God to save her/his immortal soul and who explained away unnecessary suffering by referring to the sufferers' insufficiently successful prayers and faith.

Recent philosophers of religion that might be criticized, from a pragmatist or Wittgensteinian perspective, as encouraging pseudoreligious superstition rather than genuine religious thought include, for example, analytic evidentialists,[6] reformed epistemologists,[7] as well as, obviously, creationists and other fundamentalists (though the latter can hardly even be called *philosophers* of religion). Generally, if one does not acknowledge, with William James, that religion arises as a response to something's being *wrong* or seriously *incomplete* in us,[8] and if one thinks one is "complete" and already possesses the truth, then one is pseudoreligious.

In particular, my concluding discussion aims to bring to the fore some pragmatist and Wittgensteinian-inspired ideas about what faith, in its truly religious meaning, may amount to.[9] Wittgensteinian thinkers may hold—and the issue of relativism seems to be involved in this claim—that the boundary between religion and pseudoreligion can only be marked *within* a religious form of life (or language game, tradition, or something similar), just as the distinction between moral sincerity and pseudoethical distortions of the moral point of view can only be drawn within a life already committed to the seriousness of the ethical. Although I am not going to endorse what some philosophers condemn as "Wittgensteinian relativism" (let alone fideism), I will eventually seek resources for such context-embedded demarcations from Wittgenstein's famous suggestion that a religious person "uses a picture." This suggestion should be welcomed by pragmatists as well.

"From within": The Problem of Relativism

Mere description of religious activities is clearly not enough for philosophy of religion, pragmatist or not; normative commitments are essential. And here, precisely, lies our problem. There is no God's-Eye View available to us for making such commitments; it seems that they must be made "from within" a practice defined by them—ethical or religious— unless we assume that there is an essence of religion and that our knowing it would immediately justify our normative claims. When asking, for instance, whether it is an essential feature of religion that it cannot be reduced to anything nonreligious (or religiously neutral), we encounter questions that seem to lead us to a desperate choice between essentialism and relativism. The same holds about the problem of evil: it is only from within a religious or ethical outlook that it is possible to categorize certain views, such as theodicies, as unethical or pseudoreligiously blasphemous.[10] Indeed, theodicism, critically examined in chapter 5, could and should be seen as a paradigmatic case of pseudoreligious thinking. Yet, maintaining the possibility of distinguishing genuinely ethical and religious views from pseudoethical and pseudoreligious ones seems to commit us to a form of essentialism, while at the same time we seem to arrive at relativism, realizing the hopelessness of such distinctions, when abstracted from all actual ethical and religious frameworks, traditions, or backgrounds.

In the philosophy of religion we *must* take up the issue of whether some accounts of religion, either favorable or critical, are in fact committed to pseudoreligion or superstition. It is not enough to deal with the purely intellectual adequacy of various views of religion; a critical examination of their *religious adequacy* is also constantly needed. But if this is true, then the philosophy of religion cannot simply maintain its meta-level perspective. It must also become *religiously engaged*, though of course not reducible to religion or theology. It must, at the very least, be open to the kind of religious and ethical possibilities its practitioners perceive in their own lives. Similarly, philosophical ethics cannot be removed from our attempt to live well.

It can be argued that it is possible to draw the, or any, boundary between religious and pseudoreligious language use or thought (or, analogously, between ethical language use or thought, on the one side, and its pseudoethical mischaracterizations, on the other) only *from within* a form of life or world-view that is already understood as religious (or, *mutatis mutandis*, as ethically concerned)—that is, a way of thinking *already demarcated* from ways of thinking that are not conceived as (genuinely) religious. This conclusion in a way resembles the position known as naturalism in the philosophy of science, inspired by W. V. Quine and his many followers.[11] The naturalist says that it is only from within the evolving world-picture and methodology of science itself, instead of any autonomous first-philosophical perspective supposedly prior to science, that the demarcation between science and nonscience (or pseudoscience) can be made. There is no purely philosophical way to solve the "demarcation problem." Nor is there, in the religious case, any purely philosophical way to solve the analogous demarcation problem. In neither case is there any "higher court of appeal." Genuinely religious thought is demarcated from pseudoreligion only from within a religious form of life, which obviously views itself as genuinely religious, just as science is demarcated from pseudoscience only from within science itself, which explains why the views *it* considers pseudoscientific do deserve that label, and just as morality is acknowledged as absolute and ultimate only from an ethical standpoint, which judges as unethical all attempts to step outside the moral sphere. From the perspective of religious life, or a given religious tradition, certain ideas about religion will then seem not only conceptually confused but even blasphemous.

Indeed, it is usually, or perhaps exclusively, *within* religious contexts that the issue of religion versus superstition arises as an issue for a religious believer in the first place. For example, superstition is a *sin* according to the Catholic Encyclopedia, a sin arising from an "excess of religion" instead of irreligion; specifically, it is a sin offending the First Commandment, according to which only the one true God ought to be worshipped.[12] The kinds of pseudoreligion I am primarily interested in here are not, however, superstitious religious practices but typically overly intellectualized philosophical or scientific (or, for that matter, pseudoscientific) accounts of religion that a philosopher of religion seeking to understand a genuinely religious form of life ought to resist as firmly as a Christian ought to resist the sin of superstitious practices.

Now, the problem of relativism, in a nutshell, is this. Religious institutions or practices, embodying profound perspectives on the meaningfulness of human life, are *from their own perspective* fundamental, basic, autonomous, and irreducible. For someone standing outside religion, religious views and practices may and should be intellectually and ethically evaluated, just as all other human ways of thinking and acting.[13] For the true believer, the morally right or good, however, depends on, or is determined by, God's will and becomes inconceivable if conceptualized in any other way. We again face the issue of mutual recognition, or acknowledgment, briefly invoked in the introduction to this book.

This kind of craving for a firm ground, or even an absolute starting point, is, we might say, a transcendental condition for the possibility of religious practices. If this overarching ideal of meaningful life is to *make sense* as such an ideal, it cannot be relativized or watered-down in order to accommodate other equally valuable perspectives. An inescapable condition for the possibility of religion *qua* religion is the absolute superiority of the religious point of view. There is, then, no neutral ground for making the choice between religion and some other framework critical of it. For an ethically concerned critic of religion, for instance, even the choice between ultimate foundational ("bedrock") practices or perspectives on life must be made on ethical grounds; making such choices in any other way, for allegedly primary nonethical reasons, would be immoral, because that would amount to subordinating ethical reasons for something more fundamental—and from the ethical point of view nothing can be more fundamental. But for the religious person God's grace is the ground of all our being, including our ability to engage in any morally motivated actions at all. Our capacity for moral reflection is also, according to the believer, a gift from God—if also, paradoxically, something demanded of us by God. Either way, the choice must already have been made, insofar as any framework, religious or not, can present itself as one we could legitimately choose to employ as ultimate.

Because no neutral, "purely rational" choice is possible in this dialectical situation, that is, because either a (secular) ethical or a religious perspective, considered absolute and fundamental, seems to be always already transcendentally presupposed in any choice we make, in any framework of life we find ourselves in, are we on our way to a kind of perspectivism or relativism? Should we just declare religious and nonreligious perspectives or frameworks only relatively valid, nonabsolutely correct, each from their own perspective? But subscribing to this compromise would amount to a resolution of the metalevel issue in nonreligious terms, insofar as we would now ourselves simply rationally *choose* or *decide* to view both valid "in their own terms." What is more, such a relativizing move would hardly satisfy the demands of the religious ideals, because not only religious but also other frameworks (e.g., secular ethics) represent themselves as primarily important and fundamental. Thus we would not be able to occupy a neutral ground by means of this maneuver, either. A tension remains, if not an outright paradox. No religious (or nonreligious) framework can, without begging the question, legitimate its ultimate status to those who consider some other framework more fundamental—even though religious frameworks can definitely change, and they do develop historically—and no external philosophical analysis, or relativization, can settle the issue on a neutral ground. The problem is only deepened by the observation that there is a great number of rival religious "frameworks" that are incompatible with each other.[14]

If one cannot adequately describe a religious form of life, or a religious use of language, in nonreligious terms, and if a shared religious practice thus seems to be a condition for the possibility of the meaningfulness of certain expressions, the very possibility of criticizing religious beliefs will become problematic. This, again, is one way of stating the relativism issue. Is there any way for a nonreligious person to claim that a particular use of religious language is superstitious rather than genuinely religious?[15] This question concerns (transcendentally, I am tempted to say) "the *position* from which the non-believer would be speaking" when she/he tries to make a critical comment on a religious person's utterance.[16] A pragmatist inquiry into religious practices—or, analogously, a grammatical investigation of religious language in a Wittgensteinian style—may end up with the conclusion that, for instance, superstition (or blasphemy) makes sense only on the basis of believers' sharing certain presuppositions about what is involved in "reverence to God."[17] Such presuppositions may be parts of the practice-laden background that make those people's use of language intelligible.

Lars Hertzberg, from whom I am drawing these ideas, does not say that his question is a transcendental one, but it can certainly be interpreted in such a way. Faced with the problem of how nonbelievers *can* say anything meaningful about religious language use (if they do not share the background that makes religious language meaningful), Hertzberg suggests that we might turn the problem upside down: "Rather than taking the distinction between believers and nonbelievers for granted and regarding the expression of certain religious attitudes by nonbelievers as a problem, we should perhaps take the expressions as given and instead regard the distinction itself as problematic." Then we may be led to "take a larger look" at the context in which the nonbeliever's words acquire their meaning, that is, that person's life.[18] Analogously, I want to suggest that it is our on-going normative engagement with our own and other people's language use that ought to be taken as something given. The (transcendental?) condition that makes this given actuality of our life possible is the vagueness of the normative versus descriptive distinction. It is by coming to see that describing and clarifying language use already contains a normative dimension that we can make sense of the fact that norms, rules, and limits are inevitably grounded in our factual use of words. The distinction between the normative and the descriptive should be considered as problematic and context-sensitive as the one between the believer and the nonbeliever. For pragmatist philosophers of religion, softening these traditionally sharp and dichotomous categorizations should be a natural move—and also ethically justified.[19]

Normativity now begins to look like an entirely natural—and yet somehow miraculous—"fact" about our human practices, our life with language. We should acknowledge the inescapable need for normative language use, such as the distinction between religion and pseudoreligion within the language games that philosophers of religion (and other scholars studying religious phenomena) entirely naturally engage in. This pragmatic need overcomes the less natural, less practice-facilitating, more artificial need to separate all thinkers into believers and nonbelievers. It is more important for us to be able to judge—not only as religious or nonreligious persons but also as scholars or thinkers—certain phenomena as pseudoreligious, or superstitious (and in some cases dogmatic or fundamentalist), than to be able to neatly and unambiguously classify all people, ourselves included, as either believers or nonbelievers. There can be various shades and grey areas between the side of the true believers and the one of the nonbelievers.

The relativism issue I have located is, then, expressible as the following question: Can there be any critical discussion of any particular way of drawing the limit, if all attempts to draw it are inevitably made from within a specific (religious or non-religious) perspective? Here, I suggest, a healthy dose of Jamesian pragmatism may help us again. Because pragmatism urges us to view our own practices—the very language games we engage in—with open-minded, self-critical eyes, being experimentally prepared to learn from our mistakes, including the mistake of taking something pseudoreligious to be genuinely religious (or *vice versa*), pragmatism is less vulnerable, though not entirely invulnerable, to the relativist charge than some standard Wittgensteinian views in the philosophy of religion seem to be.[20] Relativism, hence, depends on a problematic prior assumption, according to which all disagreements ought to be objectively resolvable in terms of rational grounds common to all parties to the dispute. Pragmatists may allow that there are methods and standards of reasonable discussion that fall short of full argumentative rigor but are not for this reason simply irrational or arbitrary.[21]

A Wittgensteinian thinker like Phillips might insist that when drawing the religion versus superstition boundary, we only draw this boundary *as it is articulated in our language, culture, or practice*, not absolutely, "from above," or from an allegedly neutral God's-Eye View. Here, of course, the relativism issue returns in the attempt to avoid essentialism. Could *we*, within our culture, be mistaken (or perhaps even superstitious) about how to draw the limit between religion and superstition? Could we, from within our perspective defined by the way we do draw the limit, fallibilistically acknowledge the possibility that we might be mistaken, the possibility that what we take to be genuinely religious might after all be superstitious in some more objective, practice-transcending sense? As pragmatic fallibilists we presumably should. But if so, would we again arrive at essentialism instead of relativism?

"The Religious Person Uses a Picture"

Once again there are more questions rather than answers—especially questions demonstrating the need to steer a middle course between relativism and essentialism. Before concluding this investigation, I want to briefly propose that relevant criteria (if not *the* criteria) for genuine religiosity might be found in Wittgenstein's contentions that the religious person "uses a picture," that the "gap" between the believer and the nonbeliever may result from the "different pictures" that guide them, and that the "whole *weight*" of a religious way of life may lie in its pictures.[22] Here it is important to realize that religious pictures, or religious ways of using pictures (namely, making and looking at them, and so on) are very different from nonreligious (e.g., scientific) pictures or ways of using pictures. To fail to realize this is to be in the grip of a false, misleading—perhaps pseudoreligious—picture of what religious pictures are like.[23]

But how can we distinguish between religious and superstitious pictures? We need to be able to say that a picture may be "appropriate" or "inappropriate" in its context—and that some pictures, e.g., the Muhammad caricatures that caused severe turmoil in several Islamic countries in 2006, are clearly inappropriate at least in some crucial contexts. However, appropriateness is itself a form-of-life-bound concept; so the problem of relativism seems to haunt us once again. We have to take a look at some particular religious pictures in order to find out, case by case, whether they might function as expressions of genuinely religious attitudes. Or we may look at the "pictures" of religious language-use and religious life that philosophers of religion have drawn in their writings.

For example, the picture of religion that emerges from, say, Phillips's Wittgenstein-inspired work is, roughly, of the following kind. Genuinely religious practices must be distinguished from the pseudoreligious ideas connected with the kind of traditional theism defended or criticized by mainstream philosophers of religion. Theism, as conventionally articulated, is a corrupt and superstitious form of religion, based on a false and unnecessary conception of there being a state of rivalry between science and religion (and possibly other human practices or perspectives). It is, according to Phillips, not just philosophically misleading but even religiously corrupt and blasphemous to claim, for instance, that God has reasons to allow the evil there is in the world as a necessary part of his overall plan, or even that God exists as an entity of some kind.[24] Furthermore, religion cannot be grounded in theology or dogmas but lives in people's practices.[25] Even less can religion be grounded in (analytic) philosophers' of religion superficial and often superstitious rationalizations. In the case of evil, in particular, it is blasphemous and ethically unacceptable to offer justifications on God's behalf, as I have argued (cf. chapter 5). Theodicism produces pseudoreligious pictures of religion. What is more, just as religion cannot solve the problem of evil, it cannot (when genuine) promise an eternal life; it would again be a corrupt form of religion, a false picture of salvation, to strive for one's own "place in Heaven" or to deny the full reality of death or mortality.

These aspects of Phillips's picture of genuine religion, described here only in very general terms, yield normative requirements that a person pursuing religious life ought to take seriously. The problem is, once more, whether those aspects and the norms they ground are ultimately based on a conception of the essence of religion. Does Phillips assume that the requirements for genuine religion he describes in his works are, though based on a description of what he takes to be a (family of) religious uses of language within human practices or forms of life, essential criteria that any activity classifiable as religious must meet? Or could, for example, an outlook which incorporated the idea of immortality or survival be genuinely religious, if it met some of the other criteria Phillips lists? A charitable reading would admit that the Phillipsian picture enables one to maintain a "gradualist" and possibly "family-resemblance-like" picture of religiosity, with no sharp demarcation between religion and pseudoreligion. But it is also part of this picture that in some cases the demarcation *must* be sharp. For instance, when the fundamentalist preacher comes to tell you that homosexuals will go to Hell, it is impossible, if one is serious about one's own religiosity, not to find her/his pronouncement as deeply pseudoreligious and superstitious, however admirable her/his other views might be, religiously or ethically.

Phillips's Wittgensteinian account provides us with only one—in many ways admirable, though not for that reason unproblematic—picture of what genuinely religious life and thinking might amount to. In any case, there is no way to avoid normative commitments, if one endorses this picture. Moreover, the various features of genuine religion Phillips and other Wittgensteinians take up might call for unification. Could we find a more general picture, capture the "essence" of religion in a more unified outlook?

What, in a word, might be *the* picture of genuine religious life, if seen from a Wittgensteinian perspective? Risking accusations of essentialism, I propose that one candidate for such a central, unifying picture might be found in what Wittgenstein, in the "Lecture on Ethics", described as the *wonder at the existence of the world*.[26] This powerful picture may, of course, extend far beyond religious forms of life. But religious lives not informed by it—for example, theodicist, explanatory, evidentialist views of faith—may, if the foregoing discussion is correct, be judged pseudo-religious. A religious person *ought to* (a religious "ought") be to some extent in the "grip" of this picture, be held captive by it (to borrow another familiar simile from Wittgenstein). When a person is *religiously* in the grip of the picture of existence, or the world, as something that can only be wondered at, she/he is not attempting to explain this mystery, or to solve the puzzle of existence.[27] Perhaps she/he may find it appropriate to describe this wonder in terms of the idea of the world, or life (which, according to Wittgenstein, are "one"),[28] as a "gift."[29] She/he thus acknowledges mystery in a way that her/his pseudoreligious rival is unable to, while perhaps wishing to "dissolve" the puzzle *if* it is misunderstood as an ordinary question calling for rational explanation (and thus misrepresented as a question responsive to a scientific approach).

The "mystery" invoked here—the riddle of existence and the darkest question of philosophy, as James called it[30]—might even have something to do with the topic of *skepticism*, often taken up in Wittgensteinian contexts.[31] Specifically, it might have something to do with the "Kantian" variety of skepticism, as contrasted with the "Cartesian" variety, that James Conant, one of the most perceptive recent interpreters of Wittgenstein, draws our attention to.[32] While the Cartesian skeptic doubts the truth of a particular (or even highly general) factual statement or belief, such as the statement that there is an external world, the Kantian skeptic's questions go deeper, to the point of wonder and mystery. The Kantian thinker (though not really Kant himself) may ask how it is *possible* that there is a world at all, or how it is possible that our thought and language are "answerable" to the way the world is. Insofar as genuinely religious thinking is open to the possibility of the mysterious, to the wonder that the very existence of the world, or of anything at all, may elicit in us, it must be "Kantian" rather than "Cartesian" (in this somewhat anachronistic sense of these terms). For the religious person, it is a mystery that there is a world, and it is a mystery of equal magnitude that God exists as its creator (if indeed He does). Again, a pseudoreligious account, such as traditional theism understood as a straightforward ontological postulation of a super-entity, diminishes or even totally annihilates this sense of mystery, reducing God to an entity among others whose existence is affirmed in an evidentially supportable (and challengeable) hypothesis. The mystery may, however, also be preserved in naturalistic religiosity *à la* Dewey, requiring or at least enabling an attitude of "natural piety" comparable to the classical idea (also invoked by Wittgenstein) of seeing the world *sub specie aeternitatis*.

Therefore, the religion versus pseudoreligion distinction might be reformulated as a distinction between those forms of God thought and talk that preserve our sense of mystery, our existential wonder, and those that do not. The latter, traditionally metaphysical theistic (or atheistic) pictures of divinity, are (to paraphrase Wittgenstein again) the "pictures that hold us captive" whenever we lapse into theodicies or other pseudoreligious traps. The distinction between these two *kinds* of religious picture is, fundamentally, a distinction between different forms of life or practices of living (and speaking). Transforming Conant's discussion of skepticism[33] to our specific purposes, it might even be suggested, as a rearticulation of a Wittgensteinian account of what it means to be genuinely (as opposed to superstitiously) religious, that a religious person approaches the problem of God's reality as a "Kantian" issue, not as a "Cartesian" one. That is, the truly religious person wonders, especially in the context of evil and suffering, *how it is possible* that there is a God at all—and then, perhaps, takes a Kierkegaardian and Jamesian "will to believe" leap to the mysteries faith—while the pseudoreligious person regards the problem of theism as, primarily, an epistemological skeptical issue of whether there actually is a supreme being whose existence could be adequately accounted for in terms of the evidence we possess.[34]

Another compelling suggestion for a profoundly religious picture might be the conception of religion as a response to an individual human being's "infinite despair" (*Not*), the greatest despair of all, which emerges when an individual person feels her-/himself to be lost, as articulated in Wittgenstein's remarks in *Culture and Value*.[35] Prayer, if genuine, can be seen as a search for such a response. Human mortality, arguably, lies at the root of this picture—and because it also lies at the root of the previously discussed one, as only mortals wonder at the existence of the world in which they contingently find themselves and from which they realize they will one day be gone, might these not be ultimately one and the same picture? Moreover, they might ultimately be one and the same picture precisely because it is the skeptical problem (understood in the Kantian rather than the Cartesian sense) that deeply unifies them. We have to, in Cavell's words,[36] "live our skepticism" in and through our wonder at existence, especially when it comes to acknowledging otherness—our need to acknowledge, as James insisted (see chapter 4), even those who are very different from ourselves,[37] particularly those who are in pain and agony.

We should conclude that it is as difficult to draw the religion versus pseudoreligion boundary as it may be to draw, according to Hertzberg, the boundary between the believer and the nonbeliever, although drawing the former may be far more important than drawing the latter. We should be satisfied with "soft" family resemblance concepts here. But should we then, perhaps, simply resort to the view that a substantial number of religion-making properties (from a relatively long list) will be needed, and will be sufficient, to make an activity religious, or a religion?[38] This would lead us back to essentialism, I am afraid, only a more sophisticated variety of essentialism which would have learned the basic lesson of pragmatist antiessentialism and Wittgenstein's treatment of family resemblance. We might do better by just refusing to seek the essence of religion at all, but then we would—wouldn't we?—nonetheless be committed to holding *some* sets of features as more essential than some other sets to something's being a religion or religious.

I do not believe that the essence of religion could be captured by any list of religion-making properties, any more than we could offer a list characterizing the essence of, for example, science or art. Virtually all standard properties occurring on such imagined "lists," even the theistic commitment itself, can be questioned by, say, a Wittgensteinian like Phillips, for whom most of the features characterizing traditional theistic religious thought are in fact pseudoreligious or "corrupt." The Wittgensteinian philosopher of religion is also interested in the limits of religion, but her/his approach is very different from the one relying on a predefined essence.[39]

The "limits" of genuine religion I have been exploring here, just like the limits of ethically acceptable philosophical discourse on evil explored above (see chapter 5), are both pragmatic and "transcendental" limits. As any transcendental limits, they can in the end only be drawn "from within." We must bear in mind that religious "pictures," when parts of a genuinely religious life, do not serve any allegedly more fundamental nonreligious purpose. They just express themselves.[40] Thus, they serve to mark the contrast to a life that does not have a religious quality or whose values and purposes are not appropriately described in religious terms. In this way, pictures do draw limits for us. However, contrary to essentialism, those limits may have to be *redrawn* at any time. It is up to us to draw and redraw them, "from within" practices defined (and redefined) by them.

This is what it means, in the case of the philosophy of religion, to "naturalize" and "pragmatize" transcendental philosophy.[41] If the transcendental construal of these issues is plausible, as I think it is, we cannot say that one could, as it were, "first" draw the limit between religion and pseudoreligion (from an external perspective), and only afterwards decide whether to step in the territory defined by those limits or not. Instead, one must *already be inside*, at least in a provisional way, in order to be able to draw any limit at all. Transcendental limits are self-reflectively drawn from within the practice-embedded experiential field (of meaning, cognition, and so on) they condition and constrain. At least one must be able to view certain religious options—or pictures—as *one's own* in order to assess them normatively *qua* religious. This is not to require that one is committed to any particular religious view of the world and human life. But it is to require that one is not entirely blind to the possibility of leading a religious life, or to the possibility of seeing what is depicted, always incompletely and perhaps misleadingly, in some religious "pictures." Furthermore, it is to require that one is not blind to the possibility that others may view one's conception of religiosity problematic or perhaps even superstitious and pseudoreligious: one should always be wary of construing one's own perspective on the boundary between religion and pseudoreligion as the one and only correct perspective; that is, one should admit that at least in some cases there may be gray areas and overlaps between religious and pseudoreligious thinking.[42]

Closing Remarks

Concluding both my reflection on the boundary between religious and pseudoreligious thought and the entire argument of this book, I would like to suggest that, in addition to the criterion that genuinely religious thought ought to be antitheodicist, we ought to have other criteria as well (although there can be no exhaustive list), including the criterion that genuinely religious (and therefore also ethically acceptable) thought can never regard itself as representing the one and only true religion, or the one and only true conception of genuine religiosity.

Why am I proposing this? Because, I finally want to argue, religious thought deals with such fundamental problems of human existence that no one can, without hubris, claim that others with, say, different cultural background are wrong about them. These issues include human life and death, sin, guilt, forgiveness, and many others. Distinguishing between genuine religiosity and pseudoreligious superstition is above all a *philosophical* task; religious thought itself should not condemn any other religion as pseudoreligion (even though, as has been noted above, there is a sense in which distinguishing between genuinely religious and pseudoreligious ideas is only possible within a field of not just philosophical but also religious and theological commitments—which is, however, fully compatible with the claim that the task of drawing such distinctions itself remains at least primarily philosophical).

This is also why a philosopher, even if she/he is not a believer, can, for instance, condemn an allegedly religious idea (e.g., discrimination against homosexuals) as blasphemous, just as a philosopher may reject, for philosophical and metaphilosophical reasons, as unacceptable, or even as insulting, a theodicist argument such as van Inwagen's that offers no comfort at all to human beings in their agony (see chapter 5). True, the distinction between religion or theology on the one hand and philosophy on the other in cases like these is often not entirely clear. Our practices are not as neatly categorizable as we often hope. Their proper categorization in these and other terms is a matter of continuing self-reflection. In any event, respect toward others' attempts to deal with the fundamental mysteries of life and existence—whether such attempts are understood as religious or philosophical in their primary nature—should be seen as a key religious virtue. This can be based on a pragmatic analysis of how religious thoughts and ideas are attempts to respond to human problems arising out of human practices.[43]

A critic may claim that I am arguing circularly, assuming that I am able to reach a "genuine" religious outlook. But note again that my own remarks on what is genuinely religious or pseudoreligious are *not* religious or theological but *philosophical* remarks; hence, *a fortiori*, they cannot be "genuinely religious" or intended as being so. A religious way of thinking cannot be ethically—or, given the intertwinement of ethics and metaphysics defended in the previous chapters, even metaphysically—accepted, if it claims that other religions are false, or wrong, or serve a false divinity, and so on. This is a way of rejecting an alleged religious outlook on the basis of its pragmatically unwelcome or even ethically disastrous consequences (with a broad understanding of the notion of a consequence); thus, what we have here is, again, the (Jamesian) pragmatic method at work. Tolerance and respect for otherness ought to be seen as key virtues of genuine religiosity; all major world religions, liberally and unorthodoxly interpreted, embody these virtues or can at least be seen as strongly supporting them. Yet, as virtually all facts about human cultural institutions, this is historically conditioned: *we* have come to the point in human history where *we* can no more accept intolerant "religions"—even accept them as religions.

This observation resembles the (moderately) historicist point that there can be no theodicy after Auschwitz. While it would certainly be correct to point out that one should not consider all "theodicists"— including the most important classics of Western Christian theology, such as Augustine or Thomas Aquinas—"pseudoreligious" simply because of their commitment to the pursuit of theodicy, this comes close to saying that we should not consider Aristotle or Newton pseudoscientific. In order to avoid such trivializations of the classical theologians' commitment to theodicies or to early natural scientists' commitment to whatever they found scientific, we should not forget the fundamental historicity of our struggles with religion—and, often religiously, with evil. After Auschwitz, *we* cannot be genuinely religious by relying on an Aquinian theodicy, any more than we can today be (fully) scientific by endorsing Aristotle's physical or biological theories. And the same holds for *our* need to fight against all kinds of religious (and other) intolerance, even though we may respect as "genuinely religious" also those thinkers of early Christianity, for instance, for whom religious intolerance was simply a natural point of departure. Moreover, it has been repeatedly pointed out in this book that the religious virtues of antitheodicy, tolerance, and respect for otherness were emphasized by pragmatist thinkers like James and Dewey already before Auschwitz.

Finally, it must be admitted that, through my concluding thoughts on tolerance and otherness, I have only arrived at something like a metalevel account of the ways in which religion can, and should, be philosophized about—instead of any proper philosophical theory of what (genuine) religion is or whether it can be rationally justified. Every such abstract metalevel claim, however, is just more philosophy: there is no independent metaphilosophical perspective available for us to conduct our philosophical inquiries.[44] In this book, I have put forward Jamesian pragmatism as a kind of metatheory: it is by means of employing the pragmatic method that we should inquire into the justificatory status of various philosophical views on religion, including James's own, and those of the other pragmatists, such as Dewey and the neopragmatists. I admit, of course, that this is just more philosophy. However, while we should stay away from any assumptions about there being foundationalist or absolutist metatheories, presumably there can still be metaphilosophical inquiries and reflections acknowledging their own fallible, inevitably contextual, and continuously critically revisable status. To admit this is simply to be self-critically reflexive, as any pragmatist should be. Instead of banning metaphilosophizing altogether, we should encourage meta-level reflection on what philosophy, including philosophy of religion in particular, is all about—and we should further require that such reflection is conducted in the course of actual, "first-order" philosophical inquiries. I hope that I have achieved something along those lines in this book.

Therefore, returning to the fundamental thesis of this book—the dependence of religious (and, *mutatis mutandis*, any metaphysical) ideas on prior ethical considerations—we may pause to reflect on what it actually means to evaluate religious (or, again, any metaphysical) commitments ethically, as I have urged throughout this book that we should do. At this point of the argument it should be clear that we cannot engage in such evaluation on the basis of any pregiven, substantial ethical theory (nor of any purely formal one, such as Kant's categorical imperative), because what we are presented with here is *the fundamental ethical requirement to autonomously evaluate our own life, including our commitment to ethical theories and (possibly) to religious (or antireligious) beliefs.* We must, then, evaluate our commitments from within a framework shaped and colored by those commitments themselves. This is, inevitably, a reflexive self-evaluation also continuously transcending the limits of any merely "first-order" reflection and reaching out for a metalevel critically examining our practices and criteria of critical reflection themselves. In the end, our entire lives, understood as ethically structured, must be at stake here, which again brings ethics and religion together in a deep way, as suggested in the previous chapters. Furthermore, when engaging in autonomous critical evaluation we also commit ourselves to stepping forward in order to place ourselves into a process of evaluation by others. Any substantial ethical views, or religious ones for that matter, can emerge only within such concrete self-critically evaluative engagements—thus in a sense *ad hoc*, in a "particularist" manner, rather than abstractly or generally.

This is part of what I see as a pragmatic acknowledgment, following James and Dewey, of our human finitude and fallibility. Any consideration of the boundary between religious and pseudoreligious thought should also start from such an acknowledgment.

Notes

INTRODUCTION

1. For an up-to-date summary of the realism versus antirealism dispute in contemporary philosophy of religion, see, for example, Clare McGraw, "The Realism/Anti-Realism Debate in Religion," *Philosophy Compass* 3, no.1 (2008): 254–72. For an interesting proposal to incorporate some ideas (e.g., "constructive empiricism") from recent philosophy of science, especially its debate over scientific realism and its alternatives, to the philosophy of religion, see Peter Lipton, "Science and Religion: The Immersion Solution," in *Philosophers and God: At the Frontiers of Faith and Reason,* ed. John Corwell and Michael McGhee (London and New York: Continuum, 2009), 1–20. For a recent examination of the clash between two rival views on religious language, see Anders Kraal, "The Phillips-Swinburne Debate on Religious Language: Toward a *Via Media,*" in *The Contemplative Spirit: D. Z. Phillips on Religion and the Limits of Philosophy,* ed. Ingolf U. Dalferth and Hartmut von Sass (Tübingen: Mohr Siebeck, 2010), 155–72.

2. However, John Bishop—in his "The Philosophy of Religion: A Programmatic Overview," *Philosophy Compass* 1, no. 5 (2006): 506–34—comes close to pragmatist approaches in the philosophy of religion by acknowledging a certain kind of intertwinement of epistemological (and metaphysical) and ethical issues and by considering the moral evaluation of practical commitments to the truth of religious beliefs (see especially 512–13). On the other hand, his distinction between theoretical belief and practical commitment is unpragmatic, given the pragmatists' insistence on *all* beliefs (including religious ones) being "habits of action." This topic will be revisited repeatedly in this book. For general overviews of pragmatist philosophy of religion and its history, see, for example, Ulf Zackariasson's excellent encyclopedia entries: "Religion," in *The Continuum Companion to Pragmatism,* ed. Sami Pihlström (London: Continuum, 2011); and "Pragmatism", forthcoming in *Encyclopedia of Sciences and Religions,* ed. Nina Azari et al. (Dordrecht: Springer, 2013); see also the papers on pragmatism and religion included in Sami Pihlström and Henrik Rydenfelt,

eds., *Pragmatist Perspectives* (Acta Philosophica Fennica 86, Helsinki: The Philosophical Society of Finland, 2009).

3. The best-known contributors to these debates over the place of religion in the "public sphere" include John Rawls, Martha Nussbaum, Charles Taylor, and Jürgen Habermas. For the latter's balanced account, with pragmatist inclinations (albeit "post-metaphysically" "de-transcendentalized," hence quite different from the pragmatist perspective to be developed in this book), see Habermas, *Zwischen Naturalismus und Religion* (Frankfurt am Main: Suhrkamp, 2005); and Habermas, "Religion in the Public Sphere," *European Journal of Philosophy* 14 (2006): 1–25. See also Thomas M. Schmidt, "Religious Pluralism and Democratic Society: Political Liberalism and the Reasonableness of Religious Beliefs," *Philosophy and Social Criticism* 25 (1999): 43–56. Nussbaum's influential views are readily available in her *Liberty of Consciousness: In Defense of America's Tradition of Religious Equality* (New York: Basic Books, 2008). A lucid pragmatist perspective on this debate is adopted by Ulf Zackariasson, whose work in progress on these topics, which I have been able to read in its unpublished version, will undoubtedly be a major contribution to the field: see Zackariasson, *Pragmatism, Religion and Public Life: A Critical Pragmatic Contribution to the Philosophical Discussion on the Role of Religion and Life Orientations in Public Deliberation* (unpublished ms, 2011). As Zackariasson focuses on this particular debate from a pragmatist perspective, I can safely mostly neglect the topic in my own book, which is ethico-metaphysically rather than politically oriented; in any event, Zackariasson and others have pursued the political-philosophical questions much better than I ever could. (See also Zackariasson's encyclopaedia articles cited in the previous note; I will briefly discuss Zackariasson's views as exemplifications of recent neopragmatist philosophy of religion in chapter 4.) Yet, this is not to say that I would see a gulf between the ethico-metaphysical and the political aspects of contemporary (pragmatist) philosophy of religion; on the contrary, letting different metaphysical and theological ideas enter the "public space" is a way of subordinating them to critical—not just ethical but also political—discussion and thus a way of testing them pragmatically.

4. The pragmatist, then, should be among the first to recognize that the science versus religion debate(s) today are *both* metaphysico-epistemic *and* ethico-political (see also the previous note). Cf. Thomas M. Schmidt, "The Contemporary Science-and-Religion Debate: Metaphysical or Political?," in *Scientific Explanation and Religious Belief: Science and Religion in Philosophical and Public Discourse*, ed. Michael G. Parker and Thomas M. Schmidt (Tübingen: Mohr Siebeck, 2005), 44–57. (The same book also contains other contributions relevant to the topics of my inquiry.) Moreover, the pragmatist should acknowledge these debates as addressing genuine philosophical problems instead of "immunizing" religion from scientific criticism by adopting a naive conventionalism or

instrumentalism—even though the term *pragmatism* is even today often mis-leadingly associated with such views: see, for example, Hans Albert, "Der religiöse Glaube und die Religionskritik der Aufklärung: Beschränkungen der Vernunftgebrauchs im Lichte kritischer Philosophie," *Journal for General Philosophy of Science* 37 (2006): 355–71 (see 356).

5. See, for example, Richard Wolin, "Reason vs. Faith: The Battle Continues," *The Chronicle Review*, June 15, 2009, http://chronicle.com/free/v55/i39/39wolin secularage.htm.

6. The proposal to advance pragmatism as a middle ground option in the philosophy of religion could, thus, be connected with the discussions of the concept of (mutual) recognition (*Anerkennung*) that have their roots in Hegel's *Phänomenologie des Geistes* and have been brought to the center of contemporary debates by Axel Honneth; see Honneth, *Kampf um Anerkennung* (Frankfurt am Main: Suhrkamp, 2003; first published 1992). In the theological context, I have learned a lot from my colleague Risto Saarinen's work on this matter (e.g., his forthcoming article, "Anerkennungstheorien und religiöse Überzeugungen," 2012). In this book, however, I must set the topic aside, even though my attempt to steer the middle course between various extreme positions can implicitly be understood as an attempt to challenge the often diametrically opposed conversation partners to recognize what is valuable in the opponent's position.

7. See Hilary Putnam, *The Collapse of the Fact/Value Dichotomy and Other Essays* (Cambridge, MA: Harvard University Press, 2002); and Putnam, *Ethics without Ontology* (Cambridge, MA: Harvard University Press, 2004).

8. This defense of antireductionism might be compared to Putnam's recent treatment of different kinds of Jewish philosophy, none of which is, for him, *the* correct one. See Hilary Putnam, *Jewish Philosophy as a Guide to Life* (Bloomington: Indiana University Press, 2008).

9. I have elsewhere described pragmatic pluralism in (meta)ontology as a form of "ontological tolerance." See Sami Pihlström, *Structuring the World: The Issue of Realism and the Nature of Ontological Problems in Classical and Contemporary Pragmatism*, Acta Philosophica Fennica 59 (Helsinki: The Philosophical Society of Finland, 1996); Pihlström, *Pragmatist Metaphysics: An Essay on the Ethical Grounds of Metaphysics* (London: Continuum, 2009). The concept of (ontological) tolerance could be further connected with the concept of recognition (see note 6 above), which, however, must remain the task of some other inquiry.

10. See T. L. S. Sprigge, *The God of Metaphysics* (Oxford: Oxford University Press, 2006).

11. Unless otherwise indicated, references to James's works are to the critical edition, *The Works of William James*, 19 vols., ed. Frederick H. Burkhardt, Fredson Bowers, and Ignas K. Skrupskelis (Cambridge, MA: Harvard University

Press, 1975–88). *A Pluralistic Universe* (1909) was published in this series in 1979, while *Pragmatism* (1907) came out in 1975. *The Varieties of Religious Experience* (1902) was published in two volumes in 1985.

12. Regarding relevant secondary literature on Jamesian pluralism in particular, H. G. Callaway's and David Lamberth's treatments of James should, among others, be mentioned here. See Callaway's "study edition" of James's *A Pluralistic Universe* (Cambridge: Cambridge Scholars Press, 2008), with a substantial introduction and notes by the editor; as well as Lamberth, *William James and the Metaphysics of Experience* (Cambridge: Cambridge University Press, 1999). Also other classical pragmatists' pronouncements on pluralism, especially F. C. S. Schiller's, should be taken into account in a more comprehensive study. Schiller's central writings have recently been collected in the volume, *Pragmatism and Humanism: Selected Essays*, ed. John R. Shook and Hugh P. McDonald (Amherst, NY: Humanity/Prometheus Books, 2008). Furthermore, there are general discussions of pluralism; for example, Maria Bahgramian, *Relativism* (London and New York: Routledge, 2004), interestingly yet problematically contrasting relativism and pluralism.

13. Cf. Pihlström, *Pragmatist Metaphysics*.

14. Cf. also, for example, A. W. Moore's Kantian discussion of the concept of hope in Moore, *Noble in Reason, Infinite in Faculty* (London and New York: Routledge, 2003).

15. Dewey's works will be referenced as *The Collected Works of John Dewey*, 37 vols., ed. Jo Ann Boydston (Carbondale: Southern Illinois University Press, 1967–86). *A Common Faith* is vol. 10 of *The Late Works* (LW9). See chapter 3 for more details.

16. As my choice of formulation indicates, these ideas could be compared to suggestions familiar from the work of Emmanuel Levinas, as well as to ideas in thinkers like Tillich, Wittgenstein, and Rahner.

17. Critical comparisons of Levinas and the pragmatists are rare; see, however, Megan Craig, *Levinas and James* (Bloomington and Indianapolis: Indiana University Press, 2010)—also raising the issue of "active passivity."

18. Among relevant contributions I should mention Eberhard Herrmann's account of the "existential" testing of religious ways of life; Peter Lipton's "immersion" view of religion and science (see note 2 above); and the metaphysically realistic interpretation of William James put forward by Michael Slater (see chapter 5).

19. Ultimately, such sheer unacceptability could be compared to situations in which "my spade is turned," to quote Wittgenstein's famous metaphor for our reasons being exhausted. See Ludwig Wittgenstein, *Philosophical Investigations*, trans. G. E. M. Anscombe (Oxford: Basil Blackwell, 1958; first published 1953), I, § 217. For a discussion of "unthinkabilities," see also Sami Pihlström,

"Ethical Unthinkabilities and Philosophical Seriousness," chap. 4 in *Transcendental Guilt: Reflections on Ethical Finitude* (Lanham, MD: Lexington Books, 2011).

20. I call any view that *requires* that theistic (or other religious) conceptions must provide a theodicy "theodicist," whether or not they also include the claim that a successful theodicy can be provided.

21. One highly important special concept, denoting a special practice of religious significance that should be pragmatically elucidated is the one of *prayer*. We should distinguish between genuinely religious and causally manipulative, pseudoreligious and superstitious forms of prayer (as argued, among other Wittgensteinians, by D. Z. Phillips). But we may also, when approaching religion pragmatically, understand religious beliefs, such as the ones about God's existence, as being embedded in rituals, such as prayer, roughly in the sense in which any beliefs are habits of action in the pragmatist understanding of belief James inherited from Peirce. Seeing religious beliefs as habits of action, deeply connected with prayer and other rituals, the pragmatist should also invoke the concept of *trust* in the context of religion. The believer not only trusts God but also her/his own habits, yet in a way that enables her/him to engage in a reflexive critique of them. These notions cannot be developed in any detail in this book, though.

1. PRAGMATIC ASPECTS OF KANTIAN THEISM

1. A terminological note is in order: I will not be concerned with polytheism, pantheism, panentheism, or other "nonstandard" versions of religious belief in God(s), even though I recognize the need for philosophical discussion of such varieties of theism, given the interesting alternatives to traditional religious outlooks offered, say, by process theology and metaphysics. The kind of theism I am interested in here is of the traditional (Judaeo-Christian-Islamic) monotheistic type. My discussion is, of course, philosophical in the sense of being independent of any particular religious or theological traditions (as well as the in itself ideological tradition of atheistic "free thinking"), though I do not claim to be independent of a religiously and theologically shaped background which makes only monotheistic faith a "live option" for most Western thinkers (to use an expression famously coined by William James, to whom I will more substantially return later in this chapter and in chapter 4).

2. I will not waste time for defending the view that creationism (like most other fundamentalist creeds) is pseudoscientific; a more interesting point (not argued in this chapter, either—but see the conclusion in this book) is that it may be *pseudoreligious*, too.

3. The concept of atheism requires clarification as much as the concept of theism. Atheism should be distinguished from (mere) agnosticism, which is

essentially a suspension of judgment concerning theism. While the theist believes that God exists, the atheist does not merely disbelieve this but believes that God does not exist, that is, that there is no God. Alternatively, we can distinguish between weak atheism (disbelief in the existence of God) and strong atheism (belief in the nonexistence of God). For a useful treatment of atheism and its philosophical justification, see Michael Martin, *Atheism: A Philosophical Justification* (Philadelphia: Temple University Press, 1990); for more up-to-date essays on the topic, see Martin, ed., *Cambridge Companion to Atheism* (Cambridge: Cambridge University Press, 2008). For a controversial distinction between scientific and philosophical atheism, see Raimo Tuomela, *Science, Action and Reality* (Dordrecht: D. Reidel, 1985); here, scientific atheism is the view that science can, or perhaps will, demonstrate the nonexistence of God, while philosophical atheism understands atheism as a (rational, justified) philosophical thesis never to be confirmed by science. Again, I will ignore this contrast in what follows, usually meaning "philosophical atheism" by the term *atheism*.

4. On the debate between evidentialists and fideists, see several essays in useful recent anthologies, such as Eleonore Stump and Michael J. Murray, eds., *Philosophy of Religion: The Big Questions* (Oxford and Malden, MA: Blackwell, 1999), and Brian Davies, ed., *Philosophy of Religion: A Guide and Anthology* (Oxford and New York: Oxford University Press, 2000). For a helpful overview of this issue and of major methodological controversies in twentieth century analytic philosophy of religion, see Timo Koistinen, *Philosophy of Religion or Religious Philosophy? A Critical Study of Contemporary Anglo-American Approaches* (Helsinki: Luther-Agricola Society, 2000).

5. Very little in this book depends on to whom views such as evidentialism and fideism can, or should, be attributed. Let me just note that a thinker such as Richard Swinburne is a paradigmatic example of evidentialism (see, for example, his *The Existence of God*, Oxford: Oxford University Press, 1979), while "Wittgensteinian" philosophers of religion such as D. Z. Phillips have usually, though somewhat inaccurately, been regarded as representatives of fideism (see, e.g., Phillips, *Belief, Change and Forms of Life*, Basingstoke: Macmillan, 1986). The expression "Wittgensteinian fideism" was (as far as I know) introduced by the strong atheist critic of religion, Kai Nielsen, as a pejorative term; yet, Wittgensteinians such as Phillips are not completely innocent to this (mis)characterization of their way of thinking about God and religion.

6. Note that I will usually speak about God's "reality" instead of "existence," thus honoring an important distinction made by Charles Peirce, the founder of pragmatism. If real, God may be real not in the way in which particular existing objects are but rather in the mode of generals, universals, or (Peircean-like) habits. Peirce's relevance to the philosophy of religion has recently been discussed by Robert C. Neville in his *Realism and Religion* (Albany: SUNY Press,

2009), Heikki A. Kovalainen in his contributions to the Nordic Pragmatism Conferences in 2011 (see www.nordprag.org), Vincent Colapietro (see his "The Dissenting Voice of Charles Peirce: Individuality, Community, and Transfiguration"), and Gesche Linde (see her " 'Man's Highest Developments Are Social': The Individual and the Social in Peirce's Philosophy of Religion," both presented as conference papers at the Max-Weber-Kolleg in Erfurt in 2012), as well as several theologians and scholars of religion who approach these issues from a semiotic perspective (such as Michael Raposa); I would have little to add to these scholars' learned explorations, so the major pragmatists this study will focus on are James and Dewey (as well as the leading neopragmatists). Moreover, while Peirce was indeed an interesting philosopher of religion—and among the classical pragmatists the one most knowledgeable of Kant—his central ideas in this field (e.g., agapism and the "neglected argument for the reality of God") do not seem to me to offer the kind of resources for integrating Kantian and pragmatic approaches that James's and Dewey's (and to some extent the neopragmatists') views do. See, however, chapter 5 for some references to Peircean "generals."

7. See the chapter on the "Ideal of Pure Reason" in the Transcendental Dialectics of Immanuel Kant, *Kritik der reinen Vernunft*, ed. Raymund Schmidt (Hamburg: Felix Meiner, 1990), A567/B595ff (A = 1st ed., 1781; B = 2nd ed., 1787). Regarding the cosmological argument, see also Kant's discussion of the Fourth Antinomy. The most comprehensive recent study on Kant's philosophy of religion is Peter Byrne, *Kant on God* (Aldershot, UK: Ashgate, 2007), which includes detailed discussions of Kant's criticisms of the theistic proofs as well as his "positive" account of moral faith. I will not, however, examine interpretive controversies concerning Kant's actual position; I will only provide the needed background for my own Kantian-cum-pragmatist developments. Obviously, there are philosophers of religion who view Kant's arguments very critically; see, for example, Alvin Plantinga, *Warranted Christian Belief* (Oxford: Oxford University Press, 2000). Kant's success in combating the traditional proofs is thus not at all universally acknowledged. I cannot engage in such controversies here; my argument should be read as a hypothetical one starting from the proposal to take seriously Kant's approach to theism.

8. Again, it is best to set aside here the obviously pseudoscientific arguments used by creationists and ID believers. Scientifically, there is no genuine debate between creationist "design" theories and Darwinian evolution, as the latter is the only—though of course not perfect—explanation we currently have for the development of life; religiously, moreover, a faith that needs the "make-believe" that it is science would be poor faith indeed.

9. See Michelle Grier, *Kant's Doctrine of Transcendental Illusion* (Cambridge: Cambridge University Press, 2001); and Henry E. Allison, *Kant's Transcendental*

Idealism: An Interpretation and Defense—Revised and Enlarged Edition (New Haven, CT: Yale University Press, 2004). These commentators emphasize both the hypostatization charge against the theistic proofs and the view that transcendental realism is the ultimate *proton pseudos* in the fallacious inferences reason is entangled with (not only in the theistic case but also in the Paralogisms and the Antinomy, with which we cannot deal here). Grier's reading of the "Transcendental Dialectic" seems to have influenced Allison's, who has revised some of his arguments from the first edition (1983) of his book in the second edition (2004).

10. In my terminology, fideists are (at least in most cases) theists, believing in God in a way that distinguishes sharply between reason and faith (and rejecting all attempts to provide reasons for such a faith), whereas evidentialists can be either theists (if they maintain that there are sufficient rational reasons—sufficient evidence—in favor of the theistic hypothesis) or atheists (if they maintain that there are no such reasons or evidence). In principle, evidentialists can also adopt agnosticism, if they require that theism must be supported by reasons but find no such reasons compelling, either way—at least not yet, in the present state of inquiry.

11. See, for example, Sami Pihlström, "Religion and Pseudo-Religion: An Elusive Boundary," *International Journal for Philosophy of Religion* 62 (2007): 3–32; as well as the conclusion.

12. Although I am using Allison's notion of epistemic conditions here (see Allison, *Kant's Transcendental Idealism*, especially chapter 1), I am not implying that I would agree with him that the transcendental conditions for the possibility of experience, cognition, or representation that Kant is examining would be *merely epistemic* in the sense of being entirely *nonmetaphysical*. Rather, I would urge that the critical philosophy, even in its core areas such as transcendental idealism, is (partly) a metaphysical project, though of course not "metaphysical" in the sense in which traditional precritical metaphysics was firmly rejected by Kant. Allison and some other recent interpreters—including David Carr, *The Paradox of Subjectivity: The Self in the Transcendental Tradition* (Oxford and New York: Oxford University Press, 1999)—in my view tend to read Kant too antimetaphysically, construing transcendental idealism and transcendental philosophy more generally as merely methodological or epistemological views. Such a total rejection of metaphysics (theistic or not) is not necessary for a Kantian transcendental philosopher. This is a vast issue and cannot be settled here. In contrast to Allison's and Carr's antimetaphysical accounts of transcendental philosophy, I find J. J. Valberg's identification of the transcendental self with what he calls "my horizon"—with similarities not only to Kant but to Wittgenstein and Heidegger as well—much more promising, especially because this approach is not restricted to epistemology but leaves room, within tran-

scendental philosophy, for metaphysics (which Valberg heavily engages in) and also for topics in the philosophy of religion (which he does not deal with). See J. J. Valberg, *Dream, Death, and the Self* (Princeton, NJ: Princeton University Press, 2007).

13. I am here deliberately taking some distance to Kant's actual position and redescribing Kantian views by employing Jamesian terminology; cf. James, *Pragmatism: A New Name for Some Old Ways of Thinking* (1907), ed. Frederick H. Burkhardt, Fredson Bowers, and Ignas K. Skrupskelis (Cambridge, MA: Harvard University Press, 1975). Orthodox Kantians (as well as Jamesians) would of course find my Jamesian rearticulations of Kant problematic, but I do not see any problems here, insofar as my main interest lies in the systematic issue of theism rather than in historical scholarly questions. Some work has, however, been done on the historical relations between Kant and James: see, for example, Sami Pihlström, "Synthesizing Traditions: Rewriting the History of Pragmatism and Transcendental Philosophy," *History of Philosophy Quarterly* 23 (2006): 375–90. Let me also note that Peter Byrne, in his *The Moral Interpretation of Religion* (Edinburgh: Edinburgh University Press, 1998), explicitly compares Kant's moral argument for God's existence with James's "will to believe" argument (see chapter 7). My approach is quite different, though, because I am not focusing on "The Will to Believe" (but, rather, on *Pragmatism*) and because I am proposing that we should view James's own ideas "transcendentally." Furthermore, a critic might point out that Hegel (as well as, possibly, the opposition between Hegel and Kierkegaard) would have to be taken into account when moving from Kant's philosophy of religion to James's. Again, I must simply note that not everything can be done in a single book; the role played by Hegel at the background of pragmatist philosophy of religion deserves a separate study.

14. See Kant, *Kritik der reinen Vernunft*, A795/B823ff.

15. See Immanuel Kant, *Kritik der praktischen Vernunft* (1788), in Kant, *Werke in Zehn Bänden*, ed. Wilhelm Weischedel (Darmstadt: Wissenschaftliche Buchgesellschaft, 1983), A223ff.

16. Cf. ibid., A215ff. Here, the word *ultimately*—my word in this context rather than Kant's—is crucial, because we can observe the priority of practical reason only after having done some work of theoretical reason, that is, after having become convinced of the futility of the speculative theistic proofs and having thus seen the need for a different, pragmatic, approach.

17. See Frederick C. Beiser, "Moral Faith and the Highest Good," in *Cambridge Companion to Kant and Modern Philosophy*, ed. Paul Guyer (Cambridge: Cambridge University Press, 2006), 593–99. See *Kritik der reinen Vernunft*, A810–811/B838–839, for Kant's characterization of the *summum bonum*.

18. Beiser, "Moral Faith and the Highest Good," 604. (This is not a direct quotation of Beiser's formulation of Kant's argument but my own paraphrase.)

See Kant, *Kritik der praktischen Vernunft*, A223–37. See also Byrne, *Kant on God*, especially chapters 5–6, for a critical perspective on Kant's arguments for moral faith—a perspective very different from Beiser's.

19. Beiser, "Moral Faith and the Highest Good," 606–7.

20. Ibid., 610.

21. See William James, *The Will to Believe and Other Essays in Popular Philosophy* (1897), ed. Frederick H. Burkhardt, Fredson Bowers, and Ignas K. Skrupskelis (Cambridge, MA: Harvard University Press, 1979). Beiser's misconstrual may result from the fact that he focuses only on the James of "The Will to Believe" (see ibid., chap. 1), ignoring James's discussions of our need for a moral order, and more generally of the ethically "energizing" function of theism (see the essays, "The Sentiment of Rationality" and "The Moral Philosopher and the Moral Life", also in the same volume James published in 1897; see also James, *Pragmatism*, especially chapters 3 and 8). For two excellent recent readings of James's "theological postulate" and its moral relevance (without any detailed comparisons to Kant, unfortunately), see Todd Lekan, "Strenuous Moral Living," and Michael R. Slater, "Ethical Naturalism and Religious Belief in 'The Moral Philosopher and the Moral Life,'" both available online in *William James Studies* 2 (2007), http://williamjamesstudies.press.uiuc.edu. Other important—though definitely not unproblematic or uncontroversial—treatments of James's philosophy of religion include Richard Gale, *The Divided Self of William James* (Cambridge: Cambridge University Press, 1999), and Wesley Cooper, *The Unity of William James's Thought* (Nashville, TN: Vanderbilt University Press, 2002), plus a number of more specialized studies on such issues as James's pluralism, panpsychism, radical empiricism, etc. Admittedly, James's way of arguing for the practical need or requirement of theism for the purposes of a fully moral life is—as Lekan's and Slater's papers also remind us—more empirical and psychological than Kant's a priori approach; yet, a case for a pragmatic-transcendental reconstruction of Jamesian ideas can be made, and this chapter, though no close reading of James, is part of such a reconstructive attempt. (See also chapter 4.)

22. Beiser, "Moral Faith and the Highest Good", 597, 618–19. It might be suggested, to continue the brief comparison between Kant and Jamesian pragmatism (see the previous note), that there are Kantian overtones in James's (*Pragmatism*, chap. 3) notion of an "eternal moral order" of the universe, which he sees as a deeply seated human need. Cf. also ibid., chap. 8, for a "meliorist" view of the possible though not inevitable "salvation" of the world; see also the discussion of these issues in Sami Pihlström, *"The Trail of the Human Serpent Is over Everything": Jamesian Perspectives on Mind, World, and Religion* (Lanham, MD: University Press of America, 2008). A fuller account of these issues in James would require a discussion of his famous work, *The Varieties of Religious*

Experience (1902), ed. Frederick H. Burkhardt, Fredson Bowers, and Ignas K. Skrupskelis (Cambridge, MA: Harvard University Press, 1985), which does briefly take up Kant's postulates, among other things. James's *Pragmatism*, however, is the best source for the development of "Kantian pragmatism."

23. Beiser, "Moral Faith and the Highest Good," 599.

24. Ibid., 589–90.

25. Cf. Kant, *Kritik der praktischen Vernunft*, A238–40.

26. Ibid., A244.

27. See Beiser, "Moral Faith and the Highest Good", 613, 620. It might be noted in passing that Charles Taylor's defense of theism in the closing pages of his major book, *Sources of the Self: The Making of Modern Identity* (Cambridge: Cambridge University Press, 1989), and elsewhere, is an interesting case of a modern transcendental approach to the issue of theism; cf. also his later works on religion, for example (dealing with James), *Varieties of Religion Today: William James Revisited* (Cambridge, MA: Harvard University Press, 2002). The Taylorian transcendental argument is readily comparable to the Kantian postulates. Cf. here especially the explicitly transcendental reading of Taylor by D. P. Baker, "Charles Taylor's *Sources of the Self*: A Transcendental Apologetic?," *International Journal for Philosophy of Religion* 47 (2000): 155–74; see Pihlström, *"The Trail of the Human Serpent Is over Everything,"* chap. 2, for some critical discussion. For Taylor's analysis of what transcendental arguments are, see his paper, "Transcendental Arguments" (1979), chap. 2 in Taylor, *Philosophical Arguments* (Cambridge, MA: Harvard University Press, 1995); cf. also the critical examination in Sami Pihlström, "Kant Anthropologized," in *Naturalizing the Transcendental: A Pragmatic View* (Amherst, NY: Prometheus/Humanity Books, 2003).

28. See Valberg, *Dream, Death, and the Self,* especially the introductory chapter, in which the concept of the horizon is explained.

29. See especially James, *Pragmatism*, chapters 3, 4, and 8.

30. See also Taylor's discussion of James in *Varieties of Religion Today*.

31. On James's "theological postulates," see the essays by Lekan and Slater cited in note 21.

32. Cf. here, again, the papers on James by Lekan and Slater cited above.

33. See Hilary Putnam, *The Collapse of the Fact/Value Dichotomy and Other Essays* (Cambridge, MA: Harvard University Press, 2002); Putnam, *Ethics without Ontology* (Cambridge, MA: Harvard University Press, 2004); as well as Sami Pihlström, *Pragmatic Moral Realism: A Transcendental Defense* (Amsterdam and New York: Rodopi, 2005); and Pihlström, "Putnam's Conception of Ontology," *Contemporary Pragmatism* 3, no.2 (2006): 1–13 (with a response by Putnam in the same issue). Of course, classical pragmatism—for example, the

one articulated in James's *Pragmatism*—attempts to bridge many other classical gaps, including the one between "tough-minded" empiricism and "tender-minded" rationalism.

34. See Kant, *Kritik der reinen Vernunft*, A627/B655. In their contributions to Robert Stern, ed., *Transcendental Arguments: Problems and Prospects* (Oxford and New York: Oxford University Press, 1999), Paul Franks and Barry Stroud acknowledge David Bell as the one who first observed that Kant does indeed talk about a transcendental argument in the passage cited.

35. The specific problems there might be regarding immortality can be set aside here, as this chapter focuses on the issue of theism. For Kant, the two go rather neatly together, and James, too, was deeply interested in defending the possibility of, and the legitimate hope for, immortality. See, for example, James's essay "Human Immortality" (1898), in his *Essays on Religion and Morality*, ed. Frederick H. Burkhardt, Fredson Bowers, and Ignas K. Skrupskelis (Cambridge, MA: Harvard University Press, 1982). Regarding the phrase "only if" in the first premise, it should be noted that God's existence is here regarded as a necessary but obviously not a sufficient condition for the possibility of moral pursuits. Morality might be impossible for some other reason, for example, trivially for the reason that humans or other rational beings might not exist at all.

36. For the importance of such a "how" question in Kant's theoretical philosophy, see Markku Leppäkoski, *The Transcendental How: Kant's Transcendental Deduction of Objective Cognition*, Stockholm Studies in Philosophy 12 (Stockholm: Almqvist and Wiksell, 1993).

37. I develop these issues much more comprehensively in Sami Pihlström, *Pragmatist Metaphysics: An Essay on the Ethical Grounds of Ontology* (London and New York: Continuum, 2009). See also chapter 4.

38. This worry is crucially connected with the problem of evil, to which I will briefly return in the next section. It is, above all, the undeniable existence of evil that may lead us to moral nihilism, to abandoning the pursuit of morality.

39. For this "softening" or "blurring", see Pihlström, *Naturalizing the Transcendental*, and *"The Trail of the Human Serpent Is over Everything"* (cited above).

40. A somewhat more scholarly point that could be made here is that there is a hitherto unappreciated analogy between Kantian transcendental argumentation and Jamesian "will to believe" argumentation. Both start from given human actualities and move "backward" to their conditions of possibility—in quite different ways, but analogously to each other. Just as proper transcendental arguments move from a given phenomenon backward to a condition needed for that phenomenon to be possible, the will to believe strategy (in the theistic case or elsewhere) also moves backward to the rational legitimation of the religious experiences and practices which, in turn, enable the believer to view the question about God's existence as a genuine option in her/his life, an option to

which the will-to-believe strategy can be applied. In neither case do the arguments prove anything for the radical skeptic (or the nihilist) who would dispute the starting point taken for granted. Neither Kant nor James—nor any pragmatist—sees it even possible, let alone necessary, to "respond to the skeptic" either in moral philosophy or in the philosophy of religion. This important point is often overlooked.

41. See, again, the title essay of *The Will to Believe*.

42. Here, as was seen above, I followed Beiser's account in "Moral Faith and the Highest Good," though not his account of James's relation to Kant.

43. At this point, the pragmatist developing these Kantian-cum-Jamesian ideas in the contemporary discussion may be inspired by the proposal, made by Roger F. Gibson in a very different context, that ontology and epistemology and "reciprocally contained" in each other in W. V. Quine's philosophy (see R. F. Gibson, *Philosophy of W. V. Quine: An Expository Essay*, Tampa: University Press of Florida, 1982), or perhaps even more plausibly, by Morton White's holistic pragmatism, which he has developed since the late 1940s and early 1950s. See, in particular, White's well-known *Toward a Reunion in Philosophy* (Cambridge, MA: Harvard University Press, 1956), as well as his more recent elaborations in White, *A Philosophy of Culture: The Scope of Holistic Pragmatism* (Princeton, NJ: Princeton University Press, 2002). A "Whitean" holistic pragmatist account of the relation between religion and ethics still needs to be developed, however. I am here only suggesting that this might be one interesting way to move on. For more reflections on White and his holistic pragmatism, see Robert Sinclair, "Morton White's Moral Pragmatism," *Cognitio* 12 (2011): 143–55; and Sami Pihlström, "Morton White's Philosophy of Culture: Holistic Pragmatism and Interdisciplinary Inquiry," *Human Affairs* 21 (2011): 140–56.

44. Here we may take our lead from Schopenhauer, who saw evil and suffering in the heart of the human metaphysical (and more generally philosophical) wonder at the existence of the world. See Arthur Schopenhauer, *The World as Will and Representation*, trans. E. J. F. Payne (New York: Dover, 1966; originally published 1819–44), part 2.

45. These properties attributed to God can be taken to be simply based on the concept of God. Obviously, the first premise can be disputed, as some process theologians—and, indeed, William James—have done.

46. For interesting debates over the prospects of theodicy, see the exchange between Richard Swinburne and D. Z. Phillips in *Reason and Religion*, ed. Stuart C. Brown (Ithaca, NY: Cornell University Press, 1977). Phillips, of course, argues against evidentialists' and (as we may call them) theodicists' view that evil poses an evidential problem for theism and that a successful form of theism would have to offer a theodicy. (Note that I recognize a problem in my saying that theodicist views are misleading "in religious terms." How can anyone who

does not share a religious outlook, or who does not quite consider her-/himself a believer, say anything like that? *This* is in fact part of the problem I am trying to think about, though certainly not fully resolve, here.)

47. See James, *Pragmatism*, chap. 8, and especially William James, *A Pluralistic Universe* (1909), ed. Frederick H. Burkhardt, Fredson Bowers, and Ignas K. Skrupskelis (Cambridge, MA: Harvard University Press, 1977). Process theism, advanced by philosophers like A. N. Whitehead and Charles Hartshorne, is another move in this direction: process metaphysicians and theologians tend to identify God with the world-process as a whole, thereby acknowledging that God himself "suffers" with humankind, instead of somehow endorsing or justifying human suffering from a transcendent perspective. James's flirtation with panpsychism at least occasionally come close to such a position. In this volume, I cannot further explore the very interesting relations between pragmatism and process philosophy, though.

48. See, for example, classical essays on the topic collected in William Rowe, ed., *God and the Problem of Evil* (Malden, MA: Blackwell, 2001).

49. My use of "theodicist" is intended to capture both theistic and atheistic views that regard a theodicy as necessary for theism. According to theistic theodicists, such as Swinburne, theodicies succeed, while atheistic theodicists regard the problem of evil as an atheological challenge that ought to lead a rational person to atheism.

50. On the highly insecure and easily fragmented nature of religious (and moral) faith, see David Wisdo, *The Life of Irony and the Ethics of Belief* (Albany: SUNY Press, 1993).

51. For Kant's criticism of theodicy, see Immanuel Kant, "Über das Misslingen aller philosophischen Versuche in der Theodizee," in Kant, *Werke in Zehn Bänden*, ed. Wilhelm Weischedel (Darmstadt: Wissenschaftliche Buchgesellschaft, 1983), 9:173–190. For a useful commentary essay, see Johannes Brachtendorff, "Kants Theodizee-Aufsatz—Die Bedingungen des Gelingens philosophischen Theodizee," *Kant-Studien* 93 (2002): 57–83. For James's opposition to especially Leibnizian theodicy, see chap. 1 of *Pragmatism*, in particular.

52. For insightful recent discussions along these lines, see Richard Bernstein, *Radical Evil: A Philosophical Interrogation* (Cambridge: Polity Press, 2002); Susan Neiman, *Evil in Modern Thought: An Alternative History of Philosophy* (Princeton, NJ: Princeton University Press, 2004); see also chapter 5.

53. See, again, the first lecture of James's *Pragmatism* for a discussion of evil—an often neglected starting point in James's development of pragmatism.

54. Because I want to maintain the metaphysical element of theism, though only through ethics, my remarks are implicitly oriented against the currently popular postmodern and "post-onto-theological" attempts to defend a form of religion completely independent of metaphysics. See, for example, the essays in

Mark A. Wrathall, ed., *Religion after Metaphysics* (Cambridge: Cambridge University Press, 2003), featuring work by leading antimetaphysical thinkers such as Richard Rorty and Gianni Vattimo.

55. See Sami Pihlström, "Pragmatic and Transcendental Arguments for Theism: A Critical Examination," *International Journal for Philosophy of Religion* 51 (2002): 195–213 (reprinted in Pihlström, *"The Trail of the Human Serpent Is over Everything,"* chap. 2).

2. DEWEYAN PRAGMATIC RELIGIOUS NATURALISM

1. See, for example, John Fesmire, *Dewey and Moral Imagination* (Bloomington: Indiana University Press, 2003); David L. Hildebrand, *Beyond Realism and Antirealism: Dewey and the Neopragmatists* (Nashville, TN: Vanderbilt University Press, 2003); William J. Gavin, ed., *In Dewey's Wake? Unfinished Work in Pragmatic Reconstruction* (Albany: SUNY Press, 2003); as well as the proceedings volumes of the Central European Pragmatist Forum, ed. John Ryder et al., 5 volumes published to date in the book series, *Studies in Pragmatism and Values* (Amsterdam and New York: Rodopi, 2004–11). Commentaries that do emphasize Dewey's religious concerns will be cited in due course below.

2. See especially chapters 1 and 4 in this book. For a perceptive account of Deweyan pragmatism as a naturalization of James's, also in its reconstructed conception of religion, see Randy L. Freeman, "Deweyan Pragmatism", *William James Studies* 1 (2006), http://williamjamesstudies.press.uiuc.edu/1.1/. For Dewey's own remarks on James's individualist approach to religion, which differed from his own, see his review of Ralph Barton Perry's *The Thought and Character of William James* (1935), "The Philosophy of William James" (1937), LW11:474–76. On the influence of James's functional psychology of religious experience on Dewey's views, see Steven C. Rockefeller, *John Dewey: Religious Faith and Democratic Humanism* (New York: Columbia University Press, 1991), 469–71. (Rockefeller's philosophical biography of Dewey, to be cited frequently below, is probably the best single work on Dewey's philosophy of religion.)

3. *A Common Faith* is based on Dewey's Terry Lectures, delivered at Yale University in January 1934. The slim volume was originally published by Yale University Press in 1934. Its second chapter was published separately as "The Liberation of Modern Religion" in *Yale Review* 23 (1934): 751–70. The references in the text will be made in the standard manner to vol. 9 of Dewey's *Late Works* (hereafter cited as LW9); cf. the introduction for a note on Dewey's *Collected Works*.

4. These include the "religious naturalists" in American theology, such as H. N. Wieman and the Chicago School of liberal theology, not to be considered here in detail. I will cite some contemporary religious naturalists below.

5. This conception is developed especially in *Experience and Nature* (1925/1929, LW1), *The Quest for Certainty* (1929, LW4), and elsewhere.

6. Such views are articulated in the collection, *Religion without Metaphysics*, ed. Mark Wrathall (Cambridge: Cambridge University Press, 2003). No detailed comparisons to either Continental philosophers or neopragmatists can be made here, though.

7. See John R. Shook, *Dewey's Empirical Theory of Knowledge and Reality* (Nashville, TN: Vanderbilt University Press, 2000), 68. According to Shook (ibid., 133), Dewey's early idealistic philosophy may even be close to pan(en)theism. For more details on the early development of Dewey's religious ideas, see Rockefeller, *John Dewey*, Part 1. Some of Dewey's early writings from the 1880–90s are interesting documents of his struggle to come to terms with Christianity: see "The Obligation to Knowledge of God" (1884), EW1:61–63; "The Place of Religious Emotion" (1886), EW1:90–92; "The Value of Historical Christianity" (1889), LW17:529–33; "Christianity and Democracy" (1892), EW4:3–10; "Renan's Loss of Faith in Science" (1893), EW4:11–18; and "The Relation of Philosophy to Theology" (1893), EW4:365–68. I will have to ignore these early texts and focus on Dewey's later treatments of religion. A comprehensive chronological list of Dewey's writings related to religion can be found in Rockefeller's book (633–43). See also the useful *Index* volume supplementing Dewey's *Works*. For Dewey's own later reflections on his loss of traditional religious beliefs, see his "From Absolutism to Experimentalism" (1930), LW5:147–60 (especially 149–50, 153–54). Also, there are writings by Dewey on religion that remained unpublished in his lifetime such as "Some Thoughts concerning Religion" (1910), LW17:374–80.

8. Rockefeller, *John Dewey*, 21. (Note that Rockefeller's periodization of Dewey's thought is much more detailed.)

9. Ibid., 215.

10. Ibid., 231. For example, Rockefeller quotes a 1904 poem by Dewey to the memory of his dead sons, in which Dewey refers to them as "God's blessed loan" (ibid.); see also ibid., 320–23, for later poems with symbolic references to God.

11. This chapter (or book) is not the proper place for a close reading of Dewey's major naturalist texts, such as *Experience and Nature*. A brief contextualization for the application of that naturalism to religion must be offered, though.

12. See, for example, Shook, *Dewey's Empirical Theory of Knowledge and Reality*, 203.

13. Such is, for instance, the impression one gets from reading Larry Hickman's general presentation "John Dewey, 1859–1952" in *The Blackwell Guide to American Philosophy*, ed. Armen T. Marsoobian and John Ryder (Malden, MA: Blackwell, 2004), 155–73 (on Dewey and religion, see 165).

14. Here I would suggest that the Deweyan naturalist, like John McDowell in his debated book, *Mind and World* (Cambridge, MA: Harvard University Press,

1994; 2nd ed. 1996), engages in a "rethinking" of the concept of nature. For comparisons between Dewey and McDowell in this regard, see Sami Pihlström, "How Minds Understand Their World," in *Naturalizing the Transcendental: A Pragmatic View* (Amherst, NY: Prometheus/Humanity Books, 2003).

15. Cf. Sami Pihlström, "On the Concept of Philosophical Anthropology," *Journal of Philosophical Research* 28 (2003): 259–85.

16. Cf. chapter 1 above for a preliminary discussion of the basic idea of integrating pragmatist and Kantian approaches in the philosophy of religion.

17. In addition to McDowell's work, there are important collections of articles critical of reductive naturalism but exploring the possibilities of "softer" naturalisms. See, for example, Mario de Caro and David Macarthur, eds., *Naturalism in Question* (Cambridge, MA: Harvard University Press, 2004).

18. See, for example, Ruth Walker, "Rescuing Religious Non-Realism from Cupitt," *Heythrop Journal* 47 (2006): 426–40.

19. See, for example, John Patrick Diggins, *The Promise of Pragmatism: Modernism and the Crisis of Knowledge and Authority* (Chicago and London: The University of Chicago Press, 1994), 212–17; and Rockefeller, *John Dewey*.

20. Reinhold Niebuhr's "theological neo-orthodoxy" was (at least implicitly) among the objects of Dewey's critique. See Bruce Kuklick, *A History of Philosophy in America 1720–2000* (Oxford: Clarendon Press, 2001), 192. On the religious situation in the early 1930s as a background for Dewey's project, see Rockefeller, *John Dewey*, 452ff.

21. For brief accounts of this basic message of *A Common Faith*, see Smith, *Themes in American Philosophy*, 178–180; Kuklick, *A History of Philosophy in America 1720–2000*, 192–95; and Milton R. Konvitz's "Introduction" to LW9 (1986), xi–xxxii; for detailed discussions, see Rockefeller, *John Dewey*, chapters 10–11; Michael Eldridge, "Dewey's Religious Proposal," in *Transforming Experience: John Dewey's Cultural Instrumentalism* (Nashville, TN: Vanderbilt University Press, 1998); Larry Hickman, "Cultivating a Common Faith: Dewey's Religion," in Hickman, *Pragmatism as Post-Postmodernism: Lessons from John Dewey* (New York: Fordham University Press, 2007); John R. Shook, "Dewey's Naturalized Philosophy of Spirit and Religion" (ms., 2008); David L. Hildebrand, "Religion: Religious Experience, Community, and Social Hope," in *Dewey: A Beginner's Guide* (Oxford: Oneworld, 2008); and Thomas M. Schmidt, "Empirischer Naturalismus, demokratisches Experiment und die Erfahrung des Religiösen: John Deweys Philosophie der Religion," *Jahrbuch für Religionsphilosophie* 7 (2008): 37–59. Many interpreters have argued that Dewey's main interest in *A Common Faith* is not religion as such, but social progress, democracy, and other more this-worldly topics on which he wrote voluminously elsewhere. However, for a comprehensive treatment of Dewey's theological relevance—even for Deweyan pragmatism as a theological methodology—see

Jerome Paul Soneson, *Pragmatism and Pluralism: John Dewey's Significance for Theology* (Minneapolis: Fortress Press, 1993); for a discussion of "Deweyan naturalism" (though not of Dewey's own ideas in any detail) as a stage (though not a sufficient one) on the way toward a "more open naturalism" (i.e., an essentially Whiteheadian, process-philosophical and-theological synthesis of science and religion), see David Ray Griffin, *Religion and Scientific Naturalism* (Albany: SUNY Press, 2000), 83–87.

22. However, though Dewey clearly rejects religious traditions and focuses on the functions of religious experience, those functions can also be used to evaluate the traditions in terms of how they succeed in promoting religious qualities. See Soneson, *Pragmatism and Pluralism*, 126. Instead of rejecting traditions for the good, it may be more helpful to say that no *specific* religious tradition is superior to others in serving genuinely religious functions (ibid., 134). We might perhaps talk about the multiple realizability of religious qualities in different religious traditions. Then, the communication across religious communities becomes a crucial issue (ibid., 144–45).

23. As Howard L. Parsons notes, Dewey's title "perfectly expresses his Emersonian faith in the familiar. The abstractness and fixity of dogma separate; the concreteness and fluidity of our common experience unite and integrate." "The Meaning and Significance of Dewey's Religious Thought," *Journal of Religion* 40 (1960): 173. This paper by Parsons is essentially similar to another, shorter one: Howard L. Parsons, "Dewey's Religious Thought: The Challenge of Evolution," *Journal of Philosophy* 58 (1961): 113–21.

24. Cf. also Dewey, "One Current Religious Problem" (1936), LW11:115–17; "Anti-Naturalism in Extremis" (1943), LW15:49–62, especially 56; and "Contribution to 'Religion and the Intellectuals'" (1950), LW16:390–394. The emancipatory project of *A Common Faith* and these related writings is somewhat analogous to the project of liberating aesthetic experience as a natural form of human experiencing in *Art as Experience* (1934, LW10). The explicit references to religion—and religious art—in the latter work would deserve a separate discussion. See, again, Rockefeller, *John Dewey*, chap. 11, for remarks on *Art as Experience* in relation to Dewey's evolving views on "natural piety" and "mystical intuition."

25. For the importance of the concept of (primary) experience in Dewey, see Hildebrand, *Beyond Realism and Antirealism*.

26. See William James, *The Varieties of Religious Experience: A Study in Human Nature* (1902), in *The Works of William James*, ed. Frederick H. Burkhardt, Fredson Bowers, and Ignas K. Skrupskelis (Cambridge, MA: Harvard University Press, 1985). *A Common Faith* questions, as Shook points out (*Dewey's Empirical Theory of Knowledge and Reality*, 148–49), the ideal of the moral or religious (self-)perfection of the individual. See Shook, "Dewey's Naturalized Philosophy

of Spirit and Religion," for a discussion of the relation between Dewey's concerns with religion and democracy. Hickman notes that Dewey did not reject religious institutions but argued that they should be pragmatically assessed in terms of their functioning in the enhancement of experience ("Cultivating a Common Faith," 197).

27. Rockefeller, *John Dewey*, 472. One contrast perceived by Rockefeller is to Rudolf Otto's influential theory of "the holy."

28. Thus, in "Religion in the Soviet Union" (1930), Dewey referred to communism as having the character of a religious faith (LW5:356–57). The fruits of religious experiences need not always be positive.

29. See also Konvitz, "Introduction," xiv. Furthermore, Konvitz points out that, according to some religious traditions, the relation between religious and moral experience is the opposite to the one described by Dewey: morality might be a derivative value of a more fundamental religious attitude to life, not *vice versa* (ibid., xxviii). Another question that arises here is why precisely these kinds of experience are fundamental to religious experience. Could there be other forms of experience, perhaps more banal and everyday ones (e.g., related to sports), in which religious elements could also be involved? (Think about the "religious" enthusiasm of some ice hockey fans, for instance.)

30. As Rockefeller notes (*John Dewey*, 104), all knowledge, scientific or philosophical, was religiously meaningful and valuable, according to young Dewey in the 1880s. Cf. ibid., 442–43, for Dewey's view on the religious value of the faith in the experimental method of science.

31. Ibid., 478–79.

32. He writes: "Whether one gives the name 'God' to this union, operative in thought and action, is a matter for individual decision. But the *function* of such a working union of the ideal and actual seems to me to be identical with the force that has in fact been attached to the conception of God in all the religions that have a spiritual content; and a clear idea of that function seems to me urgently needed at the present time" (LW9:35).

33. This suggestion might be compared to analogous pragmatist accounts in moral philosophy: morality, or moral experience, is so ubiquitous in human practices that it should not be "compartmentalized" in its own special department. Moral values pervade our existence as a whole; experience comes to us "screaming with values," as Hilary Putnam often quotes Dewey as saying. See Putnam, *Ethics without Ontology* (Cambridge, MA, and London: Harvard University Press, 2004); see also Sami Pihlström, *Pragmatic Moral Realism: A Transcendental Defense* (Amsterdam and New York: Rodopi, 2005).

34. See also the following writings by Dewey touching religious issues: "Christianity and Democracy" (1893), EW4:3–10; "Religious Education as Conditioned by Modern Psychology and Pedagogy" (1903), MW3:210–15; "Religion

and Our Schools" (1908), MW4:165–77; "Fundamentals" (1924), MW15:3–7; and "Religion and Morality in a Free Society" (1949), LW15:170–83. The importance for education of these and other essays by Dewey on religion is emphasized in Siebren Miedema, "The Beyond in the Midst: The Relevance of Dewey's Philosophy of Religion for Education," *Studies in Philosophy and Education* 13 (1994–95): 61–73. Again, cf. Rockefeller's more detailed list of Dewey's religious writings in his *John Dewey* (on the educational relevance of Dewey's views on religion, see especially chapter 5 of that book).

35. See also Dewey's critical remarks on the rise of "religious individualism" and its influences in *Reconstruction in Philosophy* (1920/1948), MW12:105–6; cf. *Individualism, Old and New* (1930), LW5:71–72. Rockefeller notes, on the basis of Dewey's correspondence, that he had by 1915 worked out a number of ideas central to *A Common Faith*, including his reinterpretation of the concept of God (*John Dewey*, 327–28, 513).

36. Niebuhr reviewed *A Common Faith* in *Nation* 139 (1934), 358–59. Other reviews appeared in 1934–35 in *Philosophical Review, Mind, Christian Register, Philosophy, Christian Century, Anglican Theological Review, New Republic, International Journal of Ethics, Yale Review, New Masses, School and Society, Common Sense, Social Frontier, The Monist, Journal of Philosophy, Thought,* and *Catholic World.* F. C. S. Schiller's review in *Mind* 44 (1935): 397–99, interestingly claimed that Dewey's way of justifying God by "projective imagination" appeared as strangely similar to the traditional ontological argument for God's existence. Corliss Lamont, in turn, claimed in *New Masses* 12 (1934): 23–24, that "John Dewey Capitulates to 'God'." For these reviews, see John R. Shook, *Pragmatism: An Annotated Bibliography 1898–1940* (Amsterdam and Atlanta, GA: Rodopi, 1998), 461–64; and the editors' "Textual Commentary" to LW9:452–453.

37. Henry Nelson Wieman, "John Dewey's Common Faith", *Christian Century* 51 (1934): 1450–52 (reprinted in LW9:426–34, with related reviews and other material: Edwin Ewart Aubrey, "Is John Dewey a Theist?," LW9:435–37; and Wieman's reply, "Is John Dewey a Theist?," LW9:438–40). Dewey's comments on Aubrey and Wieman can be found at LW9:294–95. See also Wieman's and Douglas Clyde Macintosh's "Converse" with Dewey (LW9:412–22), as well as Norbert Guterman, "John Dewey's Credo" (LW9:423–25). Dewey's exchange with Wieman and others started in his review, in *Christian Century* in 1932, of the book, *Is There a God? A Conversation,* jointly authored by Wieman, Macintosh, and Max Otto (LW9:213–22; cf. Dewey's response to Wieman and Macintosh, LW9:223–28; Dewey's response to Guterman's review is very brief: LW9:293). This 1932–35 debate in *Christian Century,* which cannot be analyzed here, has been later discussed in Nolan Pliny Jacobson, "The Faith of John Dewey," *Journal of Religion* 40 (1960): 191–97. Wieman returned to Dewey's views in his joint

book with Bernard E. Meland, *American Philosophies of Religion* (New York: Harper, 1936), 279–86, while Dewey continued the discussion in his "Mystical Naturalism and Religious Humanism," *New Humanist* 8 (1935): 74–75 (LW11: 84–85; reacting to Max C. Otto, "Mr. Dewey and Religion," *New Humanist* 8 [1935]: 41–47), and in "One Current Religious Problem," *Journal of Philosophy* 33 (1936): 324–26 (LW11:115–17), as well as "Religion, Science, and Philosophy," *Southern Review* 2 (1936): 53–62 (repr. in *Problems of Men*, 1946, and in LW11:454–63), reviewing Bertrand Russell's *Religion and Science* (1935). Along with the appendices to LW9, Shook's *Pragmatism: An Annotated Bibliography* has been an invaluable help in locating these references; in addition, see Rockefeller, *John Dewey*, 512–27, for a detailed account of Dewey's exchange on God with Wieman and others.

38. Rockefeller, *John Dewey*, 515. Cf. LW9:219–21, 226–27.

39. See, for example, John Wright Buckham, "God and the Ideal: Professor Dewey Reinterprets Religion," *Journal of Religion* 15 (1934): 1–9; Henry Nelson Wieman, "Dewey and Buckham on Religion," *Journal of Religion* 15 (1935): 10–21; A. Eustace Haydon, "Mr. Dewey on Religion and God," *Journal of Religion* 15 (1935): 22–25; Henry Pitney Van Dusen, "The Faith of John Dewey," *Religion in Life* 4 (1935): 123–32; Cornelia Le Boutillier, "The Religious Philosophy of John Dewey," in Le Boutillier, *Religious Values in the Philosophy of Emergent Evolution* (New York: Columbia University Press, 1936), 71–89; Orville A. Petty, *Common Sense and God: A Critique of Naturalism* (New Haven, CT: Yale University Press, 1936); Marion John Bradshaw, "A Comment on Van Dusen's Dismissal of Dewey," *Review of Religion* 3 (1938): 97–100 (responding to Van Dusen's paper mentioned above); Edward L. Schaub, "Dewey's Interpretation of Religion," in *The Philosophy of John Dewey*, ed. Paul Arthur Schilpp (La Salle, IL: Open Court, 1939; 2nd ed., 1951), 393–416 (see also Dewey's reply: "Experience, Knowledge, and Value: A Rejoinder," 594–97); and Winifred Warner, "On John Dewey's Religious Views," *Philosophic Mind* 1 (1940), 37–39. (Again, I have used Shook's bibliography for locating these various sources.)

40. For example, Francis G. Ensley, *The Naturalistic Interpretation of Religion by John Dewey* (Brown University, 1938); Bonaventure Thomas, *Deweyism in the Light of Catholic Thought* (Niagara University, 1938).

41. Dewey, "A God or the God?" (1933), LW9:213–22; "Intimation of Mortality" (1935), LW11:425–27; "Bergson on Instinct" (1935), LW11:428–31; "Religion, Science, and Philosophy" (1936), LW11:454–63; "The Philosophy of William James" (1937), LW11:464–78.

42. The book *Naturalism and the Human Spirit*, ed. Yervant H. Krikorian (New York: Columbia University Press, 1944), raised some controversy; see also Dewey's joint paper with Sidney Hook and Ernest Nagel, "Are Naturalists

Materialists?," *Journal of Philosophy* 42 (1945); reprinted in *Dewey and His Critics*, ed. Sidney Morgenbesser (New York: The Journal of Philosophy, Inc., 1977), 385–400.

43. Buckham, "God and the Ideal," 7–8.

44. Dewey, "Experience, Knowledge, and Value: A Rejoinder," 597 (LW14:77–80; responding to Schaub, "Dewey's Interpretation of Religion"). Thus, in Dewey's own words, *A Common Faith* is, puzzlingly, not intended as an argument for naturalism or against supernaturalism, but as a naturalist treatise for those who have already left supernaturalism behind.

45. Haydon, "Mr. Dewey on Religion and God," 24.

46. Corliss Lamont, "New Light on Dewey's *Common Faith*," *Journal of Philosophy* 58 (1961): 25. Lamont supports his thoroughly naturalist reading by referring to personal communications with Dewey. For example, he cites Dewey as saying, in 1940, that he has come to think his own position "as cultural or humanistic Naturalism" (ibid., 26).

47. Compare Dewey's words from 1893: "The next religious prophet who will have a permanent and real influence on men's lives will be the man who succeeds in pointing out the religious meaning of democracy, the ultimate religious value to be found in the normal flow of life itself." ("The Relation of Philosophy to Theology," EW4:367.) Rockefeller's *John Dewey* is, as a whole, a grand narrative on how Dewey sought to integrate democratic life with religious life.

48. Eliyahu Rosenow, "The Teacher as Prophet of the True God: Dewey's Religious Faith and Its Problems," *Journal of Philosophy of Education* 31 (1997): 427–37 (see 435–36). One of Rosenow's references here is Robert B. Westbrook's important commentary, *John Dewey and American Democracy* (Ithaca, NY: Cornell University Press, 1991).

49. Horace M. Kallen, "Human Rights and the Religion of John Dewey," *Ethics* 60 (1950): 169–77 (see 175).

50. Steven C. Rockefeller, "Pragmatism, Democracy, and God," *American Journal of Theology and Philosophy* 14 (1993): 263–278. Rockefeller's fuller statement about Dewey's philosophy of religion can be found in his major book, *John Dewey* (cited above); for a critical discussion of Rockefeller's reading of Dewey, see J. Wesley Robbins, "Pragmatism, Democracy, and God: A Reply to Rockefeller," *American Journal of Theology and Philosophy* 14 (1993): 279–85.

51. In his introductory essay on American philosophy of religion, William D. Dean does refer to the tension between constructivism and radical empiricism in both Dewey and James, but he hardly views the realism issue in the transcendental light I will give to it below. See Dean, "Religion," in Marsoobian and Ryder, *Blackwell Companion to American Philosophy*, 325–42 (especially 334–35).

52. In this section, I partly rely on the discussion of Dewey's pragmatic realism in Sami Pihlström, "How (Not) to Write the History of Pragmatist Philoso-

phy of Science?," *Perspectives on Science* 16 (2008): 26–69; Pihlström, "The Realism Issue from the Perspective of Deweyan Pragmatism," *Americana* 3 (2008), http://americanaejournal.hu/vol3no2/pihlstrom.

53. The entire chapter 4, "Nature, Means and Knowledge," of *Experience and Nature* (LW1) is essential to this account of the status of scientific objects.

54. See the exchanges collected in Morgenbesser, *Dewey and His Critics*, part 2.

55. On Dewey's (early) idealist views, see again Rockefeller, *John Dewey*; and Shook, *Dewey's Empirical Theory of Knowledge and Reality*.

56. For a critical discussion of such a strong conception of scientific realism, see Sami Pihlström, *Structuring the World: The Issue of Realism and the Nature of Ontological Problems in Classical and Contemporary Pragmatism* (Acta Philosophica Fennica 59, Helsinki: The Philosophical Society of Finland, 1996). According to Richard Rorty, scientific realism and religious fundamentalism are "products of the same urge," the pursuit of an absolute conception of reality. "Pragmatism, Religious Faith, and Intellectual Romance," in *Cambridge Companion to William James*, ed. Ruth Anna Putnam (Cambridge: Cambridge University Press, 1997), 92–93. It is this pursuit that the pragmatist who follows Dewey should abandon; and one need not be a Rortyan in order to appreciate these insights. (See also chapter 3.)

57. Parsons, "The Meaning and Significance of Dewey's Religious Thought," 183–84. See also Rockefeller's comment on Dewey's early position: "For Dewey, the Body of Christ is not just the church but human society at large, and it is humanity, not exclusively the man Jesus, which is the mediator between the individual and God" (*John Dewey*, 163).

58. Cf. Konvitz, "Introduction," xxiv; Rockefeller, *John Dewey*, 471. On the realism issue in Dewey, see also, for example, John E. Smith, *Purpose and Thought: The Meaning of Pragmatism* (New Haven, CT: Yale University Press, 1978), 149–54.

59. Douglas R. Anderson, "Smith and Dewey on the Religious Dimension of Experience: Dealing with Dewey's Half-God," *American Journal of Theology and Philosophy* 14 (1993): 161–76. Anderson is commenting on Smith's views on Dewey (see the previous note). In another essay on *A Common Faith*, Anderson observes that Dewey comes close to a "Peircean realism of ideals" and that his God may be "real" in this Peircean sense, "real in the power of ideals and their possibilities, but not *existent* as a being." Douglas R. Anderson, "Theology as Healing: A Meditation on *A Common Faith*," in *Dewey Reconfigured: Essays on Deweyan Pragmatism*, ed. Casey Haskins and David I. Seiple (Albany: SUNY Press, 1999), 85–95 (see 89–90). Shook ("Dewey's Naturalized Philosophy of Spirit and Religion"), in turn, explicitly calls Dewey an atheist (as well as a humanist and naturalist), arguing that his view on religion gives up the traditional assumption of God's existence. Despite Shook's admirable description of

Dewey's "broad" naturalism, this may in the end be too reductive a view on religious experience. Hildebrand (*Dewey*, 188) agrees that Dewey is an atheist, but emphasizes that he sought a middle way between militant atheism and traditional theism.

60. William L. Rowe, "Religion within the Bounds of Naturalism: Dewey and Wieman," *International Journal for Philosophy of Religion* 38 (1995): 17–36 (see 23). Rowe recognizes, however, not only this "humanist" aspect of Dewey's views on God but also a more naturalist one, according to which humankind is "continuous with nature and supported by forces in nature that are beyond our manipulation and control" (ibid.). This tension between active construction and passive dependence will be revisited toward the end of this chapter. I recommend Rowe's paper as a careful study of the different meaning that "naturalism" may receive in Deweyan or Wiemanian philosophy of religion. Rowe argues, among other things, that Wieman understandably but mistakenly took Dewey to be approaching his own conception of God as a real and superhuman yet impersonal force (ibid., 24).

61. There is much confusion, especially among Deweyan pragmatists (but also other pragmatists), with the concept of the *transcendental*. Both Dewey himself and leading commentators like Rockefeller (cf. *John Dewey*, 371–72, 468) seem to confuse it with the *transcendent*. The fact that Dewey avoided committing himself to any transcendent realm of supernatural beings does not entail that his views cannot be reinterpreted in a transcendental (Kantian) manner (his opposition to orthodox Kantianism notwithstanding).

62. Cf. Konvitz, "Introduction," xvi.

63. For a general discussion of this movement in American philosophy of religion, see John E. Smith, *Themes in American Philosophy* (New York: Harper & Row, 1970), 169–76. For a pragmatic naturalist perspective on religion inspired by Dewey, see also S. Morris Eames, *Experience and Value: Essays on John Dewey and Pragmatic Naturalism*, eds. Elizabeth R. Eames and Richard W. Field (Carbondale and Edwardsville: Southern Illinois University Press, 2003), chapters 11–12; a rich version of religiously open naturalism has also been developed by John Ryder in his "The Value of Pragmatic Naturalism," in *The Future of Naturalism*, ed. John R. Shook (Amherst, NY: Prometheus Books, 2010). In this section, I partly rely on Sami Pihlström, "Three Kinds of Religious Naturalism: A Pragmatic Critique," *Method and Theory in the Study of Religion* 17 (2005): 177–218.

64. See, for example, Jerome A. Stone, "Introduction", *Zygon* 38 (2003), 85–87; "Varieties of Religious Naturalism," *Zygon* 38 (2003): 89–93; "Is Nature Enough? Yes," *Zygon* 38 (2003): 783–800. Stone has also recently published a book-length treatment of religious naturalism: see Jerome A. Stone, *Religious Naturalism Today: The Rebirth of a Forgotten Alternative* (Albany: SUNY Press, 2008; on

Dewey, see 44–51). Also see Charley D. Hardwick, *Events of Grace: Naturalism, Existentialism, and Theology* (1996; repr. Cambridge: Cambridge University Press, 2001); Hardwick, "Religious Naturalism Today," *Zygon* 38 (2003): 111–16.

65. Stone, "Varieties of Religious Naturalism," 89. In another paper, Stone explicitly acknowledges his debt to Dewey's *A Common Faith* and to pragmatism more generally ("Is Nature Enough? Yes," 785, 790). This kind of religious naturalism, also defended by Hardwick, among others, has affinities with the Wittgensteinian tradition in the philosophy of religion, although both naturalists and Wittgensteinians tend to deny such affinities.

66. Hardwick, "Religious Naturalism Today," 113.

67. Ibid., 115.

68. Ibid., 114.

69. Another illuminating comparison might be made to the Continentally oriented reinterpretations of religion in a "post-onto-theo-logical" framework, in which the idea of God as *a* being in the world is abandoned in order to achieve a more authentic relation to divinity. See several papers in Wrathall, *Religion after Metaphysics*, especially Vattimo's and Rorty's contributions.

70. Cf. Hardwick, "Religious Naturalism Today," 112.

71. Smith, *Themes in American Philosophy*, 174.

72. Hardwick, "Religious Naturalism Today," 115–16; see also Stone's writings cited above.

73. Another thinker arguing along the same lines as Wieman, Hardwick et al. is John F. Post, who defends physicalism (roughly characterized as the view that all existing things are physical and that physical truth determines all truth) but nevertheless believes that no vocabulary or description, even the scientific one, enjoys a privileged position: scientific descriptions are not "unconditionally prior" to other descriptions, and religious discourse, referring to human emotions and evaluations, may also express an objective truth, or what Post calls a "face of existence." See John F. Post, *The Faces of Existence: An Essay in Nonreductive Physicalism* (Ithaca, NY: Cornell University Press, 1987), 338. Physicalism and theism may, then, be simultaneously true. While "all we are and all we can hope to be we owe to the disposition of physical entities," "little of what we are and can hope to be is physically or even scientifically expressible; much of it can be named only with the help of discourse that we must confess is religious." (ibid., 342–43). A theologian, unlike the physicist (with whom she/he describes the same universe), is interested in "those aspects of the whole that determine meaning and value" and in the meaning and value thus determined (ibid., 363). In a strikingly Deweyan manner (though with little explicit engagement with Dewey's views), Post views this as a value-theoretical rather than (supernaturalist) metaphysical enterprise. Richard Rorty's privatization of religion, coupled with his "romantic polytheism," might be seen as yet another

form of religious naturalism, given Rorty's generally naturalist (even physicalist) and secular outlook. The relation between Rorty's admiration of Dewey and his "turn to religion" (in a manner resembling Vattimo's) in the 1990s would deserve another study. Cf. chapter 3.

74. Yet, Dewey does not seem to go quite as far as, say, Gianni Vattimo, who argues that the "desacralizing phenomena characteristic of modernity" can be seen as "authentic aspects of the history of salvation," when interpreted in terms of the Christian idea of God's abandoning His own transcendence through *kenosis* and incarnation (see Vattimo, "After Onto-Theology: Philosophy between Science and Religion," in Wrathall, *Religion after Metaphysics*, 35), or Emmanuel Levinas, for whom a person's relation to God is best modelled in the face-to-face relation to another human being and who has persuasively argued that the ethical relation to otherness (God's or the human Other's) is prior to ontology, "otherwise than being." See Levinas, *Otherwise than Being or Beyond Essence*, trans. Alphonso Lingis (Pittsburgh: Duquesne University Press, 1981; first published in French, 1974). These reflections are often obscure, but it seems to me that their religious significance is greater than that of the religious naturalisms starting from a physicalist world picture. Paradoxically, for thinkers like Levinas and Vattimo, secularization or even atheism may be a crucial part of the development of religious life and culture. I wonder if Dewey might, to some extent, agree. In any case, the kind of atheism religiously invoked here cannot be the "militant" atheism Dewey attacks in *A Common Faith*.

75. Rockefeller, *John Dewey*, 468.

76. Ibid., 524. Note, however, that according to Habermas—a contemporary Kantian pragmatist working out a "detranscendentalized" position—religion might be primarily understood precisely as an attempt to articulate "what is missing" in our "postmetaphysical" culture and experience. See Jürgen Habermas et al., *An Awareness of What Is Missing* (Cambridge: Polity Press, 2010).

77. It is beyond the scope of this chapter (or book) to evaluate either Wittgenstein's or his commentators' views on religion in detail. Here I will only briefly note some analogies and disanalogies with Deweyan views. See also my conclusion in this book.

78. For such a Wittgensteinian approach to a Deweyan problem, see Scott F. Aikin and Michael P. Hodges, "Wittgenstein, Dewey, and the Possibility of Religion," *Journal of Speculative Philosophy* 20 (2006): 1–19. Aikin's and Hodges's paper is not actually an interpretation of Dewey but an attempt to employ Wittgensteinian resources for reconstructing pragmatist philosophy of religion. Wittgensteinianism was a major movement in Anglo-American philosophy of religion during the second half of the twentieth century, though it seems to have lost much of its energy after the deaths of its leading exponents, Rush Rhees, Peter Winch, and D. Z. Phillips. (It might be noted here that some critics

of Wittgensteinian philosophy of religion have pointed out, with some plausibility in my view, that the kind of analyses of religiosity that, for example, Phillips engages in only really apply to a "naturalistically" construed religion, not to religious ideas supernaturalistically interpreted—which is unsurprising, given Phillips's and other Wittgensteinians' project of avoiding any dogmatic supernaturalism. This would make further comparisons to Dewey and other religious naturalists especially worthwhile.)

79. Cf. Sami Pihlström, "Religion and Pseudo-Religion: An Elusive Boundary," *International Journal for Philosophy of Religion* 62 (2007): 3–32. See also the conclusion in this book. Shook ("Dewey's Naturalized Philosophy of Spirit and Religion") also repeatedly speaks about Dewey's views on "genuine" religious experience and faith, while Hildebrand (*Dewey*, 195) points out that traditional religious faith, separating humanity from nature, is "essentially unreligious" compared to the "truly religious" attitude of "natural piety."

80. These debates have often followed the interpretations given in Ralph W. Sleeper, *The Necessity of Pragmatism* (New Haven, CT and London: Yale University Press, 1986); see also Hildebrand, *Beyond Realism and Antirealism*, as well as Pihlström, "The Realism Issue from a Deweyan Perspective."

81. Cf. Wrathall, *Religion after Metaphysics* (cited above).

82. See Rockefeller, *John Dewey*, 527–39.

83. Ibid., 562.

84. Shook, *Dewey's Empirical Theory of Knowledge and Reality*, 143. On the Kantian background of Dewey's early idealism, see ibid., 140.

85. I find such an entanglement obvious in James (see chapters 1 and 4 of this book), but arguing for the point in a more detailed manner in the Deweyan case goes beyond the scope of this inquiry. At least, I think, it is clear that Dewey rejected certain traditional metaphysical (theistic) ideas primarily because of their unwelcome ethical (and political, essentially antidemocratic) consequences: for instance, the Calvinist dualism between the saved and the damned had to be replaced by the (secularized) view of "universal salvation" (see Shook, "Dewey's Naturalized Philosophy of Spirit and Religion"). There are *ethical* reasons for striving for a *via media* between, say, passive fatalism and otherworldly idealism (ibid.)—just as James argued in his defense of meliorism (*Pragmatism*, chap. 8). The Kantian aspects of Deweyan philosophy of religion are only seldom recognized, but see Ludwig Nagl, " 'The Religious': Dewey's Post-Feuerbachian 'Sublation' of Religion (and Some Critical Roycean Considerations)," *Cognitio* 12 (2011): 121–41; Nagl, however, emphasizes Dewey's "Feuerbachian" ideas.

86. Soneson, *Pragmatism and Pluralism*, 90.

87. Ibid., 126–27.

88. See ibid., 129. Soneson thus in a way defends Dewey against critics such as Schaub ("Dewey's Interpretation of Religion"), who have argued that Dewey

underestimates the contingency or "dependency" of human existence. See also Arthur Wheeler, "A Theological Support for Dewey," *American Journal of Theology and Philosophy* 3 (1982): 98–106 (especially 103–4).

89. Soneson, *Pragmatism and Pluralism*, 131.

90. See also Rockefeller, *John Dewey*, 484–90; "Pragmatism, Democracy, and God," 276–77; and Shook, "Dewey's Naturalized Philosophy of Spirit and Religion." For a dispute over whether there is a place in Dewey for the "tragic sense of life," see Raymond D. Boisvert, "The Nemesis of Necessity: Tragedy's Challenge to Deweyan Pragmatism," in Haskins and Seiple, *Dewey Reconfigured*, 151–68; Donald Morse, "Pragmatism and the Tragic Sense of Life," *Transactions of the Charles S. Peirce Society* 37 (2001): 556–72; Boisvert, "Updating Dewey: A Reply to Morse," *Transactions of the Charles S. Peirce Society* 37 (2001): 573–83; and Naoko Saito, "Pragmatism and the Tragic Sense: Deweyan Growth in an Age of Nihilism," *Journal of Philosophy of Education* 36 (2002): 247–63. Saiko's perspective on Dewey is partly an Emersonian one; cf. Saito, "Citizenship without Inclusion: Religious Democracy after Dewey, Emerson, and Thoreau," *Journal of Speculative Philosophy* 18 (2004): 203–15. On the reality of evil in James, see Sami Pihlström, *"The Trail of the Human Serpent Is over Everything": Jamesian Perspectives on Mind, World, and Religion* (Lanham, MD: University Press of America, 2008), chap. 4.

91. Soneson, *Pragmatism and Pluralism*, 166–67.

92. Ibid., 167. Anderson also admits that *A Common Faith* is "metaphysical in the sense [Dewey] allowed—he is attempting to mark the generic traits of the religious dimension" (Anderson, "Smith and Dewey on the Religious Dimension of Experience," 169).

93. See Ludwig Wittgenstein, *Philosophical Investigations*, trans. G. E. M. Anscombe (1953; repr. Oxford: Basil Blackwell, 1958), I, § 371.

94. See Rockefeller, *John Dewey*, chap. 5.

95. This is noted, for example, by Miedema, "The Beyond in the Midst," 69.

96. On Dewey's notion of natural piety, see Rockefeller, *John Dewey*, chap. 11, especially 495–501. These aspects of religious faith were present already in Dewey's early "quest for unity" (see ibid., 73). Rockefeller (ibid., 505–6) cites the closing of *Experience and Nature* (LW1:313–14) as Dewey's key passage on natural piety. Cf. Hickman, "Cultivating a Common Faith," 204. Wittgenstein's religious mysticism has recently been explored by, for example, Hanne Appelqvist, "Apocalypse Now: Wittgenstein's Early Remarks on Immortality and the Problem of Life," *History of Philosophy Quarterly* 29 (2012): 195–210; comparisons between Dewey and Wittgenstein in this regard would be most welcome. A further possibility of comparison emerges if we consider Dewey's notion of a *common* faith in relation to Wittgenstein's well-known concept of the "common human way

of acting" ("*die gemeinsame menschliche Handlungsweise*"): see Wittgenstein, *Philosophical Investigations*, part 1, § 206.

97. Therefore, from a Deweyan perspective, popular criticisms of religion such as Dennett's *Breaking the Spell: Religion as a Natural Phenomenon* (New York: Viking, 2006), or Dawkins's *The God Delusion* (London: Bantam Books, 2003), whatever their other merits, can hardly be taken seriously as *philosophical* efforts to understand religion. In particular, from a Deweyan perspective, the issue of reconciling Darwinian evolution with religion (a major issue for critics of religion like Dennett and Dawkins, somewhat understandably in the contemporary American context) hardly arises at all; from early on, Dewey saw no problem in this reconciliation (see Rockefeller, *John Dewey*, 138–40). For a perceptive critical comparison between Dewey and the "new atheists," see Robert Sinclair, "Dewey, Religion, and the New Atheism," *Contemporary Pragmatism* 6 (2009). For related reasons, the recent contributions to the "cognitivist turn" in religious studies and comparative religion—for example, in terms of Dennett's "intentional systems theory"—have only very limited relevance to the kind of pragmatic religious naturalism we have in this chapter seen Dewey as developing. See, for example, Ilkka Pyysiäinen, *How Religion Works: Towards a New Cognitive Science of Religion* (Leiden: E. J. Brill, 2001); Matti Kamppinen, "Rationality, Religion and Intentional Systems Theory: From Objective Ethnography to the Critical Study of Religious Beliefs," *Method and Theory in the Study of Religion* 21 (2009): 274–84; Ilkka Pyysiäinen and Marc Hauser, "The Origins of Religion: Evolved Adaptation or By-Product?," *Trends in Cognitive Science* (2009). From a pragmatist perspective, it should be obvious that neither "new atheism" nor "cognitive science of religion" can account for the rich entanglement of metaphysical and ethical perspectives and ways of experiencing reality that Deweyan (as well as Jamesian) pragmatism insists on. Religious beliefs, entangled with our purposive practices, are much more than mere cognitive models functioning in intentional systems. While religious beliefs—their emergence, transformations, maintaining in societies, and so on—*may* be evolutionarily explained, this explanatory strategy presupposes a prior categorization of them as individual representations internal to cognitive agents, which has been disputed from a pragmatist point of view understanding beliefs generally as habits of action, not just as cognitive representations. From the pragmatist and Kantian perspective represented by the present inquiry, it is highly unclear what it even *means* to argue that, say, morality is not based on religion. Of course it isn't and cannot be. The empirical results apparently challenging such a traditional conception of the "priority ordering" of morality and religion—however strongly substantiated they are—lose much of their philosophical (though presumably not scientific) interest as soon as we realize, with

Kant, James, Dewey, and Wittgenstein, that it is incoherent to suppose that a genuinely moral duty could be based on a nonmoral source, such as God's will. Indeed, a religious believer might simply respond to such empirically grounded suggestions that God's will is, by definition, moral. In any event, our conception of morality, whether religious or secular, must be fully nonreductive; otherwise, we can hardly do justice to our practice of moral evaluation and deliberation (which obviously is something that pragmatists are expected to do).

3. RORTY VERSUS PUTNAM: NEOPRAGMATIST PHILOSOPHY OF RELIGION

1. Cheryl Misak, ed., *New Pragmatists* (Oxford: Oxford University Press, 2007).

2. For some earlier discussions of mine on the Putnam versus Rorty contrast in philosophy generally, and on neopragmatist philosophy of religion in particular, see Sami Pihlström, "Hilary Putnam as a Religious Thinker," *Journal of Interdisciplinary Studies* 11 (1999): 39–61; and Pihlström, "Putnam and Rorty on Their Pragmatist Heritage: Re-reading James and Dewey," in *Dewey, Pragmatism, and Economic Methodology*, ed. Elias L. Khalil (London and New York: Routledge, 2004).

3. See Richard Rorty, *Philosophy and the Mirror of Nature* (Princeton, NJ: Princeton University Press, 1979); *Consequences of Pragmatism* (Hassocks, UK: Harvester Press, 1982); *Contingency, Irony, and Solidarity* (Cambridge: Cambridge University Press, 1989); *Objectivity, Relativism, and Truth* (Cambridge: Cambridge University Press, 1991); *Truth and Progress* (Cambridge: Cambridge University Press, 1998); *Philosophy and Social Hope* (London: Penguin, 1999); and *Philosophy as Cultural Politics* (Cambridge: Cambridge University Press, 2007).

4. Rorty's relation to religion can also be understood against the background of some biographical details, very interestingly explored in Neil Gross, *Richard Rorty: The Making of an American Philosopher* (Chicago and London: University of Chicago Press, 2008). Rorty's mother's Winifred Rauschenbush's father, Walter Rauschenbusch, was a Baptist minister, one of the leaders of the "social gospel movement," with a Christian motivation for progressive social reform (around 1900) (see ibid., 16). Rorty's father, James Rorty, confessed to theism late in his life (see a letter quoted by Gross, 62). There was also a tension between Winifred Rauschenbush's feminism and her father's conservative views on home and family (ibid., 65). Rorty himself, at thirteen, compared Jesus to an underground leader in a school paper (ibid., 90). In 1966 he taught a course on the philosophy of religion at Princeton, with readings of John Hick and Paul Tillich (ibid., 194–95). Clearly, however, the notion of an intellectual deeply concerned with issues of religion and theology was *not* strongly present—or was

hardly present at all——in Rorty's "intellectual self-concept," to use Gross's key expression (see ibid., chap. 9). For an excellent recent exploration of Rorty's secularism and its relation to the Enlightenment, see Carl B. Sachs, "Rorty's Disavowal of Metaphysics: Naturalism, Secularism, and 'the Enlightenment'", ms., available online at Academia.edu.

5. Rorty, *Philosophy and Social Hope*, 157.

6. See Rorty, *Philosophy and Social Hope* and *Philosophy as Cultural Politics*, as well as Rorty, "Anti-Clericalism and Atheism," in *Religion after Metaphysics*, ed. Mark A. Wrathall (Cambridge: Cambridge University Press, 2003).

7. Elizabeth F. Cooke, *Peirce's Pragmatic Theory of Inquiry: Fallibilism and Indeterminacy* (London and New York: Continuum, 2006).

8. Rorty, *Philosophy and Social Hope*, chapters 2–4. See also Richard Rorty, "Universality and Truth," in *Rorty and His Critics*, ed. Robert B. Brandom (Malden, MA: Blackwell, 2000).

9. Rorty, *Philosophy and Social Hope*, 27.

10. Ibid.

11. Ibid., 120.

12. Ibid., 88.

13. Ibid., 265.

14. Rorty, *Philosophy as Cultural Politics*, 91.

15. Ibid., 35.

16. Ibid., 91.

17. Rorty, "Anti-Clericalism and Atheism," 42.

18. Ibid., 44.

19. William James, *Pragmatism: A New Name for Some Old Ways of Thinking* (1907), ed. Frederick H. Burkhardt, Fredson Bowers, and Ignas K. Skrupskelis (Cambridge, MA: Harvard University Press, 1975), 61–62.

20. Cooke, *Peirce's Pragmatic Theory of Inquiry*.

21. For the ethical and political relevance of Rorty's views on religion (as contrasted, for example, with some Catholic dogmas), see in particular *An Ethics for Today: Finding Common Ground between Philosophy and Religion* (New York: Columbia University Press, 2011), which includes a lecture by Rorty, an introduction by Gianni Vattimo, and G. Elijah Dann's interpretive essay, "Philosophy, Religion, and Religious Belief after Rorty." See also Dann's related monograph, *After Rorty: The Possibilities for Ethics and Religious Belief* (London and New York: Continuum, 2006).

22. Rorty, *Philosophy as Cultural Politics*, 5, 8.

23. Ibid., 19.

24. Ibid., 25–26.

25. Ibid., 22.

26. Ibid., 25.

27. Ibid., 30.

28. Ibid., chap. 2.

29. Ibid., 34–35.

30. Ibid., 36. This formulation gives an indication of Rorty's conviction that religion, if it serves any legitimate purpose, should be reduced to literature. See also Wojciech Malecki, "The Unforced Flowers of Life? Richard Rorty on Religion and Literature," in *Identity and Social Transformation: Central European Pragmatist Forum* 5, ed. John Ryder and Radim Sip (Amsterdam and New York: Rodopi, 2011), 229–38.

31. Rorty, *Philosophy as Cultural Politics*, 37.

32. Ibid., 38.

33. Ibid., 40.

34. On the significance of guilt, see Sami Pihlström, *Transcendental Guilt: Reflections on Ethical Finitude* (Lanham, MD: Lexington Books, 2011). Cf. also chapter 5 and the conclusion for related reflections.

35. See especially Hilary Putnam, *Words and Life*, ed. James Conant (Cambridge, MA, and London: Harvard University Press, 1994).

36. See Hilary Putnam, *Reason, Truth and History* (Cambridge: Cambridge University Press, 1981); Putnam, *Realism with a Human Face*, ed. James Conant (Cambridge, MA: Harvard University Press, 1990).

37. Putnam's other labels—"pragmatic realism" and "realism with a small 'r'"—still apply to his views very well; cf. Putnam, *Renewing Philosophy* (Cambridge, MA: Harvard University Press, 1992); and *Words and Life* (cited above).

38. See Hilary Putnam, *The Collapse of the Fact/Value Dichotomy and Other Essays* (Cambridge, MA, and London: Harvard University Press, 2002); Putnam, *Ethics without Ontology* (Cambridge, MA: Harvard University Press, 2004). I explore this aspect of Putnam's thought in Sami Pihlström, *Pragmatic Moral Realism: A Transcendental Defense* (Amsterdam and New York: Rodopi, 2005). In a recent article manuscript, "Theology without Ontology as an Exercise in Naturalism, Or beyond Stoicism and Platonism in the Account of Religion" (forthcoming), Troels Engberg-Pedersen suggests, largely following Putnam's views on the fact-value entanglement, a way of understanding theology as a perspective on reality while maintaining naturalism and avoiding any "ontological grounding." While I obviously agree with his proposal to apply Putnam's ideas to this particular issue, I am slightly suspicious about his (and Putnam's) perhaps too strongly antiontological move. Rejecting the very idea of there being ontological grounds for our perspectives on reality (including theological ones) is not to reject ontology—as also argued in the other chapters of this book in relation to Kant, James, and Dewey.

39. See, for example, Ilkka Niiniluoto, *Critical Scientific Realism* (Oxford and New York: Oxford University Press, 1999).

40. See especially Putnam, *The Collapse of the Fact/Value Dichotomy*.

41. In addition to his 1992 book, *Renewing Philosophy*, see Hilary Putnam, "God and the Philosophers," in *Philosophy of Religion*, Midwest Studies in Philosophy 21, ed. Peter A. French et al. (Minneapolis: Minnesota University Press, 1997); "On Negative Theology," *Faith and Philosophy* 14 (1997): 407–22; "Thoughts Addressed to an Analytical Thomist," *The Monist* 80 (1997): 487–99. Putnam's most recent reflections on religious faith are set in the context of his exploration of Judaism: see Hilary Putnam, *Jewish Philosophy as a Guide to Life* (Bloomington: Indiana University Press, 2008).

42. Putnam, "God and the Philosophers," 182.

43. Ibid., 176.

44. Ibid., 178.

45. Ibid., 178–80.

46. Putnam, "Thoughts Addressed to an Analytical Thomist," 492.

47. Putnam, "God and the Philosophers," 182–83.

48. Putnam, "On Negative Theology," 419.

49. Ibid.; see also Putnam, *Jewish Philosophy as a Guide to Life*.

50. See Putnam, *Renewing Philosophy*, 190–96.

51. Putnam, "On Negative Theology," 408.

52. Putnam, "God and the Philosophers," 185.

53. Ibid., 184; original emphasis.

54. Putnam, "Thoughts Addressed to an Analytical Thomist," 498.

55. Ibid., 490.

56. Zackary Sholem Berger, "Spiritual Encounters of a Philosopher of Science," an interview with Hilary Putnam in *Forward.com* (October 3, 2008), http://www.forward.com/articles/14256/.

57. See Ludwig Wittgenstein, *Philosophical Investigations*, trans. G. E. M. Anscombe (Oxford: Basil Blackwell, 1958; first published 1953), II, section iv.

58. Ibid.

59. See Ulf Zackariasson, *Forces by which We Live: Religion and Religious Experience from the Perspective of a Pragmatic Philosophical Anthropology*, Studiae Philosophiae Religionis 21 (Uppsala: University of Uppsala, 2002); Zackariasson, "Pragmatism and Moral Critique of Religion," *American Journal of Theology and Philosophy* 31 (2010): 3–14. Cf. also Zackariasson's book manuscript on religion in the "public sphere," which is still work in progress (cited in the introduction).

60. Cf. also my review of Zackariasson's 2002 book in *Contemporary Pragmatism* 1 (2004).

61. Zackariasson, *Forces by which We Live*, 28.

62. Ibid., 12–13.

63. Ibid., 30–31.

64. Ibid., 31.

65. Ibid., 53, 79–80.

66. Ibid., 34–38.

67. Ibid., 75.

68. Zackariasson also succeeds in showing that philosophers of religion appealing to the evidential force of religious experience have not provided sufficient reasons for the analogy they draw between religious and everyday perceptual experiences. In this regard, he offers an essential contribution to the on-going critical evaluation of reformed epistemology, represented by "Christian philosophers" like William Alston, Alvin Plantinga, and others. See ibid., chap. 5.

69. Ibid., 14, 69–71, 76, 236.

70. See ibid., 100–13.

71. Ibid., 100.

72. Ibid., 185.

73. Ibid., 226.

74. Ibid., 80.

75. See Zackariasson's forthcoming essay, "Justification and Critique" (2011), ms., 17–18.

76. See Ulf Zackariasson, "What's Wrong with the Adequacy-argument? A Pragmatic Diagnosis," *Sophia* 50 (2011): 11–23 (especially 20).

77. Ulf Zackariasson, "Pragmatism and Moral Critique of Religion," 5.

78. For example, in "Public Deliberation as Separate or Embedded: Deweyan Democracy and Its Relation to Political Liberalism" (*Minerva* 11, 2007, 1–29; http://www.mic.ul.ie/stephen/vol11/index.html), Zackariasson draws on the Deweyan conception of democracy in arguing, again *contra* Rawls, that "if comprehensive doctrines are withdrawn from public deliberation, they are also withdrawn from a more general process of democratization that may be necessary if public deliberation is to remain stable over time" (25).

79. See, for example, Dirk-Martin Grube, "Refuting the Evidentialist Challenge to Religion: A Critique Inspired by William James," *Ars Disputandi* (2004), http://www.arsdisputandi.org/publish/articles/000132/index.html; and Eberhard Herrmann, "A Pragmatic Realist Philosophy of Religion", *Ars Disputandi* (2003), http://www.arsdisputandi.org/publish/articles/000092/index.html. In addition, Thomas Schmidt's works, briefly referred to in the introduction and chapter 2, are excellent examples of contemporary pragmatist philosophy of religion, as they examine, among other problems, the public versus private contrast—not only in the Rortyan context but in the broader context of the on-going discussion of the public role of religion engaged in by leading thinkers like Habermas, Rawls, Nussbaum, and others. In this sense, Schmidt should also

be included among "European neopragmatist philosophers of religion" today, as should many of his pupils and collaborators. Finally, Hans Joas—coming from sociology with a very strong philosophical orientation—has probably done more than anyone else in promoting the appreciation of pragmatist contributions to the (both philosophical and sociological) understanding of religion in Germany.

80. Malecki's "The Unforced Flowers of Life" (cited above) also helpfully elaborates on this.

4. THE JAMESIAN PRAGMATIC METHOD
IN THE PHILOSOPHY OF RELIGION

1. Note that, for pragmatists, beliefs *are* practices—or "habits of action." This is not always emphasized as much as it should. Even pragmatist reflections on religion, such as Kenneth W. Stikkers's otherwise very interesting essay, "God Works in Strange Ways, or: How William James's Pragmatism Led This Philosopher into the Catholic Church" (http://www.sju.edu/~jgodfrey/StikkersJames ianCatholicism_APA_E_2007.pdf), sometimes suffer from the failure to draw attention to this point (in Stikkers's case, that failure is manifested in his reliance on the distinction between "orthodoxy" and "orthopraxis").

2. James examines this problem at some length both in William James, *Pragmatism: A New Name for Some Old Ways of Thinking* (1907), and in his late work, *A Pluralistic Universe* (1909), both in *The Works of William James*, 19 vols., ed. Frederick H. Burkhardt, Fredson Bowers, and Ignas K. Skrupskelis (Cambridge, MA: Harvard University Press, 1975 and 1979, respectively).

3. This should be sufficient to set to rest the oft-heard allegation that James's pragmatism is simply nominalistic. He does believe that universals or generals, especially "kinds," have an important philosophical role to play, insofar as they are pragmatically cashed out.

4. James, *Pragmatism*, 73.

5. Ibid., 79. See also James's discussion of pluralism in his posthumous work, *Some Problems of Philosophy* (1911), chapters 7–8: "Pluralism [unlike monism or absolute idealism] is neither optimistic nor pessimistic, but melioristic. The world, it thinks, may be saved, on condition that its parts shall do their best. But shipwreck in detail, or even on the whole, is among the open possibilities." And further: "Towards this issue, of the reality or unreality of the novelty that appears, the pragmatic difference between monism and pluralism seems to converge. That we ourselves may be authors of genuine novelty is the thesis of the doctrine of free-will." I am quoting from the Bison Books edition, ed. Ellen Kappy Suckiel (Lincoln and London: University of Nebraska Press, 1996), 142, 145. Among the key problems of monistic idealism is, then, that it is fatalistic

(sacrificing real novelty and chance) and leads to the problem of evil (ibid., 138–39).

6. In addition to *A Pluralistic Universe*, cf. William James, *Essays in Radical Empiricism* (1912), also included in *The Works of William James* (1977). James's position here has also been described as "piecemeal panpsychism" or "panexperientialism." Here I will set aside the interpretive issue of whether James is, in some sense, a panpsychist or not.

7. When quoting James's *A Pluralistic Universe*, I am using the new edition edited and introduced by H. G. Callaway (Cambridge: Cambridge Scholars Press, 2008), which contains the editor's useful notes and his discussion of the different meanings of pluralism. For the quote, see 21. Note also that in this passage and elsewhere, James understands—somewhat puzzlingly—pluralism as a species of "pantheism," a spiritualist view that, unlike monism, understands the "spiritual substance" of the universe not as an "all-form" but as an "each-form," rejecting the "intellectually neat" picture of monistic idealism with its Absolute (see 28). In particular, the problem of evil, James argues, haunts absolutist conceptions of the spiritual universe (ibid., 72).

8. See Hilary Putnam, *Realism with a Human Face*, ed. James Conant (Cambridge, MA and London: Harvard University Press, 1990); and Putnam, *Ethics without Ontology* (Cambridge, MA, and London: Harvard University Press, 2004). See chapter 3 in this book.

9. See Nelson Goodman, *Ways of Worldmaking* (Indianapolis: Hackett, 1978). Note that pragmatism thus rejects *metaphysically realistic metaphysics* but not necessarily metaphysics as such, because metaphysics can itself be interpreted pragmatically as an inquiry into the "human world" and its (categorization-dependent and thus in the end pragmatically constructed) structure. See Sami Pihlström, *Pragmatist Metaphysics: An Essay on the Ethical Grounds of Ontology* (London and New York: Continuum, 2009). It must be kept in mind that the "world-structuring" the pragmatist metaphysician is interested in is never merely ontological but also epistemic (and, as will emerge in due course, also ethical).

10. If the phrase, "imposed on it by us," sounds too traditionally Kantian, as I am sure it will sound to many pragmatist readers, try the following replacement (kindly suggested by David Hildebrand): "a natural outcome of our lived experience." The latter retains as much transcendentality as is necessary in a Jamesian pragmatist context. More generally, it must be admitted that James is not a proper Kantian. The claim that Jamesian pragmatism just amounts to Kantian transcendental idealism in a "pluralized" and pragmatically naturalized sense must be qualified in many ways (and that is part of what I am trying to do in this chapter and book). I won't, however, be able to discuss James's negative view on the Kantian thing in itself, for instance; nor will I dwell on the

obvious difference that for Kant morality can never be a matter of feeling as it obviously is at least to some extent for James. Unlike Kant, James is skeptical not only about the transcendental philosophical system generally but about any universal moral law, in particular (as we will see).

11. Another (related) difference between Kant and James, not to be further discussed here, is the fact that, according to James, our experience always contains elements that cannot be conceptually classified or categorized. However, admitting that no categorization is final or total is not to reject categorization completely. Radical empiricism itself is *a* way of categorizing reality, however anticonceptualistic.

12. In order to properly use such a label here, we should pay attention to James's criticisms of the notion of substance in *Pragmatism*, chap. 3 (see also Pihlström, *Pragmatist Metaphysics*). Clearly, pluralism, for James, cannot just be, say, the view that there is a plurality of substances, as the concept of a substance must itself be pragmatically examined, and it may even be put to work within pluralism by emphasizing its different functions as, say, both the bearer of properties and the unchanging permanence amidst all changes.

13. James's relation to utilitarianism is critically explored in Sergio Franzese, *The Ethics of Energy: William James's Moral Philosophy in Focus* (Frankfurt: Ontos, 2008). See also the brief remark in my introduction about the relation between the metaphysical and the political aspects of pragmatist philosophy of religion (though the political ones cannot be extensively dealt with in this book). This applies to pluralism as much as to any other dimension of pragmatist philosophy of religion.

14. See José Medina, "James on Truth and Solidarity: The Epistemology of Diversity and the Politics of Specificity," in *100 Years of Pragmatism: William James's Revolutionary Philosophy*, ed. John J. Stuhr (Bloomington: Indiana University Press, 2010), 124–43.

15. William James, *Essays in Religion and Morality*, in *The Works of William James* (1982), 99; see also James's 1898 essay "On a Certain Blindness in Human Beings" in the same volume; cf. Ralph Barton Perry, *The Thought and Character of William James: Briefer Version* (New York: Harper, 1964; first published 1948), 223–24.

16. Perry, *Thought and Character*, 221.

17. The "attitude towards a soul" comes from Ludwig Wittgenstein, *Philosophical Investigations*, trans. G. E. M. Anscombe (Oxford: Basil Blackwell, 1958; first published 1953), II, section iv. The concept of acknowledgment, as distinguished from knowledge, is central in Stanley Cavell, *The Claim of Reason* (Oxford: Oxford University Press, 1979). For a discussion of James and the acknowledgment of "other minds," see Sami Pihlström, "Pragmatic and Transcendental Arguments for Theism," in *"The Trail of the Human Serpent Is over*

Everything": Jamesian Perspectives on Mind, World, and Religion (Lanham, MD: University Press of America, 2008).

18. The notion of "philosophical temperaments" is introduced by James in chapter 1 of *Pragmatism*.

19. See James O. Pawelski, *The Dynamic Individualism of William James* (Albany: SUNY Press, 2007).

20. This important essay is reprinted in William James, *The Will to Believe and Other Essays in Popular Philosophy* (1897), included in *The Works of William James* (1979).

21. Franzese, *The Ethics of Energy*, 17, 27.

22. Ibid., 26.

23. Ibid., 40.

24. James, "The Moral Philosopher and the Moral Life" (*The Will to Believe*), 141. See also Russell B. Goodman, "William James," *Stanford Encyclopedia of Philosophy* (2009), http://plato.stanford.edu/entries/james/, section 4. For recent readings of James's essay (in addition to Franzese's, which I am partly relying on here), see, for example, Deborah Boyle, "William James's Ethical Symphony," *Transactions of the Charles S. Peirce Society* 34 (1998), 977–1003; and Sarin Marchetti, "William James on Truth and Invention in Morality," *European Journal of Pragmatism and American Philosophy* 2 (2010), 126–59. Marchetti, like Franzese, makes an important point in recognizing that James's essay is not a defense of utilitarianism or any other moral theory, as James is "skeptical about the very possibility of moral theory" (128), and that, further, James's other investigations—into the mind, the world, and so on—were "driven by ethical concerns" (ibid., 129)—precisely as I have also argued in some detail in my *"The Trail of the Human Serpent Is over Everything."* In particular, Marchetti in my view accurately observes that "the appreciation of a shared moral life is a precondition on which moral reflection bears," while the moral skeptic avoids her/his responsibility of participating in a moral community (134); this is a point at which James's approach could be fruitfully compared to that of the "Wittgensteinian moral philosophers," such as D. Z. Phillips and Raimond Gaita.

25. Fallibilism, admitting human fallibility and the possibility of error in any cognitive projects we might engage, including not only scientific inquiry but ethics and politics as well, is (since Peirce's seminal works) one of the key ideas in pragmatism. No detailed definition of fallibilism is needed here, though; again, a number of fallibilisms, differing in strength, could be distinguished.

26. For further comments on James's and Levinas's similarities, especially regarding otherness, see Pihlström, *"The Trail of the Human Serpent Is over Everything,"* especially chapters 3 and 5. I should pause here to reflect for a moment on a major recent contribution to the comparison between James and Levinas: Megan Craig's *Levinas and James: Toward a Pragmatic Phenomenology* (Bloom-

ington and Indianapolis: Indiana University Press, 2010). Craig's book is not just an arbitrary comparison between two philosophers that happen to share some ideas. It is most welcome, indeed much needed, as it puts James into conversation with one of the most important Continental (post)phenomenological thinkers of the twentieth century, Levinas. These two philosophers might seem to be very different, and their divergences in writing styles, for instance, cannot be denied; yet, Craig shows convincingly that they do share a number of important philosophical commitments, many of which should make us rethink the very nature of ethics (and philosophy). She argues that "James brings Levinas down to earth, and Levinas discloses the ethics of James's pragmatic pluralism" (ibid., xvi). Breaking with both Husserl and Heidegger in his quest for a "more vital phenomenology," Levinas comes closer to James's radical empiricism than to either of his great phenomenological predecessors (ibid., 35). Thus, Craig encourages us to reflect on "pragmatic aspects of Levinas's ethics and ethical aspects of James's pluralism" (ibid., 65). Just as the Levinasian self is characterized by constant ethical vigilance, James famously rejects (eventually) the "moral holiday" the monistic idealists' Absolute could have guaranteed. One might say that the pragmatist's moral holiday is interrupted by Levinasian "insomnia"— the insomnia that "turns into ethical wakefulness" (ibid., 15) and "signifies both a risk and a hope: the risk of being subject to a day that never ends, and the hope of awakening to a world of faces that never close" (ibid., 30). James's "strenuous mood" could, then, more or less be equated with Levinas's vigilance, and with the related conception of ethics as "ongoing labor" (ibid., 93). The ethical project is endless and infinite: whatever we do in our philosophical thought, or generally in our worldly actions, may have profound ethical significance. It is precisely for this reason that ethics must, as James and Levinas both in their different ways argued, be brought "down to earth"—to the street, as Craig often puts it. Ethics is not a matter of abstract philosophical principles but of concrete human life together with others. Thus, the ethical perspective cannot be restricted; in particular, ethics cannot be a mere subdiscipline of philosophy among others. It is, rather, the point of view from which philosophy begins. In particular, reading Craig's book should help us appreciate the fact that James's life-long interest in subjectivity and experience (including religious experience) must itself be understood as ethical. The Levinasian ideas that "subjectivity *is* ethical subjectivity," openness to the vulnerable other, and that "ethics takes place in the dark" (ibid., 4), in the context of human suffering and vulnerability, are clearly Jamesian, too. Being a subject *is* to "feel uncomfortable" most of the time, or rather always; there are no moral holidays (ibid., 109)—and if there were, they would immediately end in insomnia. If ethics could be captured in a single abstract principle, we might enjoy occasional moral holidays, but no such luxury is available for us. On the street and "in the dark," one must be continuously aware of potentially ethically demanding situations, of others—or "faces"—that one is responsible for. Accordingly, Levinas's "radical multiplicity" serves, for Craig, as an "initial point of contact with James's pragmatic pluralism" (ibid., 4). What emerges here is a (what pragmatists might call fallibilistic) observation that ethics is "always at risk," without guarantees (ibid., 33). Levinas's phenomenology is, as Craig perceptively puts it, "a philosophy for the streets here below"; even its religious aspect lies in "the strictly catholic holiness of humanizing faces—a holiness descended to earth, fallen and already impure" (ibid., 63). At this crucial point, Craig also refers to Hannah Arendt's conception of the "banality of evil," noting that for both Arendt and Levinas, "to turn one's face from the banal is to risk missing everything of real importance" (ibid.). The same, again, can be said of James. No human life—and no religious experience—is too banal to merit serious ethical attention. The infinite is within the particular (ibid., 127). We must, both philosophers seem to tell us, be attentive and increasingly sensitive to, and thereby responsible for, others even in their mundane banality (ibid., 191). My only critical remark at this point is the following: Craig may here de-emphasize Levinas's (and James's) religious aspects more than is necessary. I am not quite convinced that her description of Levinas's faith as "a-religious" is correct—this strikes me as too strong, as it surely would in James's case—but there is certainly a true core to the idea of secularizing divinity in terms of the face of the other person (ibid., 92–93). If there is something like faith available to the Levinasian-Jamesian ethical subject, this must, we are told, be a faith where "the only afterlife is the life of another person who lives on after one's death, and where a holy place is a crowded street" (ibid., 93). However, this clearly would not have been enough for James, who was genuinely interested (while avoiding dogmatic belief) in the possibility of survival and immortality in a more literal sense. The topic of mortality, in any event, highlights the ethics of otherness worked out by Levinas and Craig. Just as James in "Human Immortality" discusses the prospect for immortality in a "democratic" manner, Levinas attacks Heidegger's "first-personal" approach to death focusing on the anxiety of one's "being-toward-death": "not the *thought* of death but the *fact* of dying, not anxiety but *horror*, not *my* death but the death of the *other*" (ibid., 12). Heidegger's "being-toward-death" is, Levinas on Craig's interpretation maintains, "dangerously solipsistic" (ibid.). James, we should note, struggled with a similar problem of avoiding solipsism in one's relation to the world and to the mortal others surrounding one's life, though solipsism as such is very seldom explicitly addressed in his works. (See again my chap. 5 in *The Trail of the Human Serpent Is over Everything*".) Just as James remarked that we must not be "deaf to the cries of the wounded," Levinas, and Craig following him, emphasize "the ethical importance of listening," which means that a certain kind of "passivity" is central in ethics (Craig, *Levinas and James*, 55). This, however, is a very special kind of passivity, not opposed to action. Craig notes that there is "passive activity in James" and "active passivity in Levinas" (ibid., 84); both view passivity as an ethical willingness, "getting *past oneself* in order to wake up to a reality outpacing one's intentions" (ibid.). Levinas's descriptions of fatigue and insomnia, carefully analyzed by Craig, are attempts to capture something from this special ethical mood. Vigilance, being awake, is not only to act intentionally but to remain (passively) open to others. This is not to say that I found everything in Craig's book to my liking. Occasionally, her writing unfortunately suffers from the typical problem of Levinas scholars: she seems to be rewriting Levinas all over again, saying the same in different sentences using familiar words. Sometimes it may even be a bit hard to find out who is talking—Levinas or Craig. In any event, Craig contributes in an important way to the greatly needed realization that the boundaries between philosophical traditions need not be as sharp as they are sometimes thought to be—and makes, with Levinas and James, the even more vital point that ethics should be at the center of our philosophical projects, especially when we try to reflect on subjectivity.

27. See Medina, "James on Truth and Solidarity."

28. Ibid., 124.

29. Ibid., 125.

30. Ibid.

31. Kant and James both seem to agree that the commonplace that truth is "agreement" (in Kant's terms *Übereinstimmung*) between a belief (or a proposition, an "idea," or some other truth-bearer) and reality is only what Kant calls a "nominal definition" (*Namenerklärung*) of truth. See Immanuel Kant, *Kritik der reinen Vernunft* (1781/1787), ed. Raymund Schmidt (Hamburg: Felix Meiner, 1990), A58/B82. Both philosophers maintain that the epistemically relevant criteria or standards of truth cannot be reduced to nonepistemic correspondence between beliefs and the world. Moreover, Medina's reflections on the broader ethical and political relevance of the Jamesian notion of truth could be continued by referring to Marchetti's suggestion that moral reflection, for James, is descriptive rather than prescriptive (Marchetti, "William James on Truth and Invention in Morality," 133). For example, historical writing or scholarship aiming at historical truth (as well as understanding, explanation, and so on) may itself be an engagement in moral reflection. The Jamesian pragmatist conception of truth could be applied to historical "truths" revealed or constructed in, or emerging from, such inquiries. Historical inquiry into historical truths may be morally energizing in the Jamesian sense by revealing hidden injustices simply by pointing out that *this* is what happened, urging us to take it into account ethically (for instance, by being committed to the prevention of anything like that from happening again). Mere humble truths may be pragmatically extremely

valuable. At this point, James's pragmatism could also be connected with the highly important discussions of historical and political *memory*; see, for example, Avishai Margalit, *The Ethics of Memory* (Cambridge, MA, and London: Harvard University Press, 2002).

32. See James, *Pragmatism*, chap. 3.

33. Franzese, *The Ethics of Energy*, 50. See also Marchetti, "William James on Truth and Invention in Morality."

34. Franzese, *The Ethics of Energy*, 103.

35. See Hilary Putnam, "A Reconsideration of Deweyan Democracy," chap. 9 in *Renewing Philosophy* (Cambridge, MA: Harvard University Press, 1992).

36. See, for example, James, *A Pluralistic Universe* (Callaway edition), 77, 193; cf. again Pawelski, *The Dynamic Individualism of William James*.

37. Franzese, *The Ethics of Energy*, 210.

38. Ibid., 211. This argument is developed in chapter 3 of James's *Pragmatism*; for a more detailed discussion, see Pihlström, *"The Trail of the Human Serpent Is over Everything."*

39. William James, *The Varieties of Religious Experience: A Study in Human Nature* (1902), included in *The Works of William James* (1985).

40. Or, to put the point in a more properly Jamesian manner, these needs, interests, and purposes are always already at work within our cognitive faculty itself; there is no pure cognition independently of practical orientation in the world. This is pretty much what pragmatism is all about: any experience, cognition, or representation we are capable of is inseparably embedded in human practices, or habits of action.

41. This is one of James's descriptions of the Absolute in chapter 4 of *Pragmatism*.

42. I deal with this issue concerning the ontology of subjectivity in Pihlström, *"The Trail of the Human Serpent Is over Everything"*, chap. 5. See also Sami Pihlström, "Pragmatism and Naturalized Transcendental Subjectivity," *Contemporary Pragmatism* 6 (2009), 1–13, for a more comprehensive discussion of this particular topic, in relation with more standard pragmatist accounts of subjectivity.

43. We should here take seriously James's discussions of our need for a moral order and of the ethically "energizing" function of theism (see the essays, "The Sentiment of Rationality" and "The Moral Philosopher and the Moral Life," in *The Will to Believe*; see also James, *Pragmatism*, especially chapters 3 and 8). For two excellent recent readings of James's "theological postulate" and its moral relevance (without any detailed comparisons to Kant), see Todd Lekan, "Strenuous Moral Living," and Michael R. Slater, "Ethical Naturalism and Religious Belief in 'The Moral Philosopher and the Moral Life,'" both in *William James Studies* 2 (2007), http://williamjamesstudies.press.uiuc.edu. Notably, there are

also Kantian overtones in James's notion of an "eternal moral order" of the universe, which he sees as a deeply seated human need. Cf. chapter 8 of *Pragmatism* for a "meliorist" view of the possible though not inevitable "salvation" of the world; see also the discussion of these issues in Pihlström, *"The Trail of the Human Serpent Is over Everything."* A fuller account of these issues in James would require a discussion of his *Varieties*, which does briefly take up Kant's postulates, among other things.

44. However, please keep in mind the qualification noted in chapter 1: the argument may focus on God's existence or on our belief in God's existence. This cannot always be made clear in a Jamesian context. Furthermore, the specific problems there might be regarding immortality can be set aside here. James, too, was deeply interested in defending the possibility of, and the legitimate hope for, immortality. See again, for example, James's essay "Human Immortality," in *Essays on Religion and Morality*. Regarding the phrase "only if" in the first premise, it should be noted that God's existence is here regarded as a necessary but obviously not a sufficient condition for the possibility of moral pursuits. Morality might be impossible for some other reason, for example, trivially for the reason that humans or other rational beings might not exist at all.

45. It is, above all, the undeniable existence of evil that may lead us to moral nihilism. For a discussion of the seriousness of this problem in James, see Franzese, *The Ethics of Energy*; cf. Sami Pihlström, "Religion and Pseudo-Religion: An Elusive Boundary," *International Journal for Philosophy of Religion* 62 (2007): 3–32. Cf. also chapter 5 and my conclusion to this book.

46. In particular, the notion of *prayer*—as a practice manifesting the believer's trust in God, instead of being based on the theoretical belief that a certain entity exists—might at this point be worth examining from a Jamesian perspective. Such a more specialized discussion must, however, remain the topic of another inquiry. Jamesian pragmatists should, while drawing attention to the practical results of our thoughts and ideas, be careful to avoid causally manipulative, superstitious conceptions of prayer; instead, the basis of religious prayer must be trust in God as one's general habit. (For some pragmatist remarks on prayer in connection with the problem of distinguishing "genuine religion" from pseudoreligiousness, see Pihlström, "Religion and Pseudo-Religion.") That is, a pragmatist conception of prayer, as genuinely religious, must reject too simple—or even vulgar—"pragmatist" focusing on the merely useful. Prayer must be understood as "useless self-transcendence." See Merold Westphal, *God, Guilt, and Death: Towards an Existential Phenomenology of Religion* (Bloomington: Indiana University Press, 1986) Yet this uselessness may serve a deeper purpose *internal* to religious life itself, not any allegedly more important purpose external to it. Pragmatism, thus, critically reflects on the *proper kind of usefulness and purposes* at work in our religious (and of course nonreligious)

lives. Pragmatism is, or rather should be, thoroughly antireductionist also in this sense: no reduction to (mere) instrumental usefulness is acceptable, but a pluralistic, open-ended reflection on different (kinds of) purposes our religious practices (such as prayer) may have in our lives should be encouraged.

47. See again James, *Pragmatism*, chap. 3; cf. Pihlström, *Pragmatist Metaphysics*, especially 111–15, for a discussion of James's concept of hope. While James has sometimes been compared to existentialist thinkers (e.g., Sartre), an interesting but hitherto overlooked comparison might be possible to Gabriel Marcel's notion of hope. Despite their different religious outlooks (Marcel was a catholic), there is a similar metaphysical structure in their conceptions of (religious) hope: hope is directed to something transcendent in a way that makes evidential concerns irrelevant. Thus, hope is closer to love than, say, the testing of scientific hypotheses. The comparison to genuinely religious prayer is obvious (cf. previous note). The key reference here is Gabriel Marcel, *Homo Viator: Introduction to a Metaphysics of Hope* (London: Peter Smith, 1978). Another point to be emphasized here is that, although James is (I have argued) a Kantian of sorts, there may be a tension between his views and Kant's on "what we may hope." Kant postulates the *summum bonum* (the "highest good")—the harmony of virtue and happiness. Wouldn't this be close to the "moral holiday" that the Absolute might grant us? However, for Kant there are really no holidays at all—nor are there for James, as soon as he rejects the Absolute.

48. James, *A Pluralistic Universe* (Callaway edition), 19, 31, 193.

49. Michael R. Slater, "Pragmatism, Realism, and Religion," *Journal of Religious Ethics* 36 (2008): 653–81. See also Slater's 2007 paper cited above. Slater has recently offered a more comprehensive version of his argument in his book, *William James on Ethics and Faith* (Cambridge: Cambridge University Press, 2009), but I will primarily focus on the 2008 paper here.

50. Slater, "Pragmatism, Realism, and Religion," 655.

51. See James's response to various critics of *Pragmatism* in William James, *The Meaning of Truth: A Sequel to Pragmatism* (1909), in *The Works of William James* (1978).

52. Robert Audi, ed., *Cambridge Dictionary of Philosophy* (Cambridge: Cambridge University Press, 1999). See Slater, "Pragmatism, Realism, and Religion," 658n5.

53. In addition to Putnam's works (cited above), see Sami Pihlström, *Structuring the World: The Issue of Realism and the Nature of Ontological Problems in Classical and Contemporary Pragmatism* (Acta Philosophica Fennica 59, Helsinki: The Philosophical Society of Finland, 1996).

54. See James, *Pragmatism*, 121–23.

55. See Slater, "Pragmatism, Realism, and Religion," 661.

56. D. M. Armstrong, *Truth and Truthmakers* (Cambridge: Cambridge University Press, 2004).

57. Slater, "Pragmatism, Realism, and Religion," 662.

58. See Pihlström, *Pragmatist Metaphysics*, chap. 2.

59. Slater, "Pragmatism, Realism, and Religion," 665.

60. Ibid., 663–64n16.

61. Ibid., 665.

62. James's occasional references to "humanism" must be set in the context of his exchange of ideas with F. C. S. Schiller, the somewhat more radical British pragmatist who called his view "humanism." This is not the right place to examine their similarities and differences in any detail.

63. Ibid., 665.

64. As I already suggested above, there must be something analogous to transcendental idealism at work in James's pragmatism, if, for example, the ethical argumentation in favor of theistic metaphysics is supposed to get off the ground.

65. See Goodman, *Ways of Worldmaking* (cited above).

66. Slater, "Pragmatism, Realism, and Religion," 666.

67. Ibid., 667.

68. Ibid., 670.

69. Ibid., 654. Cf. also Pihlström, *Pragmatist Metaphysics*, chap. 7, as well as the reflections in chapter 1 of this book; on James's "theological postulate," see also Slater's other works cited above.

70. Slater, "Pragmatism, Realism, and Religion," 671.

71. Ibid., 674 (original emphasis).

72. Ibid., 668, 674.

73. Ibid., 676.

74. Ibid., 655.

75. Ibid., 678.

76. Slater, *William James on Ethics and Faith*, 6.

77. One of the problems with Slater's general project is his failure to appreciate the way in which James stands outside *all* traditional ethical theories—or, to echo Franzese's and Marchetti's comments cited above, is not at all in the business of providing such a theory. For an insightful criticism of Slater's position, see Ellen Kappy Suckiel's review of his *William James on Ethics and Faith* in *Notre Dame Philosophy Reviews* (June, 2010), http://ndpr.nd.edu/review.cfm ?id=19967. Suckiel also challenges Slater's realistic reading of James, as I have done above.

78. This idea is further developed in Sami Pihlström, *Transcendental Guilt: Reflections on Ethical Finitude* (Lanham, MD: Lexington Books, 2011).

79. Peirce's famous essay, "How to Make Our Ideas Clear" (1878), is reprinted, among other places, in *The Essential Peirce*, vol. 1, ed. Nathan Houser et al. (Bloomington and Indianapolis: Indiana University Press, 1992).

80. See again Pihlström, *Pragmatist Metaphysics*.

81. What is more, I definitely do not think that any reading of James is as correct as any other; on the contrary, I have argued above against some of the mischaracterizations of James that I find in Slater's interpretation. Yet, again, we should not be too easily led to believe that any one interpretation of James is correct; here, again, pluralism should reign.

5. THE PROBLEM OF EVIL AND THE LIMITS OF PHILOSOPHY

1. Insightful recent contributions include Richard Bernstein, *Radical Evil: A Philosophical Interrogation* (Cambridge: Polity Press, 2002); Bernstein, *The Abuse of Evil* (Cambridge: Polity Press, 2005); Susan Neiman, *Evil in Modern Thought: An Alternative History of Philosophy* (Princeton, NJ: Princeton University Press, 2002); Adam Morton, *Evil* (New York and London: Routledge, 2004); Alan D. Schrift, ed., *Modernity and the Problem of Evil* (Bloomington and Indianapolis: Indiana University Press, 2005); Phillip Cole, *The Myth of Evil* (Edinburgh: Edinburgh University Press, 2006); John Kekes, *The Roots of Evil* (Princeton, NJ: Princeton University Press, 2007); María Pía Lara, *Narrating Evil: A Postmetaphysical Theory of Reflective Judgment* (New York: Columbia University Press, 2007); and Peter Dews, *The Idea of Evil* (Malden, MA: Blackwell, 2008).

2. Here, some philosophers' perhaps slightly surprising interest in the concept of a monster—as an attempt to represent the "inhuman" element in evil—is remarkable as an example of philosophical reflection on the boundary of religious and secular perspectives on evil, concerning the proper representations of evil. See, for example, Richard Kearney, *Strangers, Gods, and Monsters: Interpreting Otherness* (London and New York: Routledge, 2003); Stephen T. Asma, *On Monsters: A Natural History of Our Worst Fears* (Oxford: Oxford University Press, 2009).

3. For a more extended discussion of James's views on evil, see Sami Pihlström, *"The Trail of the Human Serpent Is over Everything": Jamesian Perspectives on Mind, World, and Religion* (Lanham, MD: University Press of America, 2008), chap. 4. It ought to be noted that James, obviously, is in his treatment of evil not concerned with the more clearly twentieth (and twenty-first) century issue concerning the limits of *language*; nevertheless, he *is*, I believe, strongly concerned with what may be called the issue of the moral limits of philosophical theorizing.

4. Cole, in *The Myth of Evil*, takes the latter line.

5. In an extended sense, also those atheist views that maintain that theism *ought to* provide a theodicy can be regarded as theodicist. The (standard) theist

and the atheist agree on the need for a theodicy while disagreeing on the ability of theism to provide one. Of course there are several problematic intermediary cases that cannot be discussed in this chapter. For instance, it is an open question whether process-theological suggestions to the effect that the divinity itself participates in the suffering and evil of the world and humanity—and thus possibly makes the suffering bearable by bearing the sufferer (a formulation I owe to Vincent Colapietro)—are theodicist or not.

6. See Sami Pihlström, "Religion and Pseudo-Religion: An Elusive Boundary," *International Journal for Philosophy of Religion* 62 (2007): 3–32. See also the conclusion to this book.

7. Illustrative works by Wittgensteinian moral philosophers and philosophers of religion include Peter Winch, *Ethics and Action* (London: Routledge and Kegan Paul, 1972); D. Z. Phillips, *Belief, Change and Forms of Life* (London: Macmillan, 1986); Raimond Gaita, *Good and Evil: An Absolute Conception*, 2nd ed. (London and New York: Routledge, 2004; 1st ed. 1991); D. Z. Phillips and Timothy Tessin, eds., *Philosophy of Religion in the 21st Century* (Basingstoke: Palgrave, 2001); and Hugo Strandberg, *The Possibility of Discussion: Relativism, Truth and Criticism of Religious Belief* (Aldeshort: Ashgate, 2006).

8. Cf. Pihlström, "Religion and Pseudo-Religion." Accordingly, an argumentative exercise such as Peter van Inwagen's *The Problem of Evil* (Oxford: Oxford University Press, 2006) is very far from my concerns with evil.

9. The ethical and political unacceptability of a dichotomous war between good and evil has been particularly emphasized by Bernstein (see his *The Abuse of Evil*) but also by many of the other contributors cited in note 1 above.

10. This project of a secular acknowledgment of certain (though by no means all) religious notions is, then, also analogous to my attempt to develop a notion of "transcendental guilt" as a secular analogy to the religious notion of original sin: cf. Sami Pihlström, *Transcendental Guilt: Reflections on Ethical Finitude* (Lanham, MD: Lexington Books, 2011). Religion, I argue in both projects, is more intimately involved in our moral perspectives and identities than we secular thinkers often want to admit. (Implicitly, this is a theme of the present volume as well.)

11. See Bernstein, *Radical Evil* (cited above).

12. See Neiman, *Evil in Modern Thought*. Again, I will get back to this issue about comprehensibility in general in due course below.

13. The classical reference here is Hannah Arendt, *Eichmann in Jerusalem: A Report on the Banality of Evil* (1963), reprinted in *The Portable Hannah Arendt* (New York: Viking, 2005). See also Bernstein's very useful discussion in *Radical Evil* and *The Abuse of Evil*. The actual historical truth about Eichmann is not, however, particularly relevant to philosophical elaborations of these notions.

14. Van Inwagen, *The Problem of Evil*, 7.

15. Ibid., 4.

16. Ibid., 12.

17. Ibid., 14–15. Van Inwagen admits that he has "a very narrow conception of philosophy" in comparison to the one at work in Neiman, *Evil in Modern Thought*. See also the discussion of Neiman toward the end of this chapter.

18. Van Inwagen, *The Problem of Evil*, 16.

19. Ibid., 65; see also 98.

20. Ibid., 72.

21. Ibid., 89.

22. Ibid., 111.

23. See also ibid., 145.

24. Ibid., 89.

25. Ibid. (emphasis in original).

26. For critical discussions of this idea, see Sami Pihlström, *Pragmatism and Philosophical Anthropology: Understanding Our Human Life in a Human World* (New York: Peter Lang, 1998), chap. 10; as well as Pihlström, *Transcendental Guilt*, chap. 4.

27. Should we, then, read, say, Boethius's *De consolatione philosophiae* as a proto-pragmatist work? Why not? Pragmatism *is* a "new name for some old ways of thinking."

28. Van Inwagen, *The Problem of Evil*, 108.

29. William James, *Pragmatism: A New Name for Some Old Ways of Thinking*, ed. Frederick H. Burkhardt, Fredson Bowers, and Ignas K. Skrupskelis (Cambridge, MA: Harvard University Press, 1975), 20. See again Pihlström, *"The Trail of the Human Serpent Is over Everything,"* chap. 4.

30. For an extended account of this process, see Neiman, *Evil in Modern Thought*. Kant's theory of radical evil is comprehensively discussed in most of the recent books on evil cited above in note 1, so I am not going to spend time on exploring this familiar topic in any detail here. The classical reference is Kant's *Religion innerhalb der blossen Vernunft* (1794), available, for example, in Wilhelm Weischedel, ed., *Immanuel Kant: Werke in Zehn Bänden* (Darmstadt: Wissenschaftliche Buchgesellschaft, 1983).

31. On the relevant notion of inexplicability—extending to our moral action generally—see Bernstein, *Radical Evil*, chap. 1; as well as Robert Louden, "Evil Everywhere: The Ordinariness of Kantian Radical Evil," *Sats* 9, no. 2 (2009): 7–27.

32. Cf. Ludwig Wittgenstein, *Notebooks 1914–1916* (Oxford: Blackwell, 1961), 79.

33. We may neglect here the contrast with the early-Wittgensteinian view according to which nothing in the world can be good or evil.

34. For these examples, see D. Z. Phillips, "The Holocaust and Language" in *Genocide and Human Rights: A Philosophical Guide*, ed. J. K. Roth (Basing-

stoke: Palgrave, 2005), 46–64; and Phillips, "Mastery, Indeterminacy, and Conversation" in *Wittgenstein and Philosophical Psychology*, ed. Cristoffer Gefwert and Olli Lagerspetz (Uppsala Studies in Philosophy, Uppsala: University of Uppsala, Department of Philosophy, 2009), 157–72 (see 167). Or perhaps, to be more precise, we *can*, but then our way of talking leads us beyond the ethical and aesthetic language game we were (or had thought of ourselves as being) committed to as the kind of beings we are.

35. Cf. Sami Pihlström, *Solipsism: History, Critique, and Relevance* (Tampere: Tampere University Press, 2004).

36. I discuss this analogy in Pihlström, "*The Trail of the Human Serpent Is over Everything,*" chap. 4; see also Pihlström, "Religion and Pseudo-Religion."

37. Cole, *The Myth of Evil*, 19. Moreover, Cole acknowledges the value of myths and literature in the task of conceptualizing those human actions that might seem to require the discourse of evil. This rich theme cannot be discussed here; see also Colin McGinn, *Ethics, Evil, and Fiction* (Oxford: Clarendon Press, 1997), and Kearney, *Strangers, Gods, and Monsters*.

38. Kekes, *The Roots of Evil*.

39. See Neiman, *Evil in Modern Thought*.

40. Dews, *The Idea of Evil*.

41. Bernstein, *Radical Evil*; and Bernstein, *The Abuse of Evil*.

42. As Schrift's volume, *Modernity and the Problem of Evil*, makes clear, a certain kind of interplay between the natural and the theological seems to be a major issue in a number of contributions to the problem of evil (including the present inquiry), with different authors seeking ways to develop a philosophical concept of evil without "falling into a theologically motivated discourse" (Schrift, "Introduction," ibid., 9). Furthermore, Lars Svendsen's recent discussion of evil in his book, *A Philosophy of Evil* (trans. Kerri A. Pierce, Champaign and London: Dalkey Archive Press, 2010; Norwegian original published in 2001), is worth recommending in this context. According to Svendsen, we all "potentially bear" the kind of guilt resulting from engaging in banal evil that people like Eichmann do (ibid., 190); contrary to the frequent suggestion that there are purely good and evil people around, we are all both good and evil, and we should also recognize that only the one who is (potentially) guilty can be innocent (ibid., 196). We are not all guilty or evil in the religious sense of having participated in something like the original sin; yet, in quasi-religious terms, Svendsen's point could also be expressed by saying that the state of the human race is "fallen." What we need in this situation, amidst evil and guilt and absurdity, is, however, moral reflection, instead of, say, supernatural grace; as Svendsen also repeatedly recognizes, we only have our reflective moral judgment to rely on when fighting the evil there is in our world.

43. On the role of the concept of evil in historical (and moral) understanding that can be expressed in the form of a *narrative*, see Lara, *Narrating Evil*. Lara, however, emphasizes the distinction between morality and religion much more sharply than I have done here (see, for example, 13).

44. For a classical treatment, see Georg Henrik von Wright, *Explanation and Understanding* (Ithaca, NY: Cornell University Press, 1971).

45. One important background idea here might be Donald Davidson's theory of actions and events: some events can be described, hence understood, in a special way as intentional actions. The same events can be described and explained both in an intentional and in a causal vocabulary. See Davidson, *Essays on Actions and Events* (Oxford: Clarendon Press, 1980).

46. The concepts of meaning and understanding are of course linked. When understanding something, that something must have a meaning that we understand. If we are able to "understand" human life, or the world in which it takes place, that life (or world) must have some kind of "meaning." One of James's most explicit treatments of this topic is his essay "Is Live Worth Living?" in William James, *The Will to Believe and Other Essays in Popular Philosophy* (1897), in *The Works of William James* (1979); the theme is, however, important in almost everything he wrote.

47. See my *Transcendental Guilt*.

48. Evil and suffering intensify the problem of the significance of life but do not exhaust it, because mere *mortality* may be taken to deprive life of meaning. These problems are, of course, connected, as death itself can be, and has often been, regarded as something evil—even though the contrary view, according to which immortality would be meaningless, has also been advanced. The present book does not directly address the issues of death and mortality; see, however, Jeff Malpas and Robert C. Solomon, eds., *Death and Philosophy* (London and New York: Routledge, 1998); as well as Sami Pihlström, "Death—Mine or the Other's? On the Possibility of Philosophical Thanatology," *Mortality* 6 (2001): 265–86. This is also a topic to which pragmatists should direct more attention (and I also hope to do so in some future work). For a promising start, see Charles A. Hobbs, "Why Classical American Pragmatism is Helpful for Thinking about Death," *Transactions of the Charles S. Peirce Society* 47 (2011): 182–95.

49. Neiman, *Evil in Modern Thought*, xviii.

50. See ibid., 42. On the "intractability" of evil, see again Bernstein, *Radical Evil* and *The Abuse of Evil*. Both Neiman's and Bernstein's books can be read as reminding us of the problem of evil as *the* challenge for any reasonable or rational attempt to evaluate philosophically the meaningfulness of life.

51. Neiman, *Evil in Modern Thought*, 7.

52. Ibid., 5. Thus, Neiman's project, focusing on evil, is to lead philosophers back to the "real roots of philosophical questioning" (ibid., 13), redescribing the

tradition of modern philosophy as a struggle with the problem of evil (rather than, say, with the problem of external world skepticism). Note that this is precisely the understanding of the problem of evil—emphasizing that evil threatens our ability to regard the world as comprehensible—that, for example, van Inwagen firmly rejects (see his *The Problem of Evil*, 15–16).

53. Neiman, *Evil in Modern Thought*, 7–8. This link could be strengthened by following Wittgenstein in regarding the world and life as, ultimately, "one." See Ludwig Wittgenstein, *Tractatus Logico-Philosophicus* (1921), trans. David F. Pears and Brian F. McGuinness (London: Routledge and Kegan Paul, 1974), § 5.621; for a useful commentary regarding this matter, see Martin Stokhof, *World and Life as One: Ethics and Ontology in Wittgenstein's Early Philosophy* (Stanford, CA: Stanford University Press, 2002).

54. Neiman, *Evil in Modern Thought*, 256.

55. Ibid., 325.

56. I am, of course, referring to James's thematization of the sick soul in *The Varieties of Religious Experience* (1902), ed. Frederick H. Burkhardt, Fredson Bowers, and Ignas K. Skrupskelis (Cambridge, MA: Harvard University Press, 1985).

57. See, for Peirce's relevant writings on this topic, Charles S. Peirce, *The Essential Peirce*, 2 vols., The Peirce Edition Project (Bloomington: Indiana University Press, 1992–98), especially vol. 2. It must be noted that Peirce, unlike the other classical pragmatists James and Dewey, has not been a central figure in this book (as already explained in chapter 1). This is not because I would find his pragmatism irrelevant to the philosophy of religion; on the contrary, there are many important insights, including realism about the generals, that could be drawn from Peirce in a more comprehensive investigation of philosophy of religion, even though I do find the Jamesian and Deweyan resources more promising. On Peirce as a philosopher of religion, see Robert Neville, *Realism and Religion* (Albany: SUNY Press, 2009).

58. Guilt, "transcendentally" analyzed, is a similar concept in this regard, though of course not the same concept. Cf. Pihlström, *Transcendental Guilt*.

59. A Peircean pragmatist might also adopt the concept of a *habit* here, but I will for now just leave that for another occasion.

60. Regarding the concept of melancholy (rather than, say, tragedy) in James, I am particularly indebted to a conversation with Thomas Schmidt. See, however, also Vincent Colapietro, "The Tragic Roots of Jamesian Pragmatism," forthcoming in *Journal of Speculative Philosophy* (2012).

61. See Albert Camus, *The Rebel: An Essay on Man in Revolt* (New York: Vintage, 1951).

62. William James, *Some Problems of Philosophy: A Beginning of an Introduction to Philosophy* (1911), ed. Frederick H. Burkhardt, Fredson Bowers, and

Ignas K. Skrupskelis (Cambridge, MA: Harvard University Press, 1977), 138. (See also the discussion of pluralism in chapter 4.)

63. James, *Pragmatism*, 20–21. James's understanding of Josiah Royce's views on evil may not have been accurate, however; see Claudio Viale, "Royce and Bernstein on Evil", ms., http://www.academia.edu/2075346/Royce_and_Bernstein _on_Evil.

64. Ibid., 20, 22.

65. Ibid., 141–42.

66. Recent historical scholarship on the Holocaust—I am thinking about the work of the young Finnish historian Antero Holmila and his work *Holokausti* (2010), in particular—tends to argue, contrary to the received political ideas of our need to prevent anything like that happening again, that there is actually nothing we can really learn from the Holocaust, no universal human message—no "meaning"—and so forth.

67. Ralph Waldo Emerson, "Experience," in *The Collected Works of Ralph Waldo Emerson*, ed. Robert E. Spiller et al. (Cambridge, MA: Harvard University Press, 1983), 3:29. Thanks are due to Dr. Heikki A. Kovalainen for his drawing my attention to the importance of this idea in Emerson. See Kovalainen, *Self as World: The New Emerson* (Diss., Tampere: Acta Universitatis Tamperensis 1568, 2010), 241; for Kovalainen's reflections on this important passage, see 242 ff.

68. Richard Rorty, *Consequences of Pragmatism* (Minneapolis: University of Minnesota Press, 1982), xlii–xliii. This crucial passage is also quoted by Robert Kraut in his insightful essay "Saving Metaphysics from the Pragmatist Onslaught" (a draft of which he kindly shared with me). In fact, part of what I will argue in this section is inspired by Kraut, though we have arrived at similar ideas—equally critical of Rorty's neopragmatism and other antimetaphysical versions of pragmatism—independently. I fully agree with Kraut that a certain degree of metaphysics is "woven into" our practices, which the pragmatist seeks to preserve, and that pragmatism therefore cannot simply get rid of metaphysics, nor should it aspire to—even when seeking an ethically acceptable response to evil and suffering.

69. Rorty, loc. cit.

70. This project is continued in Rorty's subsequent writings, including *Contingency, Irony, and Solidarity* (Cambridge: Cambridge University Press, 1989); *Objectivity, Relativism, and Truth* (Cambridge: Cambridge University Press, 1991); *Truth and Progress* (Cambridge: Cambridge University Press, 1998); *Philosophy and Social Hope* (London: Penguin, 1999); and *Philosophy as Cultural Politics* (Cambridge: Cambridge University Press, 2007). See chapter 3 for a more comprehensive discussion of Rortyan neopragmatism in the philosophy of religion.

71. See Hannah Arendt, *The Origins of Totalitarianism* (New York: Harcourt, 1951).

72. Kraut, "Saving Metaphysics from the Pragmatist Onslaught."

73. See my discussion of pragmatist metaphysics in Sami Pihlström, *Pragmatist Metaphysics: An Essay on the Ethical Grounds of Ontology* (London: Continuum, 2009), and of James's views in particular in Pihlström, *"The Trail of the Human Serpent Is over Everything."*

74. Note that when I am discussing the "ethical norms of metaphysics" (including particularly metaphysics concerned with the reality of evil), I am obviously not denying that there are other norms governing metaphysical inquiry and reflection (e.g., logical or epistemic norms, or norms of rationality, and so on), which might, however, also have an ethical dimension. It is also important to perceive that I am not inquiring into the "metaphysics of normativity" (but to the normativity of metaphysics, pragmatically understood). Nor am I simply concerned with the view that there are "moral reasons" for human actions independent of individual perspectives and preferences, which amounts to a relatively standard form of moral realism, but with the much stronger claim that there are moral reasons to accept or reject certain metaphysical positions. (In particular, there are moral reasons to reject metaphysical positions that cannot be "lived with.") In an earlier work (*Pragmatist Metaphysics*), I even suggested that certain metaphysical positions can only be properly formulated in ethical terms; this, in fact, is what James himself seems to be doing in the third and fourth lectures of *Pragmatism* (cf. chapter 4 above). Monism, from a Jamesian perspective, is morally dangerous and therefore not only ethically but also metaphysically unacceptable; moreover, what the monism versus pluralism debate is even about can eventually be cashed out (only) in ethical terms reflecting the concept of evil at the core of the debate.

75. Richard J. Bernstein, *The Pragmatic Turn* (Cambridge: Polity Press, 2010), 211. See also chap. 9 passim.

76. Ibid.

77. See ibid., 177, for an examination of Habermas's criticism of Rorty in this regard.

78. The way in which a commitment to transcendence may act as a transcendental condition of religious language can be seen by examining the problem of evil, as I have done above.

79. In this sense, the present chapter is somewhat critical of (or, perhaps rather, adopts a perspective quite different from) my own recent attempt to formulate a "pragmatist metaphysics of the fact-value entanglement" in Sami Pihlström, "Toward a Pragmatically Naturalist Metaphysics of the Fact-Value Entanglement: Emergence or Continuity?," *Journal of Philosophical Research* 35 (2010): 323–52.

80. See ibid.

81. I discuss the concept of "norms of being" from a pragmatist (and Kantian) perspective in Pihlström, *Pragmatist Metaphysics*, chap. 3.

82. See Pihlström, "*The Trail of the Human Serpent Is over Everything*," chap. 4, for further reflection.

83. See the discussion of Susan Neiman's view above.

84. Cf. again Bernstein, *The Abuse of Evil*.

85. Compare William James, "On a Certain Blindness in Human Beings" (1899), in James, *Essays on Religion and Morality*, ed. Frederick H. Burkhardt, Fredson Bowers, and Ignas K. Skrupskelis (Cambridge, MA: Harvard University Press, 1982).

86. See again my *Transcendental Guilt*, chap. 3.

87. My anti-Rortyan argumentation above could also be cashed out in terms of the claim that in Rortyan vocabularies, there is no room for *such* genuine world categorization. For a more extended discussion of the way in which the world can be regarded as a pragmatic-cum-transcendental "construction" (instead of being ready-made), see Pihlström, *Pragmatist Metaphysics*, as well as chapters 2 and 4. In particular, the pragmatist should join James in insisting that just as the world can and should be categorized in physical terms, it is for us necessary to categorize it in moral terms as well. Some of the essays included in James's *Will to Believe*, especially "The Dilemma of Determinism," are especially helpful here.

CONCLUSION

1. Cf., for example, Peter H. Hare, ed., *Doing Philosophy Historically* (Buffalo, NY: Prometheus Books, 1988).

2. These terms are not always interchangeable, though. For example, not all pseudoreligious forms of behavior can be said to be superstitious—not, at least, if superstition involves some kind of *magical* attempts to control one's fate. Someone might, for instance, have a "religious" attitude to some sport she/he is a fan of, say soccer, and others may condemn such an attitude as pseudoreligious without thereby condemning it as superstitious. Furthermore, not all superstitious forms of behavior need to be hypocritical (given that hypocrisy involves some kind of pretending or lack of serious commitment): one can be *seriously* confused in one's (pseudo)religious life. In the paradigmatic cases to be examined here, however, pseudoreligious and superstitious (though not necessarily hypocritical) attitudes are usually very close to each other or even amount to one and the same thing; hence, in my examples below I will be mainly interested in positions that can be characterized as both pseudoreligious and superstitious.

3. Note that the so-called cognitive science of religion also is, or seeks to be, antiessentialist: see, for example, Ilkka Pyysiäinen, "Cognitive Science of Religion: State-of-the-Art," *Journal for the Cognitive Science of Religion* 1 (2013): 5–28. However, as has been observed in the previous chapters, the pragmatist—and even the Deweyan pragmatic naturalist—should resist the cognitive approach if it seeks to reduce religion into mere cognitive, evolutionarily explainable mechanisms. (This, of course, is another normative claim about how religion ought to be approached.)

4. This list, of course, is by no means exhaustive.

5. Note, however, that I am not trying to define the concept of fundamentalism in any particular way. I presuppose a layman's understanding of this notion; we all can easily pick out examples of fundamentalist religious (or, rather, pseudoreligious) ideas and actions, but it is presumably as difficult to define fundamentalism as it is to define religion.

6. Especially Richard Swinburne's views on evil and theodicy might be regarded as paradigmatic here, as we will perceive. See, for example, Swinburne, *The Existence of God* (Oxford: Oxford University Press, 1979).

7. Again, the views on theodicy held by someone like Alvin Plantinga are a case in point, though Plantinga's other ideas might be taken up in this context as well. See, for example, Plantinga, *Warranted Christian Belief* (Oxford: Oxford University Press, 2000). However, discussing Plantinga's complex theory of the warrant of Christian faith is beyond the scope of this book.

8. See William James, *The Varieties of Religious Experience* (1902), available in *The Works of William James* (1985).

9. The Wittgensteinian philosophers whose views on religion are diametrically opposed to evidentialism include, among others, D. Z. Phillips, Lars Hertzberg, B. R. Tilghman, Stephen Mulhall, as well as, perhaps, Putnam (cf. chapter 3). Of course, I cannot offer any close readings of these thinkers' various texts here.

10. This idea, which comes close to the (Wittgensteinian) view that it makes no sense to ask for a source of morality more fundamental than morality itself but that the sources of morality are only available from within a form of life that is already (understood and experienced as morally committed), and that, therefore, moral duty itself is "religious" (as if commanded by God), might be spelled out—pragmatically "cashed out"—in terms of a *holistic pragmatism*, for example, along the lines proposed in another context by Morton White. See White, *A Philosophy of Culture: The Scope of Holistic Pragmatism* (Princeton, NJ: Princeton University Press, 2002); cf. chapter 2. According to the kind of holistic pragmatism that would be applicable here, we must give up the idea that either religion or morality has to be the more fundamental of the two. The holistic

pragmatist suggests, rather, that religious and ethical views (beliefs, statements, ideas) are parts of a holistic "web," both critically evaluated at the same time, analogously to, for example, analytic and synthetic sentences (Quine) or descriptive and normative ones (White). This idea can generally be extended to the relation between metaphysical and ethical statements, and religious or theological statements can be understood as a subclass of these.

11. See, among Quine's many works, his last book, *From Stimulus to Science* (Cambridge, MA and London: Harvard University Press, 1995); on analogous (though largely neglected) issues in "religious naturalism," see Sami Pihlström, "A Pragmatic Critique of Three Kinds of Religious Naturalism," *Method and Theory in the Study of Religion* 17 (2005), 177–218. Cf. also chapter 2 in this book.

12. See the entry, "Superstition", in the *Catholic Encyclopedia*, http://www .newadvent.org/cathen/14339a.htm.

13. Think, for instance, of Kant's way of arriving at the justification of religion only through the demands of morality. Or think of the ethical concerns at work in James's reflections on religion. See chapter 1.

14. The holistic pragmatist solution briefly discussed above, inspired by Morton White, would in a sense integrate religion and morality into one and the same framework. That would be the *point* of such a solution. It is somewhat doubtful, however, whether either of the two parties would accept that as a genuine solution. For a religious person, an integrated framework might be unacceptable for religious reasons, and the same could be argued to hold for the ethical framework, for moral reasons.

15. See Lars Hertzberg, "On the Difference that Faith Makes," in *Perspectives in Contemporary Philosophy of Religion*, ed. Tommi Lehtonen and Timo Koistinen (Helsinki: Luther-Agricola-Society, 2000), 114–35, especially 121ff.

16. Ibid., 127–28.

17. Cf. ibid., 129.

18. Ibid., 131.

19. See White's holistic pragmatism as developed in his *A Philosophy of Culture* and elsewhere.

20. On the other hand, I would be prepared to call the Wittgensteinian orientation "pragmatist" in a broad sense.

21. For an insightful reflection on the possibility of discussing religious issues, see Hugo Strandberg, *The Possibility of Discussion: Relativism, Truth and Criticism of Religious Beliefs* (Aldershot, UK: Ashgate, 2006).

22. Ludwig Wittgenstein, *Lectures and Conversations on Aesthetics, Psychology and Religious Belief*, ed. Cyril Barrett (Berkeley: University of California Press, 1966), especially 53–56, 72.

23. Moreover, both genuinely religious and pseudoreligious "pictures" can presumably belong to the *Weltbild* (world-picture, worldview) that is the "inherited background" I use for distinguishing between truth and falsehood, as Wittgenstein explains in *On Certainty*, trans. Denis Paul and G. E. M. Anscombe (Oxford: Basil Blackwell, 1969), § 94 (cf. also §§ 95–99, 162, 167).

24. Cf., for example, D. Z. Phillips, *Belief, Change and Forms of Life* (Basingstoke: Macmillan, 1986). In criticizing the traditional theist's conception of theism as a commitment to the existence of God, Phillips relies not only on Wittgenstein's but also on Kierkegaard's and Simone Weil's thought.

25. However, it might be argued that in a "high" religion such as Christianity, Islam, or Judaism, the content of religious practices is inseparable from theology. Thus, theology would not be an external addition to people's genuine engagement in religious practices but an integral part of those practices' being genuinely religious ones. In making theology itself part of religious practices the (contemporary) pragmatist philosopher of religion would to some extent depart from James's experience-centered and, hence, somewhat antitheological views (as spelled out in James, *The Varieties of Religious Experience*). I leave this matter aside here, however.

26. See Wittgenstein, "A Lecture on Ethics," in *Philosophical Occasions 1912–1951*, ed. James C. Klagge and Alfred Nordmann (Indianapolis, IN: Hackett, 1993), 41–42. This picture, which (like the others that Wittgenstein discusses in the same context) is a mere "simile" because it is a desperate attempt to run against the limits of language, involves a humanly impossible but (therefore) fascinating attempt to view the world *sub specie aeternitatis*, thus also touching the themes of the final pages of Wittgenstein's famous early work, *Tractatus logico-philosophicus: Logisch-philosophische Abhandlung* (1921; repr. Frankfurt am Main: Suhrkamp, 1961).

27. Thus, her/his attitude will be very different from, say, the one manifested in Bede Rundle's recent book, *Why There Is Something rather than Nothing* (Oxford: Oxford University Press, 2005). For a related discussion, see Sami Pihlström, "Wonder and Trust," chap. 6 in *Pragmatic Moral Realism: A Transcendental Defense* (Amsterdam and New York: Rodopi, 2005).

28. This theme is developed in the "solipsistic" paragraphs (§§ 5.6 ff.) of the *Tractatus*. See Sami Pihlström, *Solipsism: History, Critique, and Relevance* (Tampere: Tampere University Press, 2004), chap. 3. Cf. also chapter 5 in this book.

29. Cf. also David E. Cooper, *The Measure of Things: Humanism, Humility, and Mystery* (Oxford: Clarendon Press, 2002); and Cooper, *A Philosophy of Gardens* (Oxford: Oxford University Press, 2006). Cooper is obviously fond of the "gift" vocabulary.

30. See William James, "The Problem of Being," chap. 3 in *Some Problems of Philosophy: A Beginning of an Introduction to Philosophy* (1911), ed. Frederick H. Burkhardt, Fredson Bowers, and Ignas K. Skrupskelis (Cambridge, MA: Harvard University Press, 1977).

31. See Stanley Cavell, *The Claim of Reason* (Oxford: Oxford University Press, 1979), and several essays collected in *Wittgenstein and Scepticism*, ed. Denis McManus (London and New York: Routledge, 2004).

32. James Conant, "Varieties of Scepticism," in McManus, *Wittgenstein and Scepticism*, 97–136.

33. See ibid.

34. Given our Wittgensteinian considerations, it might be further suggested that religious thinking based on existential wonder may have to be non- or postmetaphysical, instead of relying on the kind of metaphysical frameworks that give rise to traditional theism and its alternatives. See, for example, the essays in *Religion after Metaphysics*, ed. Mark A. Wrathall (Cambridge: Cambridge University Press, 2003), cited in the previous chapters. See also the discussion of wonder, existence, and otherness in Richard Kearney's thought-provoking *Strangers, Gods, and Monsters: Interpreting Otherness* (London and New York: Routledge, 2003).

35. Ludwig Wittgenstein, *Culture and Value*, ed. Georg Henrik von Wright and Heikki Nyman, rev. ed. Alois Pichler (Oxford: Blackwell, 1998). These specific remarks were written ca. 1944.

36. Cavell, *The Claim of Reason*, passim.

37. See the discussion of otherness in Kearney, *Strangers, Gods, and Monsters*.

38. Cf. William Alston's entry on "Religion" in the *Encyclopedia of Philosophy*, ed. James Edwards (New York: Macmillan, 1967).

39. There is a further distinction to be drawn between the ways in which the contrast between genuine and confused ways of understanding religion (and thus the "limits of religion") is manifested within a particular religion (e.g., Christianity) and more generally (say, at the kind of philosophical level we have examined the matter). It is a problem—one not to be discussed here—whether philosophy of religion can ultimately remain at the abstract philosophical level, especially if it urges that normative commitments are needed instead of, or in addition to, mere descriptions of religious practices. It is clear that for scholars within religious studies, for instance, it is important to describe and explain different forms of religious behavior without relying on any prior normative understanding specific to any particular religion, but for a philosopher of religion constantly concerned with normative issues this may not be enough. Philosophical attention to specific Christian commitments, for example, may be required; however, this is obviously something quite different from recent

"Christian philosophers'" habit of relying on Christian premises in one's argumentation.

40. Cf. Wittgenstein, *Lectures and Conversations*, 71.

41. See chapter 1 in this book.

42. Cf. Anders Kraal, "The Phillips-Swinburne Debate on Religious Language: Toward a *Via Media*," in *The Contemplative Spirit: D.Z. Phillips on Religion and the Limits of Philosophy*, ed. Ingolf U. Dalferth and Hartmut von Sass (Tübingen: Mohr Siebeck, 2010), 155–72, especially 167.

43. See also Ulf Zackariasson's reflections on the "problems of religion" (cited in chapter 3 above).

44. Here I am deeply indebted to David Dilworth's critical comments on some of the papers that were the basis for the chapters of this book.

Index

Dwayne A. Tunstall, *Yes, But Not Quite: Encountering Josiah Royce's Ethico-Religious Insight.*

Josiah Royce, *Race Questions, Provincialism, and Other American Problems, expanded edition.* Edited by Scott L. Pratt and Shannon Sullivan.

Lara Trout, *The Politics of Survival: Peirce, Affectivity, and Social Criticism.*

John R. Shook and James A. Good, *John Dewey's Philosophy of Spirit, with the 1897 Lecture on Hegel.*

Josiah Warren, *The Practical Anarchist: Writings of Josiah Warren.* Edited and with an Introduction by Crispin Sartwell.

Naoko Saito and Paul Standish, eds., *Stanley Cavell and the Education of Grownups.*

Douglas R. Anderson and Carl R. Hausman, *Conversations on Peirce: Reals and Ideals.*

Rick Anthony Furtak, Jonathan Ellsworth, and James D. Reid, eds., *Thoreau's Importance for Philosophy.*

James M. Albrecht, *Reconstructing Individualism: A Pragmatic Tradition from Emerson to Ellison.*

Mathew A. Foust, *Loyalty to Loyalty: Josiah Royce and the Genuine Moral Life.*

Cornelis de Waal and Krysztof Piotr Skowroński (eds.), *The Normative Thought of Charles S. Peirce.*

Dwayne A. Tunstall, *Doing Philosophy Personally: Thinking about Metaphysics, Theism, and Antiblack Racism.*

Erin McKenna, *Pets, People, and Pragmatism.*

Sami Pihlström, *Pragmatic Pluralism and the Problem of God.*

Thomas Alexander, *The Human Eros: Eco-ontology and the Aesthetics of Existence.*